The
RIGHT
WORDS
at the
RIGHT
TIME

Other Books by Marlo Thomas

Free to Be . . . You and Me

Free to Be . . . A Family

The
RIGHT
WORDS
at the
RIGHT
TIME

MARLO
THOMAS
and FRIENDS

ATRIA BOOKS

NEW YORK   LONDON   TORONTO   SYDNEY

ATRIA BOOKS
1230 Avenue of the Americas
New York, NY 10020

ISBN: 0-7434-4649-6
        0-7434-4650-X (Pbk)

First Atria Books trade paperback printing January 2004

10 9 8 7 6 5 4 3 2 1

ATRIA BOOKS is a trademark of Simon & Schuster, Inc.

For information regarding special discounts for bulk purchases,
please contact Simon & Schuster Special Sales at 1-800-456-6798 or
business@simonandschuster.com

Manufactured in the United States of America

The
RIGHT
WORDS
at the
RIGHT
TIME

EDITOR
Marlo Thomas

EXECUTIVE EDITOR
Elizabeth Mitchell

MANAGING EDITOR
Carl Robbins

For
The Children
of
St. Jude Children's Research Hospital
and
Their Parents

CONTENTS

ACKNOWLEDGMENTS

I owe thanks to so many people for their work on this project. First of all, to my husband, Phillip, who knows a thing or two about the right words—and volumes about love and support; to my assistant Gail Newman, who never looks at the clock—but only into her heart, for ways in which she can help; to my cherished friend Kathie Berlin, a mover and shaker who always uses all her moves and shakes to help me get where I want to go. To Judith Curr, publisher of Atria Books, whose irresistible enthusiasm and intelligence told me right away that the book had found a home; and thanks to her terrific staff, especially Greer Hendricks and Seale Ballenger for their energy and expertise.

To my attorney, Bob Levine, who steered this enormous project through a thicket of negotiations and paperwork, all the while believing in it whole-heartedly.

Thanks also to Cari Ross for getting the right word out in her savvy and caring way, and to the tireless team of interviewers and writers who helped bring the magic of more than one hundred stories to the printed page: especially Bruce Kluger, who was a devoted part of our team; Sam Lipsyte, Noah Hawley, Smith Galtney, Sean Neary, Tony Karon, Josh Young, Lawrence Grobel, Dorothy Atcheson, Carl Sferrazza-Anthony, Richard Sullivan, Pat Beard, Doug Brinkley, Mara Friedman, Ted Grossman, James Higgins, A. E. Hotchner, David Huchings, Mark Katz, Elizabeth Kaye, Paul O'Donnell, D. J. Wilson, Jessica Yellin and Lucinda Franks. And a special thanks to Jen Miller, RoseMarie Terenzio, Ralph Goldman, Rochelle Korman, John Moses and Jerry Chipman.

And to Elizabeth Mitchell and Carl Robbins, whose passionate commitment and peerless professionalism made this book such a joy to work on.

"Tell me a fact and I'll learn. Tell me a truth and
I'll believe. But tell me a story and it will live in my
heart forever."

—Indian Proverb

When I was a child I loved to watch my father shave. I sat on the closed toilet seat and marveled at the sound of the razor gliding over his face, pushing aside the foamy soap like a shovel in the snow. I adored him, this grand figure who slapped lotion on his cheeks every morning, buttoned his clean white shirt and hugged me good-bye.

Once, my father made a movie with Margaret O'Brien and he often took me to the set. I would cue his lines as we drove to the MGM studios with the windows open and the heady mix of Old Spice and a Cuban cigar swirling about us as we carried on a kind of rehearsal in transit. On the set I played jacks with Margaret between takes, and when the bell rang, I would join the crew in their silence as the cameras rolled and the boom mike moved into position to record the dialogue I knew by heart.

I was in awe of my father and sinfully envious of Margaret

O'Brien. I wore pigtails. I wanted freckles. I wanted to be Margaret O'Brien. Ten years later, at age seventeen, I got my chance.

I played the lead in *Gigi* in a summer stock production at the Laguna Playhouse south of Los Angeles. The excitement of finally being a real actress was painfully short-lived. All the interviews and all the reviews focused on my father. Would I be as good as my father? Was I as gifted, as funny? Would I be as popular? I was devastated.

I loved my father; my problem was Danny Thomas.

"Daddy," I began, "please don't be hurt when I tell you this. I want to change my name. I love you but I don't want to be a Thomas anymore."

I tried not to cry during the long silence. And then he said, "I raised you to be a thoroughbred. When thoroughbreds run they wear blinders to keep their eyes focused straight ahead with no distractions, no other horses. They hear the crowd but they don't listen. They just run their own race. That's what you have to do. Don't listen to anyone comparing you to me or to anyone else. You just run your own race."

The next night as the crowd filed into the theater, the stage manager knocked on my dressing room door and handed me a white box with a red ribbon. I opened it up and inside was a pair of old horse blinders with a little note that read, "Run your own race, Baby."

Run your own race, Baby. He could have said it a dozen other ways: "Be independent"; "Don't be influenced by others." But it wouldn't have been the same. He chose the right words at the right time. The old horse blinders were the right gift. And all through my life, I've been able to cut to the chase by asking myself, "Am I running my race or somebody else's?"

The impact those words had on me made me wonder if others had such words too. What follows on these pages are the stories that changed the lives of more than one hundred remarkable people who responded to my invitation to reach back into their own lives in search of that moment when words made all the difference. Each one is a brief glimpse into the heart, a moment of awakening, a lightbulb that revealed a truth that has stayed with them for a lifetime, or a challenge that moved them to action. Muhammad Ali responded to a teacher's assertion that he "ain't never gonna be nuthin'." Billy Crystal, Walter Cronkite, Katie Couric and Kenneth Cole also received words of discouragement that goaded them on to achievement. The right words moved Al Pacino to pull out of a downward spiral. Paul McCartney's words came in a dream; Steven Spielberg's came from Davey Crockett. Chris Rock's words, like mine, came from his father; Supreme Court Justice Ruth Bader Ginsburg's from her mother-in-law on the eve of her wedding. Rudolph Giuliani, Cindy Crawford and Gwyneth Paltrow heard the words that changed their lives during a moment of crisis. Itzhak Perlman spent his entire career, almost forty years, living by a single, eight-letter word first spoken to him by a Russian music teacher when he was ten years old.

All of these stories confirmed something I've always suspected: that whether we know it or not, each of us carries our own unique slogan, a custom-made catchphrase that resonates throughout our lives.

The royalties from this book will help fund research now underway at St. Jude Children's Research Hospital, the hospital my father founded in 1962. Along with our Nobel laureate Dr. Peter Doherty, our talented physicians, researchers and nurses strive every day to save the lives of children who come to our doors from all over the world and who are never turned away because of a family's inability to pay.

I thank the men and women who offered their stories for this book on behalf of the children, and with the hope that their right words at the right time would be just that to someone else.

And I thank my father for all his words that continue to live in my heart.

Marlo Thomas

New York City
Spring, 2002

Muhammad Ali

Athlete

I was a loudmouth when I was twelve years old. I made my parents nervous. I wore my Golden Gloves jacket everywhere, strutting, bragging, shadowboxing. It was the fifties and I was what young black men were not supposed to be in Louisville, Kentucky: Loud.

That's about the time I went to the Armory to see Gorgeous George. He was a big deal then, a white wrestler who took more time parading to the ring than actually fighting. He came out all dressed up pretty and taunting the audience. "Don't mess up my beautiful hair, I am pretty," he said, swaggering all over the stage in a big red cape, his yellow hair all piled up. "Don't mess up my pretty hair," he repeated, as the audience booed and booed. That's when I noticed there were no empty seats in the Armory. The more the people booed, the more tickets he sold.

I went home and strutted even more, bragged more, and spoke even louder than before. My poor parents, they were more nervous than ever. "I'm gonna be the greatest of all time," I said as I shadowboxed everywhere. Even today, my own company is called G.O.A.T. Inc. Know what that stands for? GREATEST OF ALL TIME. I knew when I was twelve I was gonna be THE GREATEST.

In every one of my amateur fights I was floating, stinging, and winning. I pounded my chest, talked about how great I was, and all the time I knew, I just knew, I was prettier than Gorgeous George. I also knew I could sell more tickets than that ol' rassler.

I wasn't alone; there were other guys at school boxing and always talking about being the next champion. To one teacher especially, I was just another loudmouth. She kept putting us down and acting like she was disgusted with all these puffed-up boxers. She just did not believe in anyone's potential. I always thought she was sort of empty-headed. She came up to us one day while we were sparring in the hallway, looked right at me, and said, "You ain't never gonna be nuthin'."

I won the Golden Gloves in Louisville when I was seventeen. And then the next year, it happened: I won the Gold Medal at the 1960 Rome Olympics. *I was the greatest in the whole world!* First thing I did when I got home was to go straight to that teacher's classroom. "Remember when you said I wouldn't ever be nuthin'?" I said.

She looked up, sort of surprised.

"I am the greatest in the world," I said, holding my medal by the ribbon. It dangled there in front of her. "I am the greatest in the world." Then I put my medal in my pocket and walked out of that classroom for the last time.

Less than one year later I met a member of the Nation of Islam who took me to my first meeting of Muslims. Not long after that, in Detroit in 1962, I met Malcolm X, who told me that "Negro" is not a country. Chinese are from China; Russians are from Russia. Where do Negroes come from?

Malcolm also taught me how "white" in our country is always associated with good. Jesus was white. Cowboys were white; they wore white hats and rode white horses. Angel food cake is white. Tarzan, the King of Africa, was white!

It was Malcolm X who told the truth about black and white in America. Black things were bad, devil's food cake, black hats, black cats, blackmail. I began to think about the way people viewed black folks.

I learned that I didn't even know my name. Cassius Clay is a white name given to me by a white man who didn't know me. That's why we had black kids in school named George Washington. That's why we had teachers who never believed in us. Even the one who said, "You ain't never gonna be nuthin'" was black.

Malcolm X gave me my pride, my spirit. Gorgeous George gave me my plan to sell tickets, which I later used during interviews with Howard Cosell. And that doubting schoolteacher gave me all the motivation I ever needed to become The Greatest of All Time!

I knew it was true when I was twelve years old.

Muhammad Ali

Christiane Amanpour

Foreign Correspondent

I call myself "the accidental journalist" because I hadn't grown up always wanting to be one. As a child, I lived in Iran, where there's no press freedom. Consequently, there was nothing about the profession that attracted me. But journalism ended up claiming me through an odd series of events.

I was sent to high school in England and returned to Iran without a plan for my future. I'd briefly entertained the idea of becoming a doctor, but my grades weren't high enough for medical school; so I was left somewhat adrift. Then in 1979, the Iranian revolution erupted.

Not only was this cataclysmic in an international sense, but personally it turned my life—and my family's and friends' lives—upside down. Martial law was imposed, soldiers and tanks lined the streets, and a nighttime curfew went into effect across the country.

There was a great deal of uncertainty about our future as a nation. Would the Shah hang on to power? What would happen when the Ayatollah came back? Many of my father's contemporaries were rounded up and arrested, some of them executed.

I returned to England, but my circumstances were radically different. I came from a privileged background. Now my father could no longer support me; his funds had been frozen, and I needed to make my own way. At the time, my younger sister was attending a small journalism college on Fleet Street in London, but after the first term she dropped out, deciding the profession didn't interest her. Now that every cent counted, I was damned if we were going to lose this money that my family had already laid out.

I went to the headmaster's office to ask for our money back, but he said no, the fee was nonrefundable. I replied, "Then, I'll take her place." So began my journalism career.

I learned some basic skills at the school, and by the end of the first term, I'd caught the bug. *If I really want to make it in the world,* I thought, *I have to go to America.* Immediately, I began to apply to colleges in the States, with an eye toward becoming a foreign correspondent. Having lived through these unbelievable international events—including the revolution—I knew this career was perfect for me.

By the early eighties, I was finishing my education at the University of Rhode Island and doing an internship at a local television station, where I was a graphics operator. That job was fascinating, because it put me in the control room, the nerve center of a TV news program. After I'd been there awhile, a colleague said to me, "Have you heard about this new cable station called CNN? I hear they put people on the air who have English accents. Maybe you want to give them a try."

By then, I'd done the requisite pounding of the pavement—writing letters, looking for entry-level jobs at various local stations—and more than once I was told that my British accent and unconventional looks were liabilities. There was no way I'd be accepted by Middle America TV viewers, I was informed. My long and foreign-sounding name was also considered an impediment.

"Christiane Amanpour?" they would say. "That will never fly on television. No one will be able to pronounce it."

So I called the personnel department at CNN and was interviewed by phone. The woman asked me ten questions—basic information like, "What is the capital of Iran?"—and shortly afterward, I was told I got the job. I'd be working as an assistant on the foreign desk.

Although a small core of people encouraged me in my first months, several others were not so helpful. Especially my boss. Maybe my enthusiasm and eagerness annoyed her—maybe I'd done something to piss her off—but it was clear that I was not a favorite of hers, and she let me know it, belittling my ambitions at every possible turn.

"CNN is certainly not the place for you," she'd say to me. "You'll have to go off to some small market and work your way up."

One of my jobs on the desk was to telex various instructions to our overseas affiliates. Sitting at the telex machine, I faced the wall, with my back to the newsroom. Whenever senior executives strolled into the newsroom, my boss would regale them with comments about my supposedly misguided ambition—"she wants to be a foreign correspondent"—as if that were the most hilarious thing in the world! Then she would send me off to the vending machines to fetch her coffee and Twinkies.

Sometimes tears of frustration and rage would pour down my face; but I never let on and I was determined to press on. I wasted no time. The minute I found out CNN was looking for a writer, I bolted off the desk, got the job, and began writing news copy for the anchors. Then I moved up to senior writer. I kept falling into dead men's shoes, winding my way up through vacancies.

Finally, I landed my first foreign assignment. My boss had by then left and CNN needed to fill a correspondent's position in our Frankfurt office. Two or three correspondents were ahead of me, but they declined. "Hey, I'll go anywhere," I said, and suddenly I was off to Germany. A couple of months later, Saddam Hussein invaded Kuwait, and off I went to the Persian Gulf region. Before I knew it, I was in the middle of the hottest story covering the Gulf War, and in a journalistic sense, I never came back.

It's been a long and fascinating journey for me, and every step of the way has demanded hard work—but intensely enjoyable hard work. I don't believe in sailing through life. My early experience at CNN taught me to have absolute clarity of vision—to know what I wanted and to have the courage and stamina to pursue my goals.

People will always try to knock you in life—and knock your dreams. In a peculiar way, that's not such a bad thing. In the end, it gives you an opportunity to prove you want it enough, and that you're strong enough to keep going. Life isn't supposed to be too easy.

Stephen Ambrose

Historian

As I was preparing to write Dwight Eisenhower's authorized biography, he and I sat together for long interviews, stretching over five years. Of course, he said many memorable things. He had dealt with all the big men of World War II and the first fifteen years of the Cold War—Franklin Roosevelt, Winston Churchill, Bernard Law Montgomery, Joseph Stalin, George Marshall, and Harry Truman among others. I said to him once that it sometimes seemed to me that on this or that occasion Churchill and Montgomery were more concerned with preserving the British Empire than in winning the victory, or that Stalin was more devoted to preserving Communism than in defeating Hitler. I asked if he ever felt that way.

He replied, instantly, that he had long since made it a rule to "never question another man's motives. His wisdom, yes, but not his motives." As a general, a politician, and a statesman he lived by that rule. As a writer and a biographer, I've done my best to emulate him. I have been critical of some of the decisions of the men I've written about, but never because I think they were self-serving, or motivated by greed or a desire to advance some hidden motive. Only God can make such a judgment. What I can say is that this decision had this or that effect, whether for good or evil.

Dr. Samuel Johnson once said something similar to his biographer, Boswell: "We cannot look into the hearts of men, but their actions are open to observation." Like Johnson, Eisenhower always assumed that the man he was dealing with was honest and trustworthy, even if mistaken.

Eisenhower was a font of wisdom. On the day Hitler invaded Poland, in 1939, he wrote his brother Milton, "Hitler should beware the fury of an aroused democracy." World War II proved how right he was, as the democracies made war far more effectively than the totalitarian nations. In 1947, during the early years of the Cold War, Eisenhower wrote, "It is a grievous error to forget for one second the might and power of this great republic." The enduring lesson of both wars is to trust the people of democracy. When they are united behind a cause, they will become a team and nothing can stop them.

In 1959, when a group of congressmen came into the Oval Office to urge President Eisenhower to launch a first-strike nuclear attack on Moscow, to wipe out the Communists as the Nazis were wiped out, he told them they were crazy. He wasn't going to order a nuclear Pearl Harbor. Then he said, "This Cold War is going to take a long time. But if the Soviets want to keep up with us, and they do, they will have to educate their own people, and in so doing they will sow the seeds of their own destruction." That is exactly what happened.

Eisenhower was a product of and a believer in the twin pillars of democracy, universal education and the rights of every person: the right to say what he or she thinks; to vote for his or her representative; to work at whatever job suits him and live where he pleases; to worship as he chooses, freely; to be assured of a fair trial if he is accused of any crime. That is what Eisenhower said in 1944, on the eve of the D-Day invasion, to all his troops. And that is exactly what they, under his leadership, accomplished.

Eisenhower is my model and my hero. I've tried, not always successfully, but always, to live by his words.

Stephen E Ambrose

Jennifer Aniston

Actress

I think of life as a continual learning process so it's difficult for me to single out one specific moment when someone said something to me that has made all the difference. I remember many moments where my life has been turned around. The first one that comes to mind is when my dad told me, "You should become a lawyer." My father, John Aniston, has been an actor on daytime television for some twenty-five years now, and he has seen the ups and downs of the business and how many of his friends have suffered the heartache of rejection.

As a good father, he wanted to spare me that heartache. When I look back at that now, I see how complex his feelings must have been to say that. He loves acting; he derives so much satisfaction from it—yet the process can be emotionally brutal. Not just the audition and rejection process, but once you're cast, going into sometimes dark places to find a character. Of course as a good daughter, I took it as a challenge. I wanted to prove to him that I could do it. I thought he would then be unbelievably impressed and would love me that much more. I think I had a little streak of rebelliousness too. I didn't consider the hurtful end of it. And his advice really set me on my path as an actor. I tell him sometimes, "If you really didn't want me to become an actor, you should have told me to be one because then I would have chosen to be a lawyer." But sometimes, a challenge from someone who we know really loves us can be good, because we know he will love us regardless of the outcome.

As I began studying at the High School for the Performing Arts in New York City, there was another turning point. I was doing what I thought was a highly dramatic scene from *The Three Sisters* by Anton Chekhov, and I could distinctly hear laughter in the audience. I walked off stage thinking, *Huh, laughing at Chekhov; not really the reaction I was going for.*

Later when my acting teacher, Anthony Abeson, was going over the scene with me he said, "You know, Jennifer, they're laughing because you're funny."

And I said, "But I don't want to be a funny actress, I want to be a serious actress."

"No, you've got it wrong," he said. "This is a wonderful thing. You should hone it, but please don't let it become your crutch."

In performance I had a tendency to be funny instead of going deeper into a scene. And in retrospect I realize that this was something I had been doing most of my life. All through my childhood I had used humor as a survival technique. Whether it was my parents' divorce or trouble with my friends or any of a hundred problems or insecurities that kids go through, I got by through being funny and making people laugh. I think I just did what came naturally to protect myself from hurt.

That's not to say that I didn't love making people laugh; I did. And when I think about it, all the things that I loved to watch growing up depicted these women who made me laugh. Yet when I thought about acting I just always thought of myself as a dramatic actress. I wanted to be the kind of actress who had made me cry as a kid when I went to the theater. Being funny just seemed too easy for me. So this incident in high school radically changed the way I thought about acting.

I realized I had to accept this aspect of my personality—my natural tendency to make people laugh—but place it into a larger context of what I wanted to achieve. I realized I needed to strike a balance. So instead of rejecting the funny side of myself, I embraced it. And channeled it into something I love to do and that makes me unbelievably happy and, amazingly, makes other people happy too.

Another turning point in my life happened with the success of *Friends*. Here I was in my twenties, and all of a sudden I had all this perceived success, and people started thinking of me as being fabulous and famous. But all the time I was thinking: *How weird that these people think this about me. If only they knew me.*

I was really at a place where I felt undeserving. I thought about the people out there who were really making a difference in this world. I couldn't make the success and attention mean anything when I compared it to others. I was thinking that my being an actress had no larger value to anyone. Sure it gave me financial security and validation as an actress and it was fun, but initially I thought, *How could it be enough?*

I started feeling an overwhelming need to withdraw from the attention when a friend of mine, Abhi, sent me this excerpt from a Nelson Mandela speech written by Marianne Williamson. It was an epiphany for me. Part of it reads: "It is our light, not our darkness that most frightens us. . . . There's nothing enlightened about shrinking so that other people won't feel insecure around you. . . . We were born to make manifest the glory of God that is within us. It's not just in some of us; it's in everyone. And as we let our own light shine, we unconsciously give other people permission to do the same."

So with those words I realized there was nothing gained by playing small to make others feel comfortable. Who was I to deny myself the light within me, the light that is within everyone? We all need to celebrate who we are and what we have to give to the world. It doesn't matter if you're driving a truck or making television shows or movies. We all have something unique to offer.

In reading Mandela's words, I realized that I did have a value and a place in the world, and part of that was making people laugh on a grand scale. Making lots and lots of people laugh, people I would never know, but perhaps people who needed to laugh. Now I'm grateful for my achievements and happy in giving what I have to offer as a human being.

Although I feel that I am at a good place now, I'm sure there are more turning points to come. I guess that's what makes life so damn interesting.

Lance Armstrong

Athlete

M y mom is one of the most influential people in my life, if not *the* most. She wasn't an athlete like me, but she was a good lady, a strong lady—always supportive and a good example. She had me early in her life, at seventeen. Having a child at that age is tough. You gain some sort of perspective on life that's different from other kids that age, which might explain why she was so positive about everything. Whenever I wasn't happy about something, she used to say, "Well, today is the first day of the rest of your life." That was her motto. And it sounds kind of corny, but in reality, it's true. If there ever was a difficult time in my life, she always helped me to focus on what I was going to do about it, what I was going to do next, as opposed to obsessing over what happened yesterday or a month ago.

That was before I was diagnosed with cancer. I didn't really know adversity before that, necessarily. I might have had a bad grade or a disappointing sporting event, but I certainly didn't have an illness that was threatening to kill me. If you had come to me in September of 1996, a month before I was diagnosed, I would have told you I was pretty happy. It wasn't as if I needed this illness to come along and change everything, although it did, and in a good way.

By 1996, I was in my mid-twenties, single, and moderately successful as a cyclist. I was well paid, even at the age of twenty-five, and

I guess my biggest worry was having an injury or crash that would halt my cycling career.

Then cancer came along.

I had to put my career on the shelf for eighteen months. I had to stop racing for the entire time of treatment and recovery. It was always my intention to start riding again—I loved riding a bike—but I didn't know what would happen to me after the treatment, whether I would be compromised physically. And I didn't know if I would be able to find work again, because a lot of teams just figured I was history.

From day one of the diagnosis, my mom was really strong and organized, but it was tough for me to be as optimistic as she was, at first. I didn't really know what I was dealing with so I couldn't focus on what was next. I had to learn about the disease, find the best care, concentrate on getting better, and deal with any setbacks that came along, like more revelations about other tumors found in other parts of my body. Those were all speed bumps. And it's a little hard to face those things and think, *Well, today is the first day of the rest of my life.*

But the most interesting thing about cancer is that it can be one of the most positive, life-affirming, incredible experiences ever. When somebody is in that position, he starts to really focus on his life, on his friends and family, and what's really important. You experience a different emotion and feeling than the guy who has woken up for thirty years in perfect health and gone to work or school and never had to worry about anything. That guy forgets that every day when you wake up, it's really a gift.

My fight with cancer became like an athletic competition. It was me, the doctors, and the surgery versus everything the illness could stack up against us. Whether that was the tumors themselves, or the low blood counts, or all of the effects that go along with having cancer—to me, it was a big fight. That's a catchphrase, but that's what it was. And as a result, I feel even more competitive than before. I love what I'm doing by a factor of at least a hundred. It's gone from being a job to being a lot of fun. One of the best things that came out of the illness was that I met my wife. We met when I was at rock bottom—when I looked like death warmed over—and that's a good time to meet your wife, I think.

In that sense, it's impossible for me not to wake up these days and get excited about what lies ahead. But if I'm going to be completely honest, the first thing I think about when I wake up isn't *Today is the first day of the rest of my life.* It's *I'd like a nice, strong cup of coffee.* I'm a morning person, and I can't wait to get out and start my day. Whenever I go to bed at night, I look forward to waking up and starting over. So maybe a more fitting saying would be *"Tomorrow* is the first day of the rest of your life." Unfortunately, that doesn't really have the same ring.

Candice Bergen

Actress

This is an anthology of individual moments of inspiration, personal epiphanies; phrases heard that resonate so strongly that one's life course is altered. Behavioral patterns changed in the space of a few well-placed words. While I know I've often been the recipient of these transformative phrases, the trouble is *now* I can't remember them. So it's of no use to us here.

I have, however, had something else instead. Something that changed me irrevocably, turned my life and my psyche on a dime and continues to inspire me every day. On November 8, 1985, I had my daughter, Chloe.

In fact, she began inspiring me before then, during my pregnancy, when I determined to be—for her—something more. More maternal, mature, responsible. More creative, productive, protective. I wanted in any way possible to be worthy of her. To measure up to being her mom. This has proved no easy task.

In short order, she was developing into a stellar human being. In no time I came to think of her as a "Champ." A champion human being. Every year it was harder to measure up. As a baby, she was borderline hyperactive, but as a child she became compulsively creative and productive. By the age of six, she was inspiring me to make better use of my time. One weekend, as I tried to catch up on some reading, she was intensely involved in building a chapel of wooden blocks. This went on for hours. She did not want to be disturbed. When at last she asked what time it was and I answered two o'clock, she paled, burst into tears and wailed, "*Oh no!* I've wasted the *whole* day!" She gave Protestants a bad name.

She was a champion for others as well, always alert to the child who was excluded and unpopular, wasn't picked for teams, ate lunch alone, or the teacher who she felt was unjustly dismissed. She was passionate, standing in front of her preschool class, at four years old, tears in her eyes, to talk about the Valdez oil spill, the awful destruction of the wildlife and the environment (a word she could not yet pronounce).

Her self-confidence, her already unshakable sense of self-esteem awed me and boosted my own. (I am of a generation whose self-esteem was in short supply.) One morning, when she was seven, I woke her up for school. She had been up sick the night before but insisted on going. Was she sure? Why not stay home today? No. She insisted, sleepily, raising her fists above her head like Rocky: "I am Chloe Malle. I am the Mighty One—*I can do it!*"

Always physically fearless, when she was nine, I took her white-water rafting in Colorado. Stopping at a calm spot on the river, the guide announced that this would be a good place if anyone wanted to swim. The water was an icy fifty-six degrees and everyone looked at him like he was nuts. Except Chloe. She raised her hand, climbed up to the nose of the raft and promptly jumped in. She is possessed of great guts and gusto, and on that count I have stopped trying to keep up. With age, the ship has sailed on recklessness, but I am inspired constantly by Chloe's appetite for life. Her joie de vivre is contagious for everyone around her.

And she is constantly inspiring in her courage and generosity.

When Chloe was nine, her father became critically ill. Over the course of almost a year, she took care of him, she took care of me, and each morning she entered her fourth-grade classroom with a bright and cheery *"Good* morning!" while most of her classmates replied with a grunt.

She is a girl who in sixth grade was awarded the coveted school "Spirit Award," in part because of her unflagging support and encouragement of those around her and her positive outlook on life. I tend toward pessimistic, and it is her spirit that moves and inspires me most.

One evening Chloe, my brother Kris, her honorary Aunt Bee and I went to my mother's for dinner. My mom lives in a spotless pastel house of pale peaches and delicate mauves, immaculate ivory carpets. A challenge for a child.

Chloe, then eleven, came bounding into the living room clutching a huge glass of cranberry juice. Before we could suggest the white grape juice alternative, she plopped onto the sofa, accidentally tipping the full glass of red liquid onto the brand-new peach silk upholstery. For a second, we all froze. My mother had not yet come into the room, and although her love for Chloe is boundless, this might have pushed the envelope.

Then, as one, we sprang into action. Soda water, damp sponge, paper towels. Frantic mopping and blotting. Futile blowing. The sound of approaching footsteps. And Chloe adroitly flipped the large cushion over, sinking quickly into it, and announced, grinning, to no one in particular, the words, *"Life* is good!"

Jeff Bezos

Founder and CEO of Amazon.com

As a kid, I spent my summers with my grandparents on their ranch in Cotulla, Texas. I helped fix windmills, vaccinate cattle and did other ranch chores. It was hard work but a welcome change from my Houston life of school and playing Star Trek with my friends. I loved it.

One of the best, and strangest, parts of spending summers with my grandparents was caravanning with the Wally Byam Caravan Club, a group of Airstream trailer owners who took road trips together around the United States and Canada. My grandparents were members and owned a thirty-one-foot Airstream that they towed behind their 1973 Oldsmobile. Every few summers, we would join the caravan—a line of some three hundred Airstream trailers, and it was during one of these trips that my grandfather said to me the right words at the right time.

I wasn't very old, maybe ten or eleven, but I was forming my opinions about the world, and, of course, I thought I knew much more about things than I actually did.

I was then, as I am now, a big reader and a fiend for numbers. Anyone who has been on a long road trip knows that no matter how many books you bring, no matter how sparkling the conversation or beautiful the scenery, you still have too much time to think. So I spent a good deal of my extra time calculating. I calculated gas mileage. I figured out the average per-item price of groceries bought over the course of the trip. And at some point, I saw an antismoking ad on TV. The announcer declared that every time a smoker took a puff of a cigarette, he was shortening his life span by two minutes. My grandmother was a smoker. I hated it, and not just because I knew that it was bad for her. My guess is that any kid who rides for thousands of miles sitting in the smoke-filled backseat of a 1973 Oldsmobile grows to hate smoking. So on one particularly long driving day, I decided to do the math.

I don't remember exactly what the number was—two minutes per puff, twenty puffs per cigarette, twenty cigarettes per pack, one pack a day for thirty years. About sixteen years? When I was satisfied that I had come up with a reasonably accurate number, I poked my head between the two front seats and tapped my grandmother on the shoulder. "You've taken sixteen years off of your life from smoking," I said, explaining the math, and with none of the solemnity the disclosure warranted. She burst into tears.

It was not the "You're very clever—that's good math" reaction that I was expecting. But there's nothing like unintentionally stepping on a landmine to make you keenly aware of your effect on those around you. I felt terrible. I sat quietly in the backseat unsure of what to do.

My grandmother cried, and my grandfather, who had been driving in silence, carefully pulled to the side of the road. He got out of the car and asked me to follow. Was I in trouble? How much trouble was I in? My grandfather had never said a harsh word to me, but this incident was unprecedented. I had no way to gauge how severe the consequences would be.

We walked a few paces back and stood between the trunk of the car and the front of the silver trailer. I watched the parade of Airstream trailers drive by and waited for the rebuke I knew was coming. After a minute, my grandfather looked at me, put his hand on my shoulder and said: "You'll learn one day that it's much harder to be kind than clever."

With both his words and the gentle way in which he delivered them, my grandfather taught me an essential lesson. I had always admired him for his intelligence, but that day I began to understand that his intelligence was only a gift that he had been given. It was the kindness with which he chose to apply it that he could be proud of. It's something I've been working on ever since.

David Boies

Attorney

When I graduated from high school, I had no intention of going to college. As a teenager growing up in Southern California in the 1950s, high school had been a time for racing cars, playing cards, surfing, and partying with my girlfriend, Caryl. Standing five feet two with blond hair and blue eyes, Caryl had the looks of a cheerleader (which she wasn't) and the mind of a champion debater (which she was). She always seemed to be laughing and either ready for a good time or already having one.

Even after Caryl and I were married and I took a job on a construction crew, I expected the party to continue, and for a while it did. When I was laid off of my construction job, I got a job as a bookkeeper in a bank. I didn't particularly like working at the bank, but it was a steady job—indoors, no heavy lifting—and compared to being on a construction crew, it seemed an easy paycheck.

I supplemented my income by playing cards—professional bridge, mostly, and sometimes poker. I enjoyed cards, and the money wasn't bad either—I could make fifty dollars a night, or even $150 if I got lucky. (Oddly, years later I realized playing cards is similar to law: Litigation is like bridge; negotiations and settlements are like poker.) I never bet the rent money. I sometimes bet the food money, but when I lost we could always go to our parents' house for a meal.

As I continued to breeze through life, Caryl was right with me at every step, whether it was crossing the border into Mexico to go gambling or bodysurfing in the Pacific Ocean at midnight on the way back.

One day we discovered that Caryl was pregnant, and before long she grew more serious about our future. That's when she started talking to me about going to college. Until then, my wife had been a total participant in our carefree lifestyle, living for the moment and not worrying about tomorrow. Now, she was serious, with an eye on our future. Initially, I wasn't much interested in the idea of going to college. Life was treating me well, the money was coming in regularly and, frankly, I never really enjoyed high school that much, even though I had been a fair student. My main classroom interests had been history (which I had learned to love from my father, who taught it at a nearby high school) and debate (which I liked in part because Caryl was my debate partner).

Yet I also knew that with a family, things would inevitably be different. Caryl was gently relentless on the subject of my returning to school; she wasn't insistent, but she was persistent in raising the topic.

Our son David was born in March, and one Saturday night a few months later, we were all out by the pool in our garden apartment complex enjoying the evening. The sun was beginning to set, the baby was in his playpen, and Caryl and I were drinking champagne.

Jokingly, I turned to Caryl and said, "Hey, isn't it about time for you to start mentioning college?" After all, we had been going back and forth on the subject for almost eight months, and I was genuinely surprised she wasn't starting in on me again.

Caryl got very serious, very quickly.

"No," she said, "I'm not going to talk to you about this any-more."

"You're not?" I said, still smiling.

"No," said Caryl, pointedly glancing toward our son. "You just make whatever decision you would want David to make if he were in your position."

Caryl's remark brought me up short. Looking back, I don't recall responding to her immediately, but I do remember that in the silence that followed, my champagne buzz evaporated. In one moment, this protracted conversation that we had been having about college—a dialogue that had touched on such important issues as responsibility and maturity and making sacrifices—was suddenly back on me and me alone. In my heart I knew she was right about college, and I suspected that she knew that I knew she was right.

The next morning I sent in my application to the University of Redlands. By September I was enrolled there, and six years later, I was practicing law. (Later, Caryl took her own advice, went back to school, and became a lawyer herself.)

Although I didn't know it at the time, Caryl's words that spring evening in 1960 were about much more than my going to col-lege. By advising me to make whatever decision I would expect from my son—a child for whom we wanted only the best things—Caryl introduced me to a new way of thinking about my life—our life. Deciding to attend college, I soon learned, would be the first in a long line of tough decisions in which I would need to decide to do, not necessarily the easier or most enjoyable or even the most lucra-tive thing, but the right thing. I did not always make the right decision; too often I have chosen easy over hard and self-indulgent over right. However, Caryl's words have helped me make the right decision more often.

During my first year of law school, I worked as a night clerk in a motel from midnight till eight in the morning, after which I would head directly to classes. After school, in the few hours I had to myself before catching a little sleep and going back to work, it was hard to study. All I really wanted was to relax. That's when I would remember Caryl telling me to do what I would want my son to do.

Over the next forty years, I took on a number of projects—civil rights cases and other difficult cases—that were, at the time, unpopular with many of my clients and some of my partners, and that had little prospect of any significant financial payoff. In such situations I tried to decide what to do based not on what was practical, but on what was right. The same was true in 1998 when I was asked to represent the United States Department of Justice in suing Microsoft, and in 2000 when I was asked to represent Vice President Al Gore in the Florida electoral controversy. There were many reasons not to take these cases: I had just started my own firm; I hadn't been spending enough time with my family; and because of the political climate, not to mention the powerful people I was going up against, I knew I would be the target of considerable criticism. In the end though, it was impossible to say no. It was a great opportunity and it was the right thing to do.

Although Caryl and I did not stay married, we stayed best friends, and I have always been grateful to her for the right words at the right time.

David is now forty-two. He's a lawyer with a wife and four

children. Am I proud of him? Enormously. Did I set an example for him, making the kinds of decisions I hoped he would one day make for himself? Maybe, from time to time, I did.

Then again, as any good poker player knows, maybe I just got lucky.

David Boies

Tom Brokaw

News Anchor

By all accounts, I was something of a whiz kid in high school. I was a jock, got good grades, was president of the class and governor of South Dakota Boys State. As a result, there were big expectations of me as I entered college.

But in 1960, while attending the University of South Dakota, I took a steep dive off the platform of respectability, virtually ignoring my studies in pursuit of what I then believed to be the good life: drinking every night, chasing girls. I was a total screwoff. When it came to exams, I managed to pull myself together just enough to get by. I truly thought I was fooling everybody.

This precipitous slide into chaos had actually begun a year earlier while I was enrolled at the University of Iowa as a freshman. Intending to take the campus by storm, I ended up all but flaming out, not exactly flunking my courses, but not doing very well either. So I transferred to South Dakota believing I could get my act together. Instead, I continued my skid. Every morning, it seemed, I woke with a hangover, having not written some paper, wondering to myself, "Oh, my God—how am I going to work my way out of this?" I could never quite get on top of things.

It was at South Dakota that I met Bill Farber, a wonderful Mr. Chips kind of character who was the chair of the political science department. An astonishing and affable guy, Bill had been mentor to a succession of eventual Rhodes scholars. Governors and senators and people of enormous achievement had gone through his department. They came to be known as Farber's Boys.

Because I had already established political science as my major, Bill kept his eye on me.

One night in the spring of my sophomore year, Bill invited me to his home for dinner. This wasn't an unusual thing; he often asked students to drop by to discuss their coursework and politics. I figured that's what was in store for me.

"I've been thinking about you a lot lately," he said, after we finished dinner.

"Oh, really?" I said, somewhat self-satisfied.

"Yes," he said, "I've been thinking about what you're going to do with your life. And I believe I have an idea."

"What would that be?" I asked eagerly.

"I think you should *drop out.*"

I was floored. Bill's words were harsh, but he said them so cheerfully, it seemed like he was just relating what the world already knew. How could he want me to leave school? I didn't respond. What was there to say, after all? I immediately felt as if I had been caught, called on my slapdash behavior.

Before I could respond, Bill continued. "That's right, I think you should go get all the wine, women and song out of your system, and then come back when you can do some good—for the university, for your parents and for yourself. But until then," he concluded, "I don't want to see you." The whiz kid was being summarily dismissed.

If this bombshell wasn't enough, I received a devastating letter from a woman I'd been dating. Her name was Meredith, and, like Bill, she had a few choice words for me. "Look, don't bother to come around anymore," her letter began. "Why would you think I would waste my time with someone who is as unfocused as you are?"

Needless to say, Bill's comments and Meredith's letter were twin hammer-blows, and before I knew it, I left college and landed a succession of menial jobs in radio and television. I figured I could always fall back on those fields, never thinking I would end up doing broadcast journalism full-time. I learned some basics, but more important, I discovered that surviving in the real world was more difficult than I had imagined. Having always achieved at the highest levels in anything I had undertaken, I had believed I could do anything I wanted—on my own terms. Now I was learning how wrong I had been.

After about four months of living hand-to-mouth, surrounded by people whose futures were dismal—simply because they had not gone to college—I went to Bill on my hands and knees, asking him to take me back.

"Okay," he said. "But this time it's on *my* terms, not yours. Here's your new class schedule, here are the grades I expect you to get. You'll continue to keep the job that you have, working full-time and commuting back and forth to the university. And then we'll take it from there and see if you do well."

And I did. In fact, I was so focused and organized, I apparently made an impression not only on Bill but also on Meredith.

"You were right to say what you said," I told her. "I needed to hear that."

Over the next ten years, I would earn my degree, marry Meredith and launch a successful career in television. But it was this painful time in my life—in which I was always adrift—that motivated me for years to come. It taught me how easy it is to slip off into the wrong current, but also how instructive a little failure at an early stage can be.

In recent years, I've had occasion to offer Bill's advice to others. A friend once sent his nephew to me. The kid had been spending a lot of money on cocaine, and his uncle was clearly worried. "Your uncle wanted me to speak with you," I told the kid. Naturally, he rolled his eyes, but I pressed on. "I went through a similar experience when I was your age. There wasn't any cocaine around at the time, but rest assured, if there had been, I would have been using it."

"You?" said the kid, genuinely amazed.

"Yes, me," I said. "Look, I'm not going to give you a big lecture, but I am going to let you in on a little secret: It's so much easier to do it right than to do it wrong. If you do it right, you don't spend all day trying to work your way out of trouble—making up excuses, making up for lost time. I'm not asking you to go off and be a monk. I'm just telling you to get back on track and see if at the end of the month you haven't expended a lot less energy, and that you're a lot happier with yourself."

Today, that kid is an accomplished young man. Whenever we see each other, he smiles at me and says, "Hey, it's a lot easier to do it right."

And I say, "I knew that."

Mel Brooks

Director

I was sitting in my director's chair, trying like hell to decide if beating up a little old lady was funny.

The year was 1973, and I was on the set of my third film, *Blazing Saddles*. As anyone who has seen the movie can tell you, *Blazing Saddles* has more than its share of outrageous moments: A man punches a horse; a bunch of grimy cowpokes sit around a campfire, eating beans and farting. It was a dangerous enterprise, to say the least.

And yet, here I was, about to shoot a scene that left even me a little nervous. In the screenplay, a band of bad guys rides into the peaceful little town of Rock Ridge, firing off their six-shooters, tearing down hitching posts, and wreaking havoc among the locals. Included in this chaos is a quick cut of two burly cowboys accosting a little old lady: One stands behind her, pinning her arms to her sides while the other unloads a flurry of punches to her stomach. All the while, the poor old lady is letting loose a stream of *oohs* and *ows*, pausing just long enough to look straight into the camera lens and ask: "Have you ever seen such cruelty?" Then the thugs continue to beat her up.

On paper, the scene was a riot. But now I was having second thoughts.

Mind you, I had never been one to shy away from off-color humor before. My first movie, after all, had been *The Producers,* in which two schemers mount a Broadway musical called *Springtime for Hitler.* Nervy, right? But back then I was more careful about the decisions I made. I'd occasionally consider an audience's potential objections in advance—which, in comedy, is a real mistake. Once you start trying to second-guess the audience, you invariably misread them, basically because you're attaching your own fears to whatever reaction they may have. And you can never do that.

Still, this scene in *Blazing Saddles* was making me queasy.

"I don't know," I said to John Calley, who was then a senior production executive for Warner Bros., which was making the movie. "I don't mind the farting cowboys; I don't even mind socking a horse. But punching a little old lady? I think that may cross the line. What do I do?"

John just smiled and said to me, "Hey, Mel, if you're going to step up to the bell, ring it."

I instantly knew what he meant and, after a moment of reflection, yelled for the cameras to roll. Not surprisingly, the scene turned out to be one of the funniest moments in the movie.

After that, all bets were off. The set of *Blazing Saddles* became a free-for-all, as we did one crazy thing after another. At one point, our hero gallops off on his horse and runs into Count Basie, conducting his full orchestra in the middle of the desert. We broke that fourth wall, bringing reality into fantasy at just the right emotional moment, and it was perfect.

Or later on in the film, we shot a fight scene on Main Street in Rock Ridge that literally burst through a wall onto the set of another movie—a musical—being shot on the Warner lot. It was an insane,

Pirandello-like moment, not to mention the bravest thing I've ever done in my life, as a writer or as a director.

It was as if John's advice had freed up all of this creative energy. As long as our hearts were in the right place, and as long as we loved our main character—a black sheriff coping with racial prejudice—and continued to care about his feelings, we could say or do anything we damn well pleased.

John's words have frequently come back to me throughout my career, each time allowing me to get past my fears and realize my vision—nutty or otherwise. In *Young Frankenstein,* for example, I shot a scene in which the monster ravishes Madeline Kahn—and she winds up loving it, breaking into the song "Ah, Sweet Mystery of Life at Last I Found You." It was risky, to be sure, and a little scary. But while sitting in my office, asking myself, "Can I actually do this?" I spun my chair around at my desk, and looked up at the wall where I had framed John's advice—"If you're going to step up to the bell, ring it"—and there was my answer.

Ironically, I got the opportunity years later to pass John's words on to a new generation of creative artists. When we began rehearsing the Broadway musical version of *The Producers,* directed by Susan Stroman, everyone kept asking the same questions I had asked myself thirty-three years earlier while shooting the movie. "Do we really want to put a Nazi swastika up there in front of real Jews, sitting in real seats in a real theater? Won't they want to storm the stage and kill all the actors?"

But, of course, we got nothing but cheers from our audiences because they understood that we were ridiculing Hitler and the Nazis. After the show opened, Stro credited me as having taught her to ring the bell, even though that advice originally came from John Calley.

In the end, I've learned, the audience wants the best and bravest of you. They never want you to be politically correct. They want you to be fearless, honest, crazy. They want you to do something that they wouldn't do—or even think of doing—themselves.

Mel Brooks

Barbara Bush

Former First Lady

Before I met George Bush, my father, Marvin Pierce, was the wisest person I ever knew. I adored him. Even now, when I think back on all the people I met around the world as First Lady, I don't think anyone could hold a candle to him for his wit and wisdom. He laughed constantly and I think that's what people liked so much about him. That smile. That little joke that made everyone feel good about his or her day. He even had a little bit of kid in him throughout his life. I remember being gathered around the family dinner table and him making a pool for the gravy in his mashed potatoes and my mother looking across and scolding him for being so badly mannered and for eating so many potatoes. But my father just plain enjoyed life, and I always enjoyed him.

For most of my youth, my father worked at the McCall Corporation. When I was in my early twenties, he became president of the company, but long before that he knew the value of hard work. He'd been a waiter. He'd tended furnaces as a young man in Miami. He always respected people who put their shoulder to a task. Daddy introduced me to the people who worked at the McCall's plant in Dayton, Ohio, when he took me on a couple of business trips there. I loved that—an adventure with my father and an overnight train trip! And I got to see more of how he treated people. He was always decent to everyone. He used to tell me, "It's nice to be natural, so be naturally nice." He meant, "Be yourself, don't be fake, don't put on airs, don't pretend to be something you are not." And he lived it.

The other important wisdom he gave me came over a lunch when I was nineteen. I had, a few months before, happily accepted the marriage proposal of George Herbert Walker Bush, who was twenty and in the service. I was madly in love with him. One day, my father asked me to meet him in New York for a special lunch, just the two of us. This seemed extremely elegant and dignified to me.

Daddy gave me some advice there that he thought I might need in the future. "There are only three things you can give your children," he said. "One, the best education available. Two, set a good example. And three, give them all the love in the world." Those guidelines are so simple, and yet they are everything. Those are the valuable gifts he gave me. And I think how wonderful that is, how when he had wisdom to distill, it would be about his role as a father. George and I set out to give our children that same foundation.

When George and I were first starting our family, we had no idea what our lives would become. We thought we might be farmers, then immediately discarded that notion when we realized how expensive it would be and how much expertise we would need. Instead, we embarked on an unusual but ultimately wonderful adventure as pioneers in the oil fields of lonely Odessa, Texas. George started in the business painting oil rigs in the broiling sun. Around that time, I told friends George would be president one day but that was just because I had such faith in him. I didn't really have a clue how my faith would possibly translate into a reality.

Living in half a small house in Odessa with a goat tethered in the next-door yard, and a mother-daughter prostitute team sharing the bathroom, George and I had no idea what we would be able to provide materially for our family. But we knew what sort of inheritance we could pass on: the example of basic decency that our parents had given us. Education, a good example and all the love in the world.

And to those suggestions I add, give your children independence. As hard as it is. I remember dissolving in tears when our son George wrote me a letter as a teenager after one of his first weeks of high school at Andover. "Last weekend was the greatest of my life," he wrote, and all I wanted was for him to be back home with the family. But then I realized, how selfish of me. Your children's happiness should be paramount. And I tried to always hold true to that. Trust your children. George and I ultimately gave our children independence and they soared (a very biased mother's opinion).

Laura Bush

First Lady of the United States

I often think about the way my mother and grandmother lived their lives. They loved the outdoors and the majesty of God's world. And both of them had absolutely beautiful gardens. My grandmother's was a rock garden, with ocotillos and yuccas. This was the stuff of my childhood.

When I was young, my family lived in far West Texas—my grandmother in El Paso, among the deserts and mountains; and mother, dad and me in Midland, which is at the bottom of the Great Plains and perfectly flat. Midland was overgrazed one hundred years ago, so there isn't a lot of grass left, nor are there many trees. With nothing along the horizon to obscure your view, the Midland sky is huge.

From my earliest memories, I can remember sharing that sky with my mother on summer nights. We'd lie on blankets on the lawn and look up at the stars. This was something that her mother had done with her, and now she was passing along the custom to me. "Look at the sky," she'd say to me.

And what a sky it was. Because Midland was such a little town, there was barely any light reflection there, and because it's in the desert, not even a humidity haze. The heavens were perfectly clear, and the stars looked so close, it was almost as if you could reach up and touch them. Mother knew some of the constellations, and she would point them out to me.

But mostly we would just gaze up and talk. We discussed whatever was going on in our lives. Naturally, the details of those conversations have faded with the years; but the feeling I got from both my mother and grandmother—how much they loved the outdoors, what a special gift the splendor of the world is to all of us, and what perspective it gives us—is still very much alive to me to this day. Even as I grew older and discovered other beautiful parts of our country, the sky of Midland, Texas, remains vivid.

My mother's interest in nature wasn't confined solely to the heavens. One year when I was a Girl Scout—I was in the sixth grade—mother was our scout leader, and all of the girls got bird badges. For those of us in the troop, this just meant that we had completed our basic study of birds; but for my mother, it led to what would become a lifelong hobby.

Bird watching became a big part of whatever we did as a family. We often drove out to the home of a woman we knew who was a naturalist. She kept her yard entirely wild—not landscaped like the rest of Midland—just to attract birds. And more than once I can remember driving to see my grandparents in El Paso when I was in high school, trying to sleep in the backseat of the car, when suddenly my mother would gasp, pull out her binoculars and announce, "Look, there's a hawk!" or "Did you see—it's a painted bunting!" At the time, of course, I didn't want to be bothered. I only wanted to sleep. But eventually, I too would develop an interest in bird watching and being outside.

In fact, it was through bird watching that I learned a little bit about community. One year Mother actually identified a varied thrush in her own backyard. This was a rare bird for Midland, and he had evidently blown in on a norther. During his stay in Mother's backyard, a lot of bird-watchers in Midland—geologists, mostly, and some of the scientists from the town's oil businesses—would come over on their lunch hour with their sack lunches, sit at the counter in Mother and Daddy's kitchen and patiently wait for the bird to show up. Of course, a lot of times the bird would never come; but when he did, everyone would jump up and hug each other, so thrilled that they had added this new bird to their list. And my dad would watch it all and say to me, "You know, bird-watchers are really good people."

Today, I continue to let the outdoors inspire me, even as life gets busier. I find going for walks to be the most relaxing, most comforting times of life. If I feel unhappy or anxious about something—if I'm sad or bored—a walk outside always wakes me up and makes me feel good. When I lived in the Texas governor's mansion, I would go for a brisk walk every day along the beautiful trail next to the Colorado River, which runs through downtown Austin. And even though I can't do that sort of thing at the White House, the president and I still enjoy walks when we're at Camp David and our ranch.

I've also scheduled regular trips with a group of women I grew up with in Midland. When we all turned forty, we celebrated by traveling up the Colorado River in the Grand Canyon, then hiked down the South Rim. When we turned fifty, we set out along the Yampa River in Colorado, and into the Green River in Utah. On our last trip, we hiked in Yosemite.

But no matter where I am, I'm always somehow drawn back to that big Midland sky, lying beneath it with my mother. I've tried to pass that very ritual along to my daughters. I remember one time in particular: The girls were about four years old, and we had been in

Maine for the summer. It was our last night there, and the sky was a magnificent turquoise, with a turquoise ocean beneath it, and thin lines of pink gracefully running through. The sun had just dropped, and our part of the world was awash in twilight.

"Look at the sky," I said to the girls, echoing the words my mother had said to me so many years before. "Look at the sky and remember it, because you won't see a sky like this for another year."

And I know they remember that. I'm sure they remember.

Laura Bush

President Jimmy Carter

Mediator, Statesman and Humanitarian

My life was profoundly influenced by my school superintendent, Miss Julia Coleman, who encouraged me to learn about music, art, and especially literature. I was one of about 250 elementary and secondary school students whom she closely supervised each year at Plains High School.

Miss Julia was short and somewhat handicapped, yet graceful as she walked through the rows of desks each day, telling us about the world beyond the peanut and cotton fields surrounding us in Plains, Georgia. Her face was expressive, particularly when she was reading one of the poems she loved, or presenting to a class the paintings of Millet, Gainsborough, Whistler, or Sir Joshua Reynolds. Miss Julia had poor eyesight, and the discipline in her classrooms evaporated during her later years of supervising schoolwork, but this certainly was not the case when I was her student.

She urged all of us to seek cultural knowledge beyond the requirements of a normal rural classroom. Those of us who attended Plains High School became highly competitive in debating, an essay contest called "Ready Writing," music appreciation, one-act play productions, and spelling bees. Every student in the classroom was required to memorize and recite long poems and chapters from the Bible. Each of us had to learn the rudiments of music and play some instrument—even if it were only a ukulele, harmonica, or piccolo.

Miss Julia prescribed my reading list as I grew up and gave me a silver star for every five books I finished and a gold star for ten book reports. When I was about twelve years old she called me into her office and stated that she was ready for me to read *War and Peace.* I was happy because I thought that finally Miss Julia had chosen a book for me about cowboys and Indians. I was appalled when I checked the book out of the library. It was about fourteen hundred pages long, written by the Russian novelist Tolstoy, and of course not about cowboys at all. It turned out to be one of my favorite books, and I have read it two or three times since then. But without Miss Julia, it would have been a long time before I discovered that remarkable book, if I even chose to read it at all.

I think Miss Julia was superlative in every way and represents the finest of teachers. She made us all feel that we were special whether we would never leave the cotton farm or instead go on to be president of the United States.

Remarkably, for a woman who never moved out of her small house in Plains, Georgia, and never married, her most important lesson was pertinent to every student who passed through her classrooms, regardless of which far-flung direction life took him. "We must adjust to changing times," she told us, "but cling to unchanging principles." I never forgot that. We have to analyze new situations repeatedly, she said, but whether it was choosing a spouse or selecting a career or making difficult decisions during times of stress or trial or temptation, we not only have to accommodate those new challenges but never deviate from certain ideals that we were taught, such as justice and integrity and peace and truthfulness and loyalty. The frontiers she took us to in literature and art were a way to test out those core beliefs, to practice thinking them through before we got out into the world and faced them alone.

Miss Julia never had her own family but gave herself instead to her students. She actually died a local hero in 1973. She is buried in the Plains cemetery, and there is a monument to her on the high school grounds. If you go into the school building, which is now a visitors' center and museum run by the National Park Service, her portrait is prominently displayed. Everybody who goes in and out of the building now sees Miss Julia Coleman's picture. I live in Plains, and she is a preeminent spirit here because just about all of my contemporaries, as well as people both younger and older than I am, had their lives affected by her. Whenever we have a meeting of our historical society or the Plains Better Hometown group we think and talk about her. This past spring she was instated in the Georgia Hall of Fame as one of the greatest citizens of our state.

When I ran for president, I had many private conversations about what theme I should choose as my most ardent promise to the American people. I didn't want to go into complexities like supporting one specific House bill or another in my bigger speeches. My competitors did, but I said instead that I would never lie and that I would adhere to the basic principles that Miss Julia and my parents taught me. I quoted Miss Julia in my inaugural address—"adjust to changing times but cling to unchanging principles"—committing myself and all Americans to real ideas of justice and truth, no matter what difficulties faced us.

Jimmy Carter

Hillary Rodham Clinton

United States Senator and Former First Lady

No human being is immune to adversity or personal setbacks. We all have our share of difficulties and challenges, and we all look for sources of inspiration to carry us through. In my case, inspiration has always started with my parents, especially my mother. Today she remains a woman of remarkable strength and common sense who always seems to know what to do in every situation.

I remember one of her earliest lessons. I was about four years old and my family had just moved to the Chicago suburb of Park Ridge. I was eager to make new friends, but I soon discovered that it wasn't going to be easy. Every time I went out of the house to play, the kids in the neighborhood would tease and bully me and occasionally push me or knock me down. Each time this happened I'd burst into tears and run back into the house and refuse to come out for the rest of the day.

My mother witnessed this for several weeks and finally, one day, she stood waiting for me as I barreled through the door. She took me by the shoulders and told me there was no room for cowards in our house. She sent me back outside to confront my tormentors. Out I went, shocking myself, as well as the other kids, who didn't expect to see me return so quickly. The next time they challenged me I stood up for myself and I won some new friends. Only much later did my mother confess that she had watched the whole episode from behind the drapes, worried sick about what would happen to me.

My father also taught me some important lessons. Sometimes when I would bring home a good report card his response was: "Well, that must be an easy school you go to." While that approach might not be appropriate for all kids, it taught me not to think too much of myself, or too little. And that perspective has been invaluable later in life, particularly during political campaigns when I've heard everything from the nastiest smears about myself to the most inflated and overheated praise.

My general rule is to disregard comments that are at either extreme and focus on what I believe to be true for myself. I try to take criticism seriously, but not personally. Above all, I think it's important to remember what you are trying to accomplish and how you are going to do it, rather than spending a lot of time answering uninformed or misinformed critics or gloating over compliments handed out too lightly.

At difficult times, particularly when I've been in the public eye, I've also drawn support and strength from family and friends. When Chelsea was growing up, Bill and I always tried to have breakfast with her before school and break from work to have dinner in the early evening. It didn't always work out, but it was our goal each day. And it was an important way of keeping our world centered when events around us felt chaotic or pressured.

Like most Americans, I also have relied on my religious faith to get me through life's challenges, losses, and setbacks. And I've found that faith in God and tapping into one's own spirituality is often the best way of getting beyond events—like the tragedy of September 11—that seem inexplicable, unfair, or horrible.

In his marvelous book *The Return of the Prodigal Son,* Henri J. M. Nouwen talks about "the discipline of gratitude," suggesting that in times of crisis we need to work hard to remember the gift of life and take stock of the goodness around us. I like to think of adversity as a test of our capacity for love and forgiveness. Being grateful for what we have is often our greatest balm.

Hillary Rodham Clinton

Chuck Close

Artist

Handicapped people hate phrases like physically challenged. We like to call ourselves cripples and gimps. It helps take the sting out of it. It helps us accept the handicapped part of us.

I became a quadriplegic thirteen years ago, at the age of forty-eight, when an artery in my spine collapsed. I had already had a great career as an artist, with paintings in museums around the world. I knew who I was. The problem was getting back to what I loved. The two great fears of any artist are that you're going to lose your eyes or you're going to lose your hands. I always thought of them as equally bad. Turns out if you're going to lose one, it had better be your hands. Which is exactly the way of thinking that helped me in my life, weighing out what makes any situation positive relative to another state of affairs.

My father died when I was eleven, so I think I learned early on that you could suffer a terrible tragedy and still be happy again. We didn't have any money but my father was extremely handy and he made all my toys—bicycles from scratch, model trains. It was very intimidating because he could do anything with his hands.

I've always been a gimp in some sense. When I was a kid I had a lot of problems. Back then no one thought there was such a thing as learning disabilities. You were just dumb, or lazy, or a shirker. I couldn't memorize anything, didn't know the multiplication tables, didn't know how to add six and seven without using my fingers. I couldn't even recognize faces. I was a klutz. My eyes didn't converge enough for me to catch a ball. But art gave me something to do that made me feel special. Probably had my father lived, I might not have even tried a lot of projects, but when he died I inherited his tool kit and all his power tools and I got started trying to make stuff myself.

After I suffered the artery collapse, I wasn't sure how I was going to be able to go back to my work. Lying in the hospital bed, I thought maybe I would have to be a conceptual artist. I got enough movement and then thought, *Well, I can paint holding a brush in my teeth.* Eventually I could move my arms a little bit. I remember my wife and my occupational therapist got me this device to hold a brush. They put a piece of shirt cardboard in a vise and I tried to draw a grid on it to divide the space into smaller, more manageable sections. I was totally exhausted. I mixed some paint and jabbed a stroke at the painting and said, "See, I can't do it!"

I started crying. But there was a little piece of me that thought, *Well, you know, it doesn't look* that *bad.* My assistant tells me I cried every day I painted in the hospital. I don't remember that at all. I just remember those words coming to me when I thought I was lost. "It's not *that* bad."

I've been very lucky all along. People think that if you're in a wheelchair and you have to paint with brushes strapped to your hands, "luck" is not a word you should be using. But I am fortunate in many ways. When you're a gimp, you don't envy able-bodied people. You envy people who are one notch above you. Quadriplegics envy paraplegics. I look at someone like Chris Reeve; he was dealt a much more devastating blow. He must look at me and think, *Well, it's like he has a hangnail.*

I'm not a hero. I have a wife who fought for me, and I'm an optimist by nature. But that's not all it takes. You have to be lucky with your body, too. I don't believe in the punish-the-victim mentality I saw in the hospital. This was the notion that if you didn't get better it was because you didn't have the right attitude. But, you know, life isn't always fair. Some people in the hospital refused to go to therapy and would lie around and whine and be shitty to the nurses and they got better. And some other people had wonderful attitudes, worked their butts off, but didn't get better at all.

In life, you have to deal with your fear, the part of you that says, "I can't do it." You have to rely on the part of you that says, "Well, it doesn't look *that* bad." And you have to keep going even though there are no guarantees. I've found a way to work for myself by breaking everything down to the smallest pieces. I just keep working at each little unit of the painting. Today I'll do what I did yesterday and tomorrow I'll do what I did today, the same thing in pieces small enough for me to handle.

For people who are handicapped, if you can keep from being destroyed by what happened, or pigeonholed by what happened, you're certainly going to be different, but you have a chance to be more interesting as a person, because you're not like everybody else. I know a lot of people who are paralyzed in other ways, even if they can walk.

Chuck Close

Kenneth Cole

Designer and Entrepreneur

When I was a child, my father seemed enthusiastic and excitable. As I got older, he seemed stubborn as a mule and tough as the ex-marine that he was. He also could be as caring and generous as anyone I have ever known, which is why, I suppose, working with him was so exhilarating and leaving him was so difficult.

My father owned a factory in Williamsburg, Brooklyn, that manufactured women's shoes. The factory was a brick box in a gray industrial landscape, heavy with the smell of shoe leather and diner cooking. Working at the factory was not my ideal career choice, but when I graduated from Emory University with plans to start law school in September, I felt a responsibility to postpone this decision to briefly learn the family business, in case anything ever happened to my father, who was truly the hand that fed us.

We were different men, my father and I. He was tall and handsome; a man with a ready smile who wore a jacket and tie on almost every occasion. I, on the other hand, threw on a button-down shirt and jeans every workday.

Two years went by and I was still working with my father. Law school had fallen by the wayside. My father and I then started a new venture, Candie's Footwear. We closed down the factory and opened an office in Manhattan, importing wood-bottom shoes from

Europe. This is when our differences became clear. We disagreed on so much. From how many people to hire, to how much we should pay them; how much advertising to do, if any, to whether we should buy ten thousand pairs of one shoe or fifteen thousand of another. I believed that his ideas were right for a business that had once existed. But the present market was different.

Every time I'd walk away from one of these tangles, my voice hoarse and my blood pressure racing, I wondered, *Why am I doing this? Why am I aggravating this relationship? Why can't I just go along with what he says—he deserves that much—and leave it at that?* After all, I realized, I could simply do everything his way and probably remain quite comfortable.

However, at the ripe old age of twenty-eight, I decided to venture out on my own.

I broke the news to my father at his kitchen table. I told him that, in the interest of our relationship—which to me was bigger than the business—and to quench a personal thirst I had to see if I could succeed on my own, I needed to take my shot. *Now.* I was single, unattached, and full of energy and desire. I had no idea where this move would take me—whether I'd end up running a women's shoe company, making men's underwear, or selling peanuts at baseball stadiums—but I knew that if I didn't make the move right away, I might never have the courage or opportunity again.

"We had a great success," I told my father, "and built a wonderful business together. But I need to move on. I need to keep growing and you're not ready, nor should you be, to give me the room I need." I thought this was an elegant little speech.

My father's response was, in retrospect, predictable. He played his last card. "You'll be back," he said.

Those angry but resigned words were obviously a big vote of no confidence in me. I was stunned. Looking back I can see that my father might have been warning me. He was telling me, "You have no idea what's ahead of you, and you can't make it without me. But don't worry, your office will always be waiting for you."

Needless to say, I knew I had only one option—to succeed. I was *not* going to go back. I would make "it" work. I wasn't quite sure what "it" was, but I knew I would figure "it" out along the way. . . . I walked out. And, of course, never looked back.

Six months later I was making money. I got lucky—the success for Kenneth Cole Footwear came quickly, and that usually doesn't happen with a new business. When I succeeded, my father was proud of me, again in his own way. He liked to take part ownership of my achievements, pointing out to everyone how much he had taught me. Observing him acknowledging my success and connecting himself to it, in even the smallest way, is the thing I am most proud of. I learned a lot from him. Always. Up until the day we lost him.

With a wonderful foundation I have developed my own business and life philosophies separate from my father's. My company's involvement with social and political issues, for example, was born from the idea that so much can be gained by making the business of selling shoes be about more than just business. Because in the end what you stand *in* is less important than what you stand *for*. I can't work sixty hours a week; I can't give so much of my soul to my business and, at the end of the day, have it just be about money. I knew then that what I was doing overall would never be truly meaningful unless I found a way to make it part of something bigger than it was.

I needed a more healthy balance in my life. One morning, I

woke to realize that I was routinely heading off to work before my kids were up, and coming home just before they went to bed. I wasn't connecting with them. I wasn't a part of their lives. So I decided to work at home every Friday, which permitted me to take the kids to school, pick them up, visit with their teachers, and have meals with them. I went from having no relationship with my daughters to having a meaningful one, practically overnight.

So how will I respond if, one day, for whatever reason, my children need to leave me the way I left my father? Hopefully, I've learned from my experiences and will say the right thing. I think it was Rabbi Hillel who said, we should hold on to our children the way we would hold a dove, tight enough to keep them safe and secure, but not so tight as to smother them.

And to that I add: not so tight as to keep them from spreading their wings.

Kenneth Cole

Bill Cosby

Comedian

During one's lifetime, one ought to be able to turn to more than twenty people who have said something that is common sense. Even if a person is self-assured, a significant sentence or symbol causes changes in one's behavior and life. No matter how small, muddled or great one feels about one's self, there is always an influence that is important.

I believe that we find strength in the horse that can applaud the person who led it to water. It is probably very good for the horse. If the horse is thirsty and chooses not to drink, then the *horse ought to have a good reason.* The obvious explanation is that the water is poisoned or something floated by and the horse didn't like what it saw. In this case, the horse can say, "No, I don't want to drink now; I'll wait." Conversely, the horse certainly should not fall back on the logic that many human beings use, which is, "I'm not drinking because you brought me to this water." Herein lies the problem for humans—to look and know that one is being led to or shown the best place to drink the water, but to employ a feeling of callous stubbornness to reject it simply because of the person who led them to the water.

Having written all of that, my point is that every great thing that was ever said to me was not necessarily, and this is a word I made up, "drinkdeded." I think it is all right and very fair to make up and use one's own words. My reasoning for this is having listened to the speech of the president of the United States several days ago. The president used a word that I'm quite sure does not exist.

Some people said, "OK, we know what he means," because he used the correct word, "underestimate," twice in the same speech. For example, the enemy "underestimated" us. I think it was the third time after using this word, the president said, "misunderestimate"; my wife and I both ran to our American dictionary and an Oxford dictionary just in case our English is too hip for the *English* English and we found that even the king had never used the word. So somewhere along the line, I feel justified in using the word "drinkdeded." I still think it is all right for the president to say "misunderestimate," because we still have not gone through the United States of America to clear people of their use of the word "irregardless." I feel if people want to say "irregardless," they should put the prefix "dis" in front, so that the negatives will cancel each other out and we can get back to "regardless." However, I am wandering.

There was a time in the 1940s when teachers in the state of Pennsylvania had to get permission from parents to strike a child. That was a law. Not only did my mother sign the doctrine for my fourth-, fifth- and sixth-grade teachers, but she also cut the stick and put my name on it before she gave it to each teacher. However, there were rules. There was only one area my mother allowed the teachers to strike me and that area is called the buttocks or, in those days, the behind. There were no conditions on the number of times I could be struck and my mother requested that it not be a public striking. So I was brought into a room then called the "cloakroom," which always confused me because I never wore a cloak. Later, I learned that room was where topcoats were hung and that was also where I learned firsthand Pavlov's theory. There was always some sort of philosophy and behavioral modification that accompanied the striking of the behind. "Will . . . you . . . do . . . that . . . again? Do . . . you . . . understand . . . why . . . you're . . . being . . . punished?"

They called it punishment and of course there was always an agreement at the end. In a child's mind, something very strange happens. In other words, when told, "You will not chew gum in class anymore" followed by *"whack! whack!"* one will promise not to chew gum in class. The promise, one would have to believe, is made in earnest because one does not want the stick placed on the behind at a rapid rate of speed where two solid objects cannot occupy the same space.

However, it has been known that there are children and grown-ups who have received punishment of the highest degree who would then repeat the act, doing the same thing again. You'll notice that I do not write *exact* same thing, which I find "redumbdant."

Anyway, having said that, I will not end this piece in typical humorous American fashion by saying that I did hear something from my fourth-grade teacher that changed my life. I remember Ms. Sarah McKinney, an African-American woman, saying to me, "You are more important to yourself than you think you are." However, this did not register until twenty years later. So the moral of this story is, to all the teachers, just keep saying it. Maybe, just maybe, it will register. Not now necessarily, but twenty years is good enough; thirty years is good enough but forty years is questionable because you're possibly looking at dementia. The good news is that I never altered what she said. It stuck. Perhaps the enforcement of Ms. McKinney's words interrupted my having fun—and that's me.

Bill Cosby

Katie Couric

Morning Anchor

Ever since I was a little girl, people have called me "smiley"—a ubiquitous half-moon has appeared on my face for as long as I can remember. Not the kind from the Pepsodent commercials . . . mine is big, gummy and slightly lopsided. But more often than not, it is really a true indication of how I am feeling. But when I was just ten years old, that smile got me into some trouble, in an experience that still sticks with me today.

It was a crisp fall morning at Jamestown Elementary School, and as the hall monitor, I had to deliver a message to Mrs. Barton's fourth-grade class. As I walked in the classroom door, the entire room was standing, reciting the Pledge of Allegiance. Everyone turned to look at me, and I will never forget how I felt. With so many pairs of eyes on me, I did the first thing that came to mind: I smiled. Not a happy smile, but a sheepish, embarrassed smile.

Instead of smiling back, everyone in the class just stared. Mrs. Barton looked at me with disgust and said, "Katie, you smile too much."

My embarrassment only deepened with that remark. I had made an honest mistake, and a teacher responded with an unkind observation that felt like an uncalled-for personal attack.

My unease stuck with me all afternoon, and I went home still smarting from the incident. "I can't help the way I smile," I told my father later that night, after bending his ear with the details of the story. "What should I do?"

My father is an intelligent man, a journalist himself by trade, and the kind of guy who encouraged his kids to come to the dinner table every night with a new vocabulary word. He knew more than a few things about the power of words, and he was quick to respond to my dilemma.

"Just use her words to your advantage," he said, explaining that it isn't the words themselves that hurt us, but instead the way we react to them.

I thought about this idea for a while, and before I knew it, I was able to put my dad's advice into action. As it so happened, at the time I was running for Jamestown's student council presidency, and I was in the process of writing my speech. My dad, who helped all his children with their various campaigns, suggested these opening lines:

"Hello, my name is Katie Couric. People wonder why I am always smiling. It's because I am happy. Happy to go to such a wonderful school. Yes, Jamestown is a wonderful school and I'd like to keep it that way."

While President Bush may not be calling me or my dad to write his next state of the union address, it was just what the doctor ordered. I won the election by a lucky thirteen votes.

My father's words have come back to help me time and again throughout my life. When I first began to look for work in television, the president of CNN, seeing me on the screen for the first time, called the assignment desk and said, "I never want to see her on the air again." Relying on my father's theory that even the most critical words can bring about the most positive results, my boss's bleak forecast of my future only fueled my ambition. I'm part of a generation of women who don't take no for an answer, and I was willing to work doubly hard to get where I wanted to go.

My run-in with my boss at CNN (and my subsequent success at NBC) serves not so much as an "I told you so" story, but instead as proof that determination and grit can get you past even the most ardent naysayers. (Okay, fine—so maybe I do enjoy a bit of the "I told you so," too.)

I often think of the naysayers I have met along the way, and whenever I give young people advice, I implore them not to take critics and their negativity to heart. There are many people who will try to stand in your way, even cut you off at the knees for whatever reason, but it is often more about them than about you. Learning this early on helped me believe in myself, even when some of those around me did not.

And by the way, I'm still smiling.

Katie Couric

Cindy Crawford

Actress and Model

I was eight when my two-year-old brother, Jeff, was diagnosed with leukemia. My parents had noticed that he was getting bruised from the slightest touch so our family doctor sent him to a specialist in Chicago. There he was diagnosed with acute lymphocytic leukemia, which was pretty much incurable at the time. It really wasn't a matter of whether he would live but for how long. I don't think my parents ever sat down and explained that to the rest of us but somehow we picked up on it.

For the next two years, our family's life was filled with hospitals and doctors and Jeff's health. He was undergoing chemotherapy and radiation so he had a lot of bad days, but there were some good days in there as well. Although the severity of his condition wasn't discussed, my sisters and I knew something was seriously wrong. In retrospect, I remember feeling not so much that we weren't allowed to be bad or give my parents trouble, but somehow we just knew we couldn't put one more thing on their plate.

The day Jeff died we had spent the night at my grandparents' house. I remember seeing my parents come over early in the morning and they didn't have my brother with them. They didn't have to say anything. I knew. Being surrounded by family members got us through that day. There was a lap for every kid and we cried in each one of them. The day of the funeral was a blur.

Coping with the loss of a child is always tragic. Somewhere during the course of those difficult days my mother said to me, "Who are we to say that his life was not full?" I understood my mother was drawing on her faith and spirituality to help grieve the loss of her son. She believes we are all born on this earth to do something, and when we have finished what we were put here to do, we will be with Jesus. And in his four short years, Jeff must have done it already.

Jeff had a very direct relationship with God even as a three-year-old. I remember my uncle was sick and my mother and Jeff were saying their prayers as she put him to bed. My mother said, "Jeff, let's pray for Uncle Orville." My brother looked at my mom and said, "Mom, I've already talked to Jesus about him." I witnessed his faith and saw how accessible he felt God was. You didn't have to say the right words in the right order. God loved each of us and would take care of us.

The way I've come to articulate it for myself is that I picture my brother as the booster engine on a rocket that falls off once it reaches the sky. I see Jeff as a booster engine for my life. His strength and spirituality empowered me in so many ways. I do believe there is a plan for each of us and I know that Jeff *really* lived. The quality and fullness of our lives is not measured in length, but in the love and examples we leave those we have left behind.

Walter Cronkite

News Anchor

Ibecame interested in journalism when I was just a kid. I used to read a magazine called *American Boy,* which, among other things, ran a monthly novelette about various professions. The idea was to give boys some sense of what the outside world was like, and what they might find interesting. One month, the featured vocation was that of a foreign correspondent, and boy, I took to it, deciding then and there that this is what I wanted to do with my life.

But it wasn't until I met Fred Birney that I got the opportunity to exercise those dreams.

Fred was a newspaperman from Texas, a dedicated guy who worked as the city editor for one of the daily papers in Houston. When I was about fourteen years old, Fred talked our local Board of Education into permitting him to teach one hour of journalism per week, on a volunteer basis, at each of the five area high schools.

Because only twelve or fifteen students attended, Fred was able to give each of us personal attention. We all worked on the school paper, *The Campus Cub,* and sometimes Fred would take us off-site on special trips. He took us to the printing plant where *The Cub* was made. We saw the Teletype machines and rotary presses; we watched the paper roll off the press, its ink still wet, the wonderful smell of newsprint in the air.

It was during one of these regular visits by Fred that he imparted a bit of wisdom that has stuck with me for more than seventy years. I had been working on a story for *The Cub* about our school's track coach, Cap Harding, who was also the teacher-sponsor of the ROTC. Cap specialized in training students for the high hurdles, and because I was trying to become a hurdler myself, I figured I could curry favor with Cap if I wrote a piece about him that was, let's say, more entertaining than it was journalistic. In other words, I did a puff piece on Cap Harding.

Fred read the story and instantly recognized that I'd done a slapdash job on it. He called me into a borrowed classroom—he didn't have an office because he was in the school only a few hours a week—and asked me to sit down. This wasn't out of the ordinary: Fred picked favorites, and I was one of them. He knew that I was dedicated to being a journalist, that this wasn't some extracurricular course that I had stumbled into. For my part, I hung on Fred's every word. I looked up to him enormously, imbuing him with all the attributes of a great professor, even though he was, in fact, just a solid newspaper guy.

Fred reread the piece quietly to himself, then looked up at me and casually tossed the manuscript back across the desk.

"Cronkite," he said without hesitation, "this is a *terrible* piece. Simply terrible. You didn't ask him the right questions; you didn't tell his whole story. You didn't find out what this man is all about."

As Fred spoke, I felt myself sinking deeper into my chair. That's when he said the words I'll never forget:

"Just remember something, Cronkite. If anything's worth doing, it's worth doing well."

Although I felt a bit shaken by Fred Birney's words, I immediately understood what he was telling me. I wasn't a scholar by any means, but even as a young man I appreciated the value of good advice, particularly when it came to journalism.

"Well, he couldn't be that mad at me if he's suggesting ways I could do better," I consoled myself as I gathered up my manuscript and headed for the door.

Naturally, I rewrote the piece—this time to Fred's satisfaction—and continued working on *The Campus Cub,* ultimately moving my way up to editor. Fred then got me a job as a copyboy on *The Houston Post,* where I occasionally got to write stories no one else wanted to cover—Kiwanis meetings, business luncheons, that sort of thing. When I went off to college in Austin, *The Post* gave me a job as the paper's campus correspondent, paying me fifteen cents an inch for every article. Then I moved to *The Daily Texan,* which doubled as the university journal and the city paper. Each new job fueled my journalistic ambitions further. (Although I must confess, for a moment I also entertained the idea of becoming a mining engineer, but I was dissuaded from that after flunking first-year physics. I figured that if I couldn't understand how a pulley works, I probably shouldn't go down into a mine.)

But throughout it all—with each new assignment, each new job—Fred Birney's advice stuck with me.

Case in point: My first full-time job on a newspaper was with *The Houston Press.* During my cub year, one of my chores was the church beat, with a feature story every Saturday. One week, I was covering a small laboring community on the outskirts of Houston that had fallen on hard times but had worked its way out. A local Pentecostal minister preached from the pulpit the words "community involvement"—in organizing, housing, and policing—until the town was so excited and energized that it acquired public works funding and virtually turned itself around. In effect, the minister had saved this little neighborhood.

But when I wrote up the story, I emphasized the poverty of the area, and the crime that had befallen it prior to the minister's arrival. As I was polishing my final rewrite on that Friday afternoon, all ready to submit the story for the next day's paper, I decided to give it one more read. Only then did it dawn on me that by focusing on the wrong things, I had made these people out to be losers—when, in fact, they were winners. They had coalesced around this minister and brought themselves back to life. This remarkable achievement was the real story, and I had missed it entirely.

That's when Fred Birney's words came back to me yet again. The story was worth doing, I knew, so why not do it well?

I did a lot of rewriting that afternoon and got the story to my editor just in time to make the deadline for Saturday's paper.

Fred Birney died not long after the time we spent with him, and I never got a chance to thank him personally for inspiring me. But it goes without saying that I've called on his words countless times over the course of my long career.

Fred's credo applies to everything in life, of course. Just the other morning I was shaving in my bathroom, and when I felt my cheek, I noticed that I had missed a spot. My first inclination was to put the razor down and say to myself, "Oh, to hell with it—I'm not going anywhere today, anyway." But then Fred's voice came back again, just like it was yesterday: "Wait a minute, Cronkite—if it's worth doing, it's worth doing well. Go back and shave that spot!"

Walter Cronkite

Cameron Crowe

Director

It was the winter of 1968 when my fifteen-year-old sister decided she wanted to have a weekend getaway with her boyfriend. The plan was to go up to Idyllwild for a few days of snow and possible romance and bring me, her ten-year-old brother, as a sort of chaperone. Our parents didn't like the idea. In fact, they grounded us for even suggesting something so creative, and that's how we ended up spending a Friday night imprisoned in our bedrooms while my mother held one of her study groups upstairs.

My mom was a teacher at San Diego City College from the late 1960s to 1993. She taught self-designed courses in psychology, speech arts, and philosophy and regularly held study groups in our small, book-stuffed two-story condo. That particular Friday, I sat in my bedroom, sulky and glum, and listened to my mother and her students talking in the living room above me.

About halfway through the study session, one of the students appeared in my bedroom doorway. She had navigated the narrow stairway and stacks of books in search of a bathroom, but, instead, found me. She looked like a vision of early beatnik style in her over-sized glasses; big, maroon sweater; and her long, brown hair. She was cool—a beautiful egghead.

"Well, hello," she said, curiously.

"Hi," I replied, and the sounds of life brought my sister from her room next door.

"Bummer to be here on a Friday night," my sister said, "isn't it?"

The young woman shook her head, her Joan Baez hair flowing, her eyes earnest and wide behind her giant glasses. "We're here by choice," she said. "We wanted to come and talk and hang out." My sister and I looked at each other in utter confusion, waiting for her to reveal the joke. "Your mom is really cool," the girl offered excitedly. "She's the best teacher I've ever had. I wish she was *my* mother."

We were aghast and fascinated. It's striking to hear someone that cool finding greater cool in your own mother. Cool? *Mom?*

In that blinding moment, I knew that we had to give our mom a chance. Hearing this student made me realize that my mom was also a person in the world. She was a valuable teacher, and I decided that I would try to listen, not just as a kid but as a person too.

I knew my sister still had her journey to go on before she would be ready. She would one day follow too. From that moment on, sometimes reluctantly, I listened to my mother. Her basic message was to value humanity with good humor and live up to yourself in the world. And always, she dispensed most of her wisdom in the form of painstakingly culled quotes.

She could read volumes of dense philosophy and distill the essence into two or three electrifying sentences. Even now she has quotes for every situation. When I'm facing a particularly rough time, I'll often hear the buzz of a fax coming in. Inevitably, it's a fax from my mother with some words or thoughts about strength and positivity. She's on constant spiritual alert for her kids.

Now I'm a parent with two-year-old twin boys, and I often think about what great parenting really means. I think it requires more than just love and support. All parents have a responsibility to teach and inspire their children, and all kids have a responsibility to let their parents teach, and to be a good listener. There's nothing more important or, dare I say it . . . cooler.

For more than forty years, my mother has been an amazing parent and an on-duty teacher. In November 2001, March of Dimes named her one of the mothers of the year. She deserves it. Here are a few of her greatest hits:

Alice Crowe's Top Five Favorite Quotes

In the depth of winter, I finally learned that within me there lay an invincible summer.

—Camus

Wherever there is a human being, there is an opportunity for kindness.

—Seneca

I am not full of virtues and noble qualities. I love. That is all. But I love strongly, exclusively, and steadfastly.

—George Sand

Become the most positive and enthusiastic person you know.

—H. Jackson Brown Jr.

Ten percent is what life brings to you. Ninety percent is what you do about it.

—Alice Crowe

Cameron Crowe

Billy Crystal

Comedian

I was just starting out as a comedian. I'd been in an improv group called Three's Company for four years, on the coffeehouse circuit, traveling to colleges, staying for three or four days, doing several shows a night. We did sketch stuff, improvs with the audience. I think of it as my vaudeville.

Though I was learning a lot and doing what I wanted to do, I knew it was time to move on. I was twenty-seven years old, with a child, and the only real money I was making came from my work as a substitute teacher. As a comedian, I was frustrated because I knew I was hiding behind the other two guys in the group.

So in 1974, I got up the nerve to head out on my own. I threw together a hunk of stuff. Imitations of Muhammad Ali and Howard Cosell. Mr. Rogers doing a striptease. Spoofs of commercials. These were conceptual pieces—very effective, very funny.

Once I got the act together, I tried it out at Catch a Rising Star, which at the time was a kind of gymnasium for comics to work out their material. A wonderful group of new comedians was starting out then—Jay Leno, Richard Lewis, Richard Belzer, Freddie Prinze. As the new kid on the scene, I was giddy. I was hot as a pistol. I'd come onstage, go into these bits, and by the time I finished, the audience was screaming. I was killin' 'em.

Along the way, I'd caught the attention of the best manager for comedians in the business—Buddy Morra, who worked with Jack Rollins and Charlie Joffe. Rollins in particular was, taste-wise, the most respected man in the industry. This was the fellow who said to Woody Allen, "You should not only write, you should perform." He practically forced Woody onstage at little clubs in the Village and went on to produce his movies. I knew if I could get Rollins to see me perform—and like me—I was set.

Finally, Jack came in one night to watch me work. I went up onstage and saw him settle in at the back. He's a very interesting-looking man—like a slightly unkempt Brooklyn College law professor. Duke Ellington's eyes, aristocratic. He looks less like a comic's manager than a guy who would lecture on Chaucer.

So I did my twenty-five minutes; the crowd went crazy. Afterward I headed straight out to Rollins. We made small talk, and then he said, "Let's grab a bite." We headed next door to a coffee shop and sat down. All that time I was expecting him to say, "I'm giving up Woody. Now that I've seen you, there is no one else for me to handle. I want to spend all my time working for you."

Instead, he started with a question. "So how did you feel about your performance tonight?"

"Great!" I said. "I felt hot from beginning to end."

He stared at me.

"What did you think?" I asked hesitantly.

"Effective?" he said. "Yes. Good? I don't think so."

I was astounded. I couldn't even get my fork near my mouth. I was shocked and surprised and hurt and trying like hell not to reach across the table and choke him.

Then, very gently, Rollins said: "Let me explain. You got up onstage tonight and made the audience laugh—and don't get me wrong, these were big laughs. You did wonderful impressions. You entertained. But never once did you say how *you* felt about anything. You never gave your point of view."

I was silent.

"Listen," he continued, "I already know how Muhammad Ali feels about things. But as good as your imitation is, there wasn't one inch of you in that show. You didn't leave a tip."

"I didn't what?"

"You didn't leave a tip. You didn't leave a little something on the table that the audience will remember you by."

I still didn't understand.

Jack leaned forward. "Look, these people tonight, they saw razzle-dazzle," he said. "They saw fireworks. They saw toys and games. But when they left, I guarantee you they didn't remember your name or anything you said. Why? Because you didn't take risks. A comic's job is to take risks, and you're playing it too safe. Throw everything out and start from scratch. Get up there and just talk. Read the paper. Tell us what you think. Tell us what you feel.

"And most important," he said, "don't be afraid to bomb. Leave that tip."

Needless to say, I was dumbfounded. I lived about an hour outside of Manhattan, and on the drive home I played the tape of my performance over and over. I was angry and confused, but at the same time I wanted to understand what Jack meant.

Oddly enough, those words started to sink in the next night. I walked onstage and gave Rollins's idea a try. I didn't do very well. But ultimately, this singular piece of advice vaulted me into a whole different state of mind. I began to change the way I looked at the world, my thought process, my writing, the way I valued my time onstage. That's when I began to let my work get personal. That's when I began taking chances. That's when I became a comedian.

Now if I meet one person on the street who says, "Your work meant something to me"—that comment makes the work worthwhile. It means that I left a tip, and those people's gratitude is the tip I wind up getting back.

Billy Crystal

Ellen DeGeneres

Actress and Comedienne

As a young girl I didn't know I was gay. I was boy crazy. I look back now and realize how much I liked girls and identified with guys when they talked about having a crush on girls, but I never experimented back then.

When I finally told my parents I was gay, I was lucky they didn't throw me out of the house or disown me because that sort of stuff happened to lots of kids. A lot of boys' fathers beat them up. It's horrible.

I told my mother that I was gay when we were walking down the beach in Mississippi when I was twenty-one. She initially didn't understand my homosexuality and was in shock. But she went to a library and started reading about the topic and ended up writing books to help other parents deal with their own kids being gay. My father didn't say anything when I told him, but no one in my family turned against me.

Even though my family knew I was gay, I did not come out to a wider circle, particularly not professionally, for a long time. In fact, I was terrified people would find out. The first fifteen years of my career I was doing stand-up. I *had* to hide this big part of who I was, because I was doing my routine in bars with a lot of drunk people, following guys who did antigay jokes. My goal was to win the crowd over in the first few minutes, and if they knew I was gay, I wouldn't have a chance. I was conditioned to understand that being gay was not accepted. So I always pretended to be straight.

But it got more and more uncomfortable. It got to a point where I realized that there is something wrong if you're always thinking you're supposed to live your life to fit into some type of popular consensus. Most people live their lives like that. They dress a certain way because it's acceptable; they act a particular way because they've been conditioned and domesticated. They've been taught by reward and punishment what's going to be tolerated and what is not. But I finally realized that this is my one and only life. It's my obligation to be true to my soul, my being. So I had to clear a space from all society's rules and admit who I was.

In 1995, I was doing *Ellen,* and my manager gave me a present of a weeklong seminar at Esalen Institute, in Big Sur. The topic of the seminar was "Changing the Dialogue of Your Inner Subconscious." He went along too. I didn't think I would last a day, much less the entire week on this hippie, spiritual retreat, but I was wrong.

There were fifteen strangers from all over the country. The instructors convinced us to open up and listen to ourselves. There were three classes a day, three hours each, for seven days. There we talked and meditated. Everybody seemed so normal when we first met; they would say what they did for a living, whether they were married or not. By day three, we were all so broken down; I was listening to people's stories thinking, *God, they're so screwed up.*

Then it was my turn. I was afraid through my whole life that people would find out that I was gay. Even in this seminar, I was paranoid that all these strangers would go back to their jobs in Michigan or wherever and say to somebody, "By the way, did you know Ellen DeGeneres is gay?" It was a huge fear of mine.

But I stood up. I said the words that I was most terrified to say throughout my whole life. "I'm gay," I admitted, "and I'm afraid for people to know I am." I started crying. Those words changed my life.

What came out of that seminar for all of us was that whatever you tell yourself, your body—your every cell—is listening to you, whether your inner monologue says "I'm fat," or "I'm stupid," or whatever the words are. My monologue was constant—don't let people know you're gay or they won't like you. Once I spoke that truth at the seminar, I couldn't live the false version of myself anymore.

Everyone I knew said, okay, that's fine to come out at the seminar and to your friends, but whatever you do, don't come out publicly. Nobody on television was out. Some of my friends were—Melissa Etheridge, k. d. lang—but they were singers. It's okay to be gay if you sell a few million records, but not if you're in a few million living rooms on television. At that time, to keep a show on the air you needed to get 20 million viewers every single week, and everyone worried that if I admitted I was gay, viewers would start changing the channel.

Everyone warned me not to come out, except, oddly enough, my manager, who supported me completely. We decided together to use my character to educate people in a creative way. What did it matter if I said I am gay offscreen? To say it onscreen would be a great opportunity to show the process of when someone starts to realize she's gay, then comes out, then deals with it.

Coming out on the show proved to be a huge success: We had 46 million viewers. People held parties around the country to watch.

It became a cultural event. My heart felt good. Many people have told me that they came out after watching that show with their parents.

But on a personal level, it was brutal. I had been in therapy and one of the things I talked about before I made this very public announcement was that I had a huge fear of being killed if I came out. Then, horrifically, I got death threats. Jerry Falwell called me Ellen DeGenerate. People boycotted the show and Disney, the parent company of my network. Coming out was like having an open wound and instead of people being tender, they threw salt on it or poked at it.

I eventually lost the show but, more important, I lost a lot of fans. People really changed their minds about me. It didn't help that I met someone at the time who encouraged behavior in me that would not have happened had I met someone else. I often wonder, as in *It's a Wonderful Life,* where my life would have gone if I hadn't met her that night. I don't regret it, because history will show that there was an openly gay couple that walked down the red carpet holding hands. It was an important visual symbol, but there was a price that I paid.

It makes people really uncomfortable when someone is honest. It intimidates people that I don't have anything to worry about now. My ratings diminished and are starting to pick up only now, after five years. What I did in coming out became bigger than my career, bigger than my talent, bigger than whether I'm funny or not. Everything that I had worked for over fifteen years was pushed aside, and I became an unintended icon.

To be honest, I'm glad I didn't know then how everything would play out, because as freeing and as amazing as the experience of saying those words has been, it has also caused a lot of pain. I'm a sensitive person, and the sadness from years of feeling bad about myself is only just starting to balance out by—now, finally—feeling really, really good about who I am.

Barry Diller

Businessman

I grew up in a completely unstructured, antiauthoritarian environment in Beverly Hills. My father was in the real estate business, and my mother quite naturally did nothing—quite happily. Our economic circumstances allowed me to feel that I was born lucky. I had an active life and a lot of friends, and a lot of them, like me, never did anything. Most of my friends went on to college but I didn't because I was so unstimulated by the whole schooling process. My family took this teenage sloth and lack of direction to the conclusion that I'd just never go to work in any organizational structure. Then, when I was nineteen, from a heretofore unknown reservoir of ambition came the idea that I was really interested in the entertainment business and wanted a real go at it.

My curiosity was always buried there, but I didn't contemplate issues of the future. For my entire career, I have never thought about futures as such. I've never thought, *This is what I want to be when*. . . . I've had no such imagery fantasy, and actually I've always mistrusted people in the entertainment business who come to see me when they're nineteen or twenty-two or twenty-seven and say, "I want to run a studio." I just look at them and smile at the foolishness of it. In my own life, I never had any kind of clarified ambition. My interest in entertainment was always there, rolling around under the surface, submerged until that one day when somehow I got energized.

I was friends with Marlo Thomas and her sister, Terre. I spent endless amounts of time with their family. When I decided to learn about the entertainment business I called their father, Danny Thomas, who was at the Sands Hotel in Las Vegas, and I said, "Would you do me this favor?" And he said, "Of course." He called the William Morris Agency, and they interviewed and then hired me to work in the mail room. Very quickly I came under the influence of Phil Weltman, who was a senior agent there. He was the first person of any authority who I ever listened to in my life. Not that he said anything remarkable, but what was remarkable were his standards, his values, and his decency. Having someone in your life who is in authority take a stern interest in your development at almost any early age is great good luck.

William Morris was like a rigid church, and Phil Weltman was quite authoritarian. He was the epitome of the drill sergeant with the secret, mush heart of gold. He made me aware that there were values and qualities in business relationships, that there was so much to be learned from organization and hierarchy.

There are lessons about all sorts of things that come if you are lucky enough to find somebody who is not only desirous of teaching you, but is somebody that you are open enough to listen to what they're telling you. And if you're really lucky—and I've been shockingly lucky in my life—at an early and totally impressionable age you get somebody like Phil Weltman to be your first light. He was the seminal business experience in my life, because he laid down, as the strongest law, a mode of behavior that is consistently ethical.

There were no particular "right words"; it was more his qualities—his values and stern decency—that meant so much to me.

As I started to meet people in my late teens and twenties, there was no one who ever said to me, "You're great, kid." Phil Weltman was the first person who actually confirmed any emerging sense of self that I had. Never directly, but indirectly, in the most powerful way. He was my first confirmation that there *was* any self.

Leaving William Morris was like graduating for me. I grew up, thanks partly to him. I went to ABC, then to Paramount, then to Fox, and I always stayed in contact with him. Not necessarily with great frequency, but he was wondrously proud. Of me, and so many others he influenced.

There were certainly others who have felt about Mr. Weltman the way I do (there's a plaque on a wall at CAA dedicated to him). Because I've had a noisy career, and because he was a father figure to me, I know how sustaining my accomplishments were for him and how much real pleasure he took in that during the last period of his life.

So I guess my right words come from me—"thanks, Mr. Weltman."

Dr. Peter Doherty

Nobel Laureate in Medicine, St. Jude Children's Research Hospital

As a boy in the suburbs of Brisbane, Australia, I often found myself, not on a sunny rugby field or out in the bush, but sitting happily before an open book. This was due, in part, to my fair Irish skin as well as my father's emphasis on the value of education. About this time I discovered the works of Sartre, Hemingway, Shakespeare, and others. I recall that it was Shakespeare's *Hamlet* that served up a bit of wisdom that has carried me through the years. Among the advice that Polonius gave his son Laertes on the eve of his journey was:

> This above all: to thine own self be true,
> And it must follow, as the night the day,
> Thou canst not then be false to any man.

Say what you will about Polonius and his son—they are both complex and dubious characters—but the profound utility of the statement is undeniable: Believe in yourself, above all else. It's good counsel for not just any journey, but the journey that is life.

My own journey has taken me around the world several times. I received a scholarship in veterinary sciences at the University of Queensland that required me to work for several years after graduation for the Queensland Department of Agriculture and Stock. I traveled to Edinburgh, Scotland, for a Ph.D. in immunology. In 1972 I returned to Australia to work as a research fellow at the John Curtin School of Medical Research in Canberra. It was here that Rolf M. Zinkernagel and I did the work for which we would, twenty-three years later, be awarded the Nobel Prize in 1996. By the time I moved to the United States in 1975 to accept a position at the Wistar Institute at the University of Pennsylvania I felt at the top of my game, writing grants, working with outstanding graduate students—basically I was an established scientist and academic.

I was so confident that I decided to return to Canberra to attempt to revive the once vibrant research environment there. It was disastrous. For six years I struggled to bring together all the pieces, but in the end I had to admit to myself that Canberra's golden era had passed. So in 1988 I took a position as chairman of the Department of Immunology at St. Jude Children's Research Hospital in Memphis, Tennessee, where I have been for the last thirteen years. There's no place like St. Jude for a scientist. There is a terrific atmosphere in the highly interactive clinical and basic science programs, and the tremendous levels of funding make it all possible for me to do my research without interruption.

Establishing and running a successful research lab is a complex and difficult, but challenging, task. The decision to leave Canberra and move halfway around the world again to Memphis was not easy, but the alternative would likely have been a life dominated by mediocrity and failure. You have to believe in yourself to make such choices. A well-known Frank Sinatra song from the 1960s pretty much describes what it takes:

Now nothing's impossible, I've found, for when my
     chin is on the ground,
I pick myself up, dust myself off, and start all over
     again.
Don't lose your confidence if you slip, be grateful for a
     pleasant trip,
And pick yourself up, dust off, start over again.
Work like a soul inspired until the battle of the day is
     won.
You may be sick and tired, but you be a man, my son.
Will you remember the famous men who have to fall
     to rise again,
So take a deep breath, pick yourself up, start all over
     again.

This catchy tune has stayed in my head over the years, and I came to realize that the song bore strange resonance with not just my career, but all of science. In scientific research, the public hears only of the grand accomplishments, the newsworthy discoveries. Untold years of toil, dead ends, wild goose chases, and erratic funding all pock the road to great scientific achievements. You have to have confidence in yourself. You have to be willing to get up when you're knocked down. Success in scientific research is built upon failure. If you don't fail, you aren't trying to do anything new. In fact, the scientific method requires that you struggle exhaustively to disprove, or falsify, your best ideas. You actually try, again and again, to find the possible flaw in your hypothesis. Sometimes the consequences are disastrous, disproving weeks or months of work. We scientists are rather accustomed to falling flat on our faces!

The course of science and understanding depends on getting up from where failure has left us. The quest for knowledge is endless and we must be tireless if we hope to improve our lives and world. If we allow setbacks and failures to stop us in our tracks then we have already lost. To our own selves we must be true, to our passions and curiosities. And it must follow, as the night the day, that mankind will benefit.

Phil Donahue

Talk Show Host

Five years after graduating from college I found myself on the side of a mountain in West Virginia peeing behind a railroad boxcar. A mine collapse had trapped thirty-eight men underground, and I was on the scene with my cameraman Andy Cassells as a reporter for my employer, WHIO radio and TV, in Dayton, Ohio.

I was also offering radio reports for CBS News. One phone call to New York had deputized me as a stringer for The Tiffany Network, the most respected enterprise in broadcast journalism, home to Murrow, Friendly, and Cronkite. I was twenty-seven years old and playing with the big boys. I was reporting for a *national* network. Okay, it was only radio, but by God, it was *CBS*.

I phoned my nightly reports to both New York and Dayton on the tragedy unfolding in the snows of Holden, West Virginia. Anxious family members gathered at the entrance to the doomed mine. Prayers were offered as the snow fell all day and night, covering the Salvation Army coffee station and the phone booth set up for the media.

Each night, I called CBS Radio and offered my report to Blair Clark and *The World Tonight,* an 8:00 P.M. weekday program carried by the whole network. "Miners are a tough breed . . . ," I reported earnestly. I listened to my own voice and imagined it soaring across

America's heartland; Phil Donahue's voice in farmhouses, urban high-rises, and taverns throughout the Western Hemisphere, all over the free world, and most important, flowing into my parents' radio in hometown Cleveland. Me and Blair Clark.

For three days, Cassells and I survived on Salvation Army donuts, taking turns warming the camera. Then my shot at the television network suddenly materialized.

As miners took their break from the rescue effort in the depths of the shaft, they gathered around an old barrel filled with burning scrap wood. The flames shot above the rim, embers flying off through the snowflakes and the heat and smoke, rising like the prayer of a thirty-something preacher who spoke without notes.

"Dear God, we ask your blessing at this troubled time. . . ."

The preacher was surrounded by the sooty faces of miners whose lamp-caps framed workingmen's features. What followed was the most beautiful and moving drama I had ever seen:

". . . In your name and for your sake we offer this prayer. . . ."
As he preached, the miners began to sing:

> What a friend we have in Jesus,
> All our sins and grief to bear,
> What a privilege to carry
> Everything to God in prayer.

"Bless us, Lord, hold us in your arms . . . ," he said.

The most profoundly beautiful and inspiring reality TV was taking place before my eyes. It was all right there: The rock-of-ages faith of mountain folk, the fearful eyes of the women and children, the snow falling from heaven, and a Protestant hymn I never heard sung at mass. A hymn that made its way straight to my heart, sacred music I can sing from memory to this day. I was already producing this fabulous film feature in my mind. Our camera would pan from face to face revealing a very private moment in an Appalachian winter. Here was one story that would make it on the television news schedule of CBS, a riveting look at the truth of the coal miner's life. I was going to appear on the CBS Television Network! Murrow, Friendly, Cronkite, *Donahue*.

Then the panic set in. Our camera made a grinding sound; the oil had thickened in the freezing temperatures. I stood helplessly as this most spiritual moment ended.

". . . In your name and for your glory, Amen."

No film, no feature, no world fame. We moved the camera closer to the barrel of flames, stroked it like an infant, and offered our own prayer for its recovery. When it finally did, I made my move.

"Reverend," I began reverently. "I'm Phil Donahue from CBS News. We had some camera problems and were not able to record your wonderful prayer. Our equipment is ready now; may I ask you to repeat that prayer and I will ask the miners to sing again."

The preacher looked troubled. "But I have already prayed, son," he said.

"Reverend, I am from *CEE BEE ESS NEWS*," the emphasis impressed me greatly.

"I have already prayed," the reverend repeated. "It wouldn't be right to pray again. Wouldn't be honest."

I couldn't believe what I was hearing. Would not pray? C'mon. I had witnessed many retakes for the Lord; at plane crashes and all manner of mayhem, ministers and monsignors threw holy water a second time for the news crew that arrived late to the scene. What was the problem with this guy?

"Reverend," (never give up) "Your prayer will appear on more than two hundred television stations of CBS News. Millions of people will see and hear your prayer and join you in petitioning God's help for these trapped miners. You will be seen by millions of viewers throughout the free world, demonstrating the deep religious faith of West Virginians and reminding viewers everywhere that God is good." I was begging shamelessly, no level to which I would not stoop for the ambitious purpose of getting on national television.

"No," he said, "it wouldn't be right. I have already prayed to my God." Then he turned and walked away, leaving CBS News standing in the snow in the ruin of total defeat.

I closed the door of the phone booth, dropped the dime in the slot, identified myself for the collect call, and waited. My teeth were clenched, the phone clutched so tightly my knuckles were turning color. When the assignment editor accepted the call I got right to the point:

"The son of a bitch won't pray."

I had finally come to grips with my own reality: Phil Donahue was *not* going to appear on his parents' TV, nor in any taverns, nor be seen by millions of viewers throughout the free world.

Why the dawn came slowly to me I cannot explain. It was months before it hit me: That preacher demonstrated more moral courage than I had ever seen in my lifetime. In a world of posturing and religious pomp, here was a man of God who refused to perform for television. His prayer had already been offered, and repeating it would have been phony. "It wouldn't be right," he said resolutely.

I have thought about that preacher many times since. If he doesn't go to heaven, nobody is going. No matter my pleadings, he would not do "take two" for Jesus. Not for me, not for all those taverns, not for "millions of people throughout the free world."

Not even, praise the Lord, for CEE BEE ESS NEWS.

Michael Eisner

President and CEO of the Walt Disney Company

Three weeks in the wilderness.

Three weeks in the wilderness with prospects of seeing absolutely nobody other than seven other boys and two staff men. Three weeks in the wilderness carrying food in "wanigans," pitching tents, paddling on and on through seeming unending lakes in Algonquin, Canada. Carrying canoes over three-mile portages and carrying myself as the youngest boy at age fifteen. The senior wilderness trip . . .

AND NO PROSPECT FOR GETTING OUT OF IT! Only two days were left, two days before I would climb onto a truck with seven much older boys (nine months older at least!), towing five canoes, hundreds of pounds of supplies and shovels and bumwad and elephant bumwad (toilet paper and paper towels to the layman) and dehydrated stuff and first-aid kits, transporting all this equipment twelve hours from Vermont to Canada. Two days to go . . . and now I had fear and stomachaches and dizziness and thinking: HOW DO I GET OUT OF IT? Maybe faking getting sick (but I really did feel sick) and hiding those feelings and becoming quiet and sitting at the lake to plot a phone call to suggest to a parent that . . .

But I couldn't think clearly what to suggest.

I was fifteen years old at a wilderness camp on Lake Dunmore in Vermont, preparing to go on the most cherished trip the camp had to offer. I had begged and pleaded to go on the trip. I could think of no higher honor, no greater status than to be among the select few who would be picked. Then I was picked.

And I became petrified. I had nobody to tell because all the other boys were obviously excited as they packed the food and the canoe paddles and their duffel bags and their gear. I was silent. I was scared. I was too old to be homesick. That was for the little kids. I was trapped, and the more trapped I felt, the more I panicked and the more my thinking failed me . . . a fog set in . . . and I got quiet.

I was in a fog of confusion for good reason. I had wanted so badly to be picked for the trip because it signaled that my adult heroes, those who could chop wood and pole down a river and read the stars, thought I had leadership ability. When I found out I had made the cut, my lungs pushed against my ribs trying to force out a cheer. Unfortunately, no sound came out because it suddenly dawned on me that I was going to have to display some leadership ability. Sitting by the lake, I went from petrified to paralyzed. I tracked the activities of others. I stared at the island on the other end trying to figure out how to get to a phone in those pre–cell phone days to call my parents. How can I get a fast appendicitis? It would be worth it. Even if they operated I would be safe, safe in Middlebury, Vermont, rather than the wilderness, the far wilderness of Canada in storms and rapids and danger.

The eight boys would be divided into four teams for this trip. At each campsite one team would pitch the tents, one would build the campfire, one would cook the meal and one would "wallop" the dishes. The next day, responsibilities would rotate. My partner, Baird Morgan, was the best boy to have as a partner. He was the strongest, oldest and best stern canoer in the camp. He and I, as a team, were supposed to do our share in getting ready to go. We were assigned to patch the tents. But it's hard to patch tents when one is immobilized.

Brownie, our trip leader, a man at least one hundred years old in my mind but actually more like forty, with a strange hole behind his ear that I was always afraid to look into, came over and sat down. "You know," he began. "I'm always nervous before these big trips."

I stared away from that hole.

"Sometimes I get afraid of things that I build up in my mind," he said.

I looked directly through him. "I sometimes think things are more dangerous than they really are, but then I calm myself down and work through the problem and realize that I'm safe and I'll have a good time. Then I always end up laughing at myself and wonder why I got afraid in the first place."

"Yeah," I responded.

"Funny, isn't it," he said and walked away.

We left for Canada two days later. The trip up in the back of the army surplus truck was windy and disporting. The sightseeing in Quebec City was "cool" but just set the stage for the big act of going into the wilderness. By then, I had butterflies.

But my paralysis had somehow disappeared after my lake talk with Brownie. I didn't know why. I even survived clearheadedly (no hyperventilating) after capsizing while going over a waterfall—a small waterfall that is. A little later, even the butterflies disappeared, as the three weeks of not seeing another person, of shooting rapids and creating campsites, with no parents or siblings became a nonstop adventure of self-reliance, of teamwork . . . yes, of leadership. The only time I sat alone again by the lake was to brush my teeth.

We arrived back at our camp in Vermont to a hero's welcome from one hundred fifty more junior campers. After putting away the tarps from the trip, Brownie came up to me.

"Mike" (people called me Mike in those days), "we had a great trip, don't you think? It's great you were on the team." I now tried to look into that little hole in his head to see if I could fathom what was inside. I looked, but only gleaned my last lesson of that trip: that wisdom can't be seen.

It was nice to hear his praise, but it was what he said before the trip that stayed with me. I can't say that anxiety was removed forever. Dentistry, open-heart surgery or a major commencement address can bring it back. But with a few brief words, Brownie got me to see that everybody gets nervous; everybody is vulnerable; everybody must deal with it. How did he know I had to hear that?

Funny, isn't it.

Daniel Ellsberg

Activist

In the 1960s, I worked as a high-ranking civil servant in the Pentagon working on Vietnam and, after that, at the embassy in Vietnam for two years. Back then, I believed in the Vietnam War—above all, in our not losing it. On coming back from Vietnam in mid-1967, I returned to my pre-Pentagon job at the RAND Corporation, a private think tank that received government contracts. As a consultant from RAND, I took part in a classified Pentagon study of the history of U.S. decision making in Vietnam. I was later authorized access to the entire top-secret study for my research at RAND.

The American war in Vietnam had been going on for four years. There were 475,000 Americans fighting in the country. Tens of thousands had already been killed. In 1968 Americans had voted for Richard Nixon because they thought that as president he'd end the Vietnam War faster than Hubert Humphrey would if he were elected. But I became aware in 1969 from a colleague in the White House that the war wasn't ending and was almost surely going to get bigger. By this point a majority of people viewed the war as immoral. It was hopeless. It was killing people to no end. The question was what should a citizen do about that? I was moving closer to direct opposition.

What can be done? I thought constantly. What can anyone do to shorten a war? That was my preoccupation. In late August 1969, I attended a conference of the War Resisters League at Haverford College. The WRL was started by former conscientious objectors, and Albert Einstein had been the chairman at one point. I was there because I wanted to meet people who were living this life. I had never met a draft resister before. I had been a Marine. I wasn't a pacifist.

One of the people I met, Bob Eaton, was actually going to prison for resisting the draft. I stood vigil for him, rather reluctantly, outside the Philadelphia courthouse while he was sentenced. It was the first time I had publicly announced my position on the war. If I had been seen, it would have jeopardized my position with the government-affiliated think tank. I was nervous about being photographed. I wouldn't even have gone to the vigil except that I was ashamed not to go with the others. But that very act of supporting a draft resister on a downtown street corner liberated me from a great fear, which was the fear of looking absurd. I discovered I wasn't made of sugar after all. That's what civil disobedience does for people; it gives them back their own courage.

I found myself the next day at this international conference listening to a young man named Randy Kehler, who was the head of the War Resisters League in San Francisco. I was taken with what a good impression of America this young man gave. He was very articulate, very sincere in his speech, and very earnest. And I was thinking, *I'm glad the foreigners in this audience are seeing him. What a good example of an American he is, the best we have.* And in the course of his speech he said, "Last month our friend David Harris went to prison [for draft resistance]. Terry and John are gone. Yesterday our friend Bob went to jail." He said, "Soon there will be no men left in the office, only women. And I'm very excited that soon I'll be able to join them."

And he said this very calmly. I hadn't known that he was about to be sentenced for draft resistance. It hit me as a total surprise and shock, because I heard his words in the midst of actually feeling proud of my country listening to him. And then I heard he was going to prison. It wasn't what he said exactly that changed my worldview. It was the example he was setting with his life. How his words in general showed that he was a stellar American, and that he was going to jail as a very deliberate choice—because he thought it was the right thing to do.

There was at this time no question in my mind that my government was involved in an unjust war that was going to continue and get larger. Thousands of young men were dying each year. I left the auditorium and found a deserted men's room. I sat on the floor and cried for over an hour, just sobbing. The only time in my life I've reacted to something like that. And there were words that kept coming through my head. Words that his action had put in my head. The first sentence was, *We are eating our young. We are consuming them whether in the jungles or on the barricades.*

And I thought of a line from a song by Leonard Cohen, "Dress Rehearsal Rag." The line was: "So it's come to this. And wasn't it a long way down. Ah, wasn't it a strange way down."

And I was thinking, *My country has come to this. That the best thing a young man can do is go to prison.*

And then I thought—and these were the words he put into my head, the words that changed my life—*What can I do to help end this war, if I'm ready to go to prison?*

I knew that I was ready to go if need be once I thought of it, because when I had believed in the war, working in the field in Vietnam, I had risked my life many times. And so, it was obvious that if I could risk my body driving the roads of Vietnam when I believed in the war, I could risk my freedom the same way when I didn't, to oppose it. I saw that it was a duty to take risks in civilian life just as we'd expect a soldier to do.

So I knew I was capable. The question was, What can I do given that? And it so happened that I had in my safe seven thousand pages of what came to be known as the Pentagon Papers—forty-seven volumes of top-secret documents. Of lies and violations of treaties and crimes. Ultimately, I gave the newspaper those papers, for which I was put on trial facing twelve felony counts with a possible sentence of 115 years. And, ironically, President Nixon was so afraid that I would release documents on his own secret policy in Vietnam—which unfortunately I didn't have—that he took criminal actions against me, which in the end were crucial in bringing him down and helping to end the war. So it turned out to have a good effect.

I never for a moment thought my releasing those papers would by itself end the war. I just thought giving the people the information of what was really going on might help. And it did.

In the same way, Randy Kehler never thought his going to prison would end the war. If I hadn't met Randy Kehler it wouldn't have occurred to me to copy those papers. His actions spoke to me as no mere words would have done. He put the right question in my mind at the right time.

Daniel Ellsberg

Betty Ford

Former First Lady

For three days in that hot summer of 1974, Richard Nixon went back and forth about whether or not he was going to leave the presidency—whether to depart office willingly, or stay and go through impeachment. My husband had been serving as a nonelected vice president for nine months since Spiro Agnew resigned. In early August, after much anguish and anxiety, my husband Jerry said to me, "You better forget about moving into the vice president's house—it looks as though it's not going to happen."

I knew what that meant. We would not be occupying the vice president's residence because we would enter the White House as President and First Lady. I remember thinking, *Good Lord, this is going to change our lives.* We never expected to be in that position. Not only would Jerry be assuming that demanding office, he would be doing so at a time when the country was in absolute chaos.

There had never been a time in our lives when we so much needed a source of strength beyond ourselves. We would be overwhelmed otherwise. So Jerry reminded me of the fifth and sixth verses of chapter three of the Book of Proverbs, a prayer he learned as a boy, which reads: "Trust in the Lord with all thine heart; and lean not unto thine own understanding. In all thy ways acknowledge Him and He shall direct thy paths." And this became our prayer.

When I was confronted with breast cancer that September of 1974, a month after his swearing in, those words became especially important. With them I was able to release my concerns for the outcome of my surgery (whether I had a mastectomy or a biopsy). Treatment options were so different then. Relying on the strength of my family, I knew all would be manageable at that time. There was still such a stigma associated with breast cancer. It was not discussed, and people held in all their anguish and anxiety. Thank you, Lord, that things have changed.

The Biblical verses were also a great source of strength for me as I underwent alcohol and prescription drug recovery in 1978. It was a difficult time, as you can imagine, but one that ultimately brought me even closer to my family. At first, of course, there was a lot of denial, a lot of soul searching. But that faith, that belief in whom I call "God" sustains me through recovery—an ongoing process.

There are periods in life when we realize more than ever our life is not totally in our control. Being an Episcopalian, I have always looked to God. He is what I believe in. But you don't have to be a religious traditionalist to understand the meaning of a Higher Power. It is a force larger than yourself, greater than your ego. It provides a sense that no matter what happens, you will be okay, that you will ultimately survive any crisis, any horror, any difficult time in your life.

Now, there is one critical lesson I learned early, when I was attending Central High School in Grand Rapids, Michigan, and was asked to perform a modern dance solo for our annual variety show. Somewhat overextended, perhaps overconfident, I whipped something together without much effort and didn't spend a lot of time rehearsing. After watching the performance, my mother said it was great that I danced, but that I shouldn't do it in the future unless I did it to the best of my ability. I realized how right she was and her words stayed with me.

These two ideas form the bookends of how I approach things. If there is something over which you have control and to which you have committed, you must do it to the best of your abilities or not at all. However, when something unexpected happens over which you have no control, you must have the faith to trust that something greater than yourself will guide you.

Betty Ford

Diane von Furstenberg

Designer and CEO

I was born in Brussels, Belgium, and although I had a perfectly nice childhood, I did not enjoy being a child. I wanted to be a grown-up and be in control of my own life. So when my mother suggested that I go to boarding school in Switzerland at age thirteen, I was ecstatic. Finally, I would have my own life, independent from my family, and maybe, I thought, if I was lucky, something exciting might happen to me in my new world.

It was a beautiful sunny day in Lausanne, Switzerland, when we arrived at the Pensionnat Cuche where I would spend the next three years of my life. We dropped my luggage off in my room, and before saying good-bye, my mother took me down to Ouchy, a town by the Leman Lake, to have tea. She told me about life and love and she tried to talk about serious things, such as the fact that I would become a woman soon. She tried to speak to me about sex.

Very embarrassed to discuss such matters with my mother, I promptly said, "Don't worry, I know everything." My mother smiled and said something I never forgot and repeated many times afterward. "Remember, we all do the same things . . . we work, we eat, we cry, we make love. . . . What makes you different is how you do it."

I loved her for saying that to me, for trusting me, for telling me that all that mattered is that I had to take responsibility for myself, and if I could do that, my life would be about more than the things I did; it would be about how I did them.

Recently, I was having lunch with Vartan Gregorian, a man I admire greatly. He came to the United States as an Armenian immigrant many years ago and became an important scholar. He was the president of The New York Public Library, the president of Brown University and is now the president of the Carnegie Foundation. We had a long and wonderful lunch during which I asked him about his youth.

He told me he lost his mother at age six, and that his grandmother raised him in Tabriz, in the mountains of Iran. That lady had lost all of her children to the wars and various illnesses, and she raised the little Vartan by herself. She told him: "Boy, there are two things to remember. The first one is kismet, destiny, and there is nothing you can do about that. The second thing is your character, and there, you have all the control. You can lose your beauty, you can lose your health, your wealth, but you will never lose your character; it is in your own hands."

What my mother told me, and what Vartan's grandmother told him, are the same thing. It deals with your character; it's about how the way you live your life and the kind of person you are will always be more important than the things that happen to you along the way. It's ultimately how you make destiny divine.

Frank Gehry

Architect

I'm concerned with form and structure and images in my work. These are things that resonate for me. I've never been a verbal person. But the power of words is something I learned to appreciate when the psychologist Milton Wexler said one sentence to me more than thirty years ago that stopped me in my tracks.

I was just starting out in my profession, and, of course, it was more than a profession to me. I was enamored with architecture. When I look back, it seems I had a new favorite architect every week: Le Corbusier, Frank Lloyd Wright. These were the innovators. I didn't measure myself against them. They were in their own sanctified realm.

I didn't know then what I would be capable of achieving in my own career. I had no idea I would have the career I came to have. I certainly possessed ideas and confidence that I could produce the designs, the buildings. But at the time, my career wasn't going the way I wanted it to. Projects fell through. I didn't understand why. I was certain that it wasn't the work itself. It was something I couldn't identify.

I was quite an isolated person then. And that's undoubtedly one of the reasons that my friend pushed me into therapy with Milton Wexler. And pushed is the word for it. I went reluctantly because, like a lot of people who rely on their creativity, I had a mystical sense of what it is to be an artist. You recognize that the source of your talent is your identity, so you don't want to tamper with yourself. I was stubborn about this. I would rather be myself—for better or for worse—than alter myself in any way, even if other people saw the alterations as improvements.

But I went.

Dr. Wexler led a therapy group of fifteen people twice a week. There were artists and writers and businesspeople. They were all talented and successful to one extent or another. For the next two years, I went to the group and never talked, never said one word.

Everyone else seemed to talk easily. I was surprised by their fluidity. I have to say, I was somewhat envious of it. I was shy by nature. I had no confidence in my ability to express myself in words. So two years went by while I sat there in silence. Then one night, the entire group turned on me. They said things that stunned me. They attacked me, really, saying who did I think I was, sitting there, never talking, judging them, withholding. If it was one or two people I could have dismissed it. But it was all of them.

Afterward I had a talk with Dr. Wexler. And he said the words that changed everything for me. What he said was, "You asshole, don't you see what they see?"

I didn't. It never occurred to me that they took my shyness for judgment, my silence for withholding, my inability to take part in the group for refusal to engage. They saw me as something I wasn't. It struck me that I was giving the exact same impression to clients. Projects were falling through not because people didn't like my work but because they were uncomfortable with me.

Nothing was the same after that. It wasn't even that I talked that much more, though I did. The change went deeper. I was able to dismantle the wall I had built around myself. I began to listen. I don't think I had ever listened before. But I heard what people were saying, heard it clearly. The more I listened, the more interested I became in them. I got to know them.

Knowing my clients opened up the world for me. The relationships I developed over the years have become the part of the architectural process I value most. In some cases, I've designed buildings for corporate institutions, and the people I originally worked with have moved on by the time the project is completed. Those are the buildings I don't go back to look at, because without the people who inspired them, they aren't the same to me.

In my profession, clients generally want what is new but what is truly new often daunts them. Many times you find that they're walking a line between wanting to go far enough with a design to have something original, something enviable, but to not go so far that they might be laughed at. This means that they are entrusting you with a balancing act. And that's when the words come back again, in another context, but one critical to my work. To design a building for them with any measure of success, you have to, in fact, see what they see.

Richard Gephardt

Minority Leader of the House of Representatives

I learned one of the most important lessons of my life early in my childhood. As a child, I can remember whenever my mother Loreen wanted to talk to me, she would not tower over me, but would make herself level with me and meet my eyes when we talked. She was not a highly educated person—she hadn't finished high school—but she had a better understanding of people, and of life, than anyone I've ever met. Her moral values, commonsense approach to life, and religious convictions were the foundation of my upbringing. It wasn't until I grew up that I realized how much her values shaped my life.

I grew up in a typical South St. Louis small bungalow. We didn't have a lot of money; my dad was a milk truck driver and my mom stayed at home with us until I was in the fifth grade, before she became a secretary. Ours was not a fancy life. Since we didn't have a car, we walked to school and every Sunday took the streetcar or bus to the Third Baptist Church. That was my world, and I thought it was terrific.

Of all the life lessons that my mom taught me, I remember the one that shaped my life the most: I was around five years old when my mother sat me down, looked me in the eye, and told me how to *listen* to people. "When people talk to you, look them in the eyes and focus on what they're saying. Really listen. Do your best to understand what they're trying to say." When you listen, you show respect. And to get respect, you have to give respect. It doesn't mean you have to accept all of what they say, or even a part of it. But try to understand where their ideas come from.

My mother reinforced this message throughout my childhood: "Put yourself in the other person's shoes." "Think about how you like things said to you." "When you're talking to people, ask them questions. People want you to ask them questions and get to know more about them. Not the other way around."

I have tried to carry these basic principles into my life in Washington, D.C. Nearly every day, I host a "Democratic leadership meeting." It is an opportunity to listen to what members are saying about the topics of timely concern. This has caused a huge transformation in the way the group operates. I'm amazed at how my own thinking evolves when I sit and listen to a group of people for just an hour a day. Since arriving in Congress, I have met people from different walks of life, people with different backgrounds than my own, and people who share a different set of beliefs than me. The Democratic Party represents many different people from across this great nation. All members of Congress feel strongly about the issues their constituents face, and they want to be heard. Sometimes, just listening to their concerns and trying to understand their point of view results in a way to compromise that helps us move forward. I've never gone wrong by putting everybody in a room and listening. I have found consistently that any person, organization, or business that upholds the values my mother taught me has always ultimately proved to be successful in their goals.

My mother is still alive and I have tremendous love and respect for her. Her advice has applied to everything that I've done and every success I've had. One of the reasons I think I've been selected to lead the Democrats in Congress is that I've tried to give them the time and attention they need to say what they think. Some say I'm a good listener. If that is true, I credit my mother. It's my mother who reinforced that—and, thankfully, I listened when she told me.

Dick Gephardt

The Honorable Ruth Bader Ginsburg

Associate Justice of the Supreme Court of the United States

It was June 1954. I had just graduated from Cornell University and was about to marry Marty Ginsburg, the only young man I dated who cared that I had a brain. Marty and I had met on a blind date at Cornell in 1951 when I was seventeen. He was then eighteen and a year ahead of me at the Arts and Sciences College. We were best friends through all of my Cornell years. On school breaks during my senior year, I would often dine at Marty's parents' house in Rockville Centre, New York. My mother died just before my graduation from high school, and Marty's mother acted as a substitute parent for me. She and Marty's father were there whenever we needed them, never judging, always loving us.

Marty and I planned a small, traditional Jewish ceremony in his parents' living room. We limited attendees to eighteen, which represents the Hebrew symbol for life. The morning of the wedding, I was upstairs, making last-minute adjustments, when Marty's mother put something in my hand and said, "I am going to give you some advice that will serve you well: In every good marriage, it pays some-times to be a little deaf." She had placed in my hand a set of wax earplugs.

I was puzzled. What was she trying to convey? I put her words in the back of my mind for a time, a rather short time as it turned out. When Marty and I were on our honeymoon, I began to appreciate the wisdom of her advice. That appreciation has grown enormously over the years.

My mother-in-law meant simply this. Sometimes people say unkind or thoughtless things, and when they do, it is best to be a little hard of hearing—to tune out and not snap back in anger or impatience. In my forty-seven years of marriage I have recalled that advice regularly. When Marty and I were temporarily miffed by something one or the other of us said or did, I would take several deep breaths and remember that tempers momentarily aroused generally subside like a summer storm.

I have given mother's advice to my own children, and it has helped in their marriages as well. But the idea behind the words reaches far beyond family. I grew up in a time when there was much more anti-Semitism and gender discrimination in the United States than there is today. I drew upon Mother's words when I was told I was not welcome in certain places because I am Jewish or that I could not do certain work because I am a woman. In the years I was campaigning for the ERA, and arguing cases on behalf of women in the nation's courts, many an unkind or thoughtless word was uttered from the bench or by opposing counsel. Mother's advice helped me to remain unruffled and to prevail.

Every day at the Supreme Court my colleagues and I decide important issues. We sometimes divide sharply and have animated conversations about our opposing views. While I have abiding respect and affection for all of my colleagues, I sometimes find myself alone in chambers momentarily distressed or annoyed, thinking if not saying, *I'd like to strangle Justice So-and-So.* Then I smile, thinking of Mother's words.

Anger, resentment, envy, and self-pity are wasteful reactions. They greatly drain one's time. They sap energy better devoted to productive endeavors. Of course it is important to be a good listener—to pay attention to teachers, coworkers, and spouses. But it also pays, sometimes, to be a little deaf. I still use the brand of earplugs my mother-in-law gave me.

Ruth Bader Ginsburg

Rudolph Giuliani

Former Mayor of New York City

On August 28, 2001—exactly two weeks before the most painful day in American history—a rookie firefighter named Michael Gorumba had a heart attack while fighting a blaze in a Staten Island auto body shop and died. When I became mayor, I vowed that whenever a city employee was injured on the job I would go to the scene immediately. It was the least I could do for the people sacrificing their own safety to serve the people of New York. So when I heard about Michael Gorumba, I headed to the hospital.

The young man's mother arrived and was, of course, inconsolable. But this tragedy wasn't the only one she had suffered that year. She had also lost her father and her husband—both suddenly—over the course of the past ten months. And now, her son was gone too.

But I sat in the waiting area with the family and watched, amazed, as Mrs. Gorumba, crushed by sorrow, slowly became the calmest person in the room. She consoled her relatives. She bravely moved to the unhappy business of discussing funeral plans. Suddenly, someone brought up the fact that the wedding of Mrs. Gorumba's daughter was planned for the following month.

"You have to postpone the date," insisted one relative. "You can't go through with a wedding at a time like this."

Mrs. Gorumba didn't even pause. "I will not put off this wedding," she said. "We are going to go through with it."

I was amazed. Here was a woman in the throes of the worst tragedy possible—the loss of a child—yet she was speaking calmly, drawing her words from a reservoir of courage that was unimaginable to me. Later, I asked her how she could handle all this. "How do you deal with such a horrible loss?" I asked. "Where do you get this strength, this focus?"

Mrs. Gorumba looked at me. "When terrible things happen," she said, "I try to concentrate on the good parts of life and celebrate them even more than I had before. Think about it. At this very moment I have two things in front of me: dealing with my son's death—which I have to do and will do—and dealing with my daughter's wedding. I choose to focus on the wedding. Why? Because life is a combination of great tragedy and great beauty. This family will deal with our tragedy. But we will also celebrate the beauty of this wedding with even greater joy. This is what my son would want, and this is what my daughter needs." I hugged Mrs. Gorumba. I kissed her good-bye and left the hospital.

The next day, I went to the wake. Mrs. Gorumba approached me with her daughter by her side. "This girl has lost all of the male relatives in her life," Mrs. Gorumba began, "and there's no one left to give her away on her wedding day. Even before this tragedy, our family admired you, so I want to ask a favor: Could you walk my daughter down the aisle?"

"I would be honored," I told Mrs. Gorumba. I also said what was in my heart: This was one of the most beautiful things anyone had ever asked of me. She told me that the wedding was scheduled for Sunday, September 16, in Gerritsen Beach, Brooklyn.

"I can't wait," I told her.

Then, on the morning of September 11, I went to a breakfast meeting in Midtown to begin a regular day of work.

That first day of horror was to me—as it was to most of the world—a series of rapid-fire events, a blur of tragic images, frantic activity and excruciating heartbreak. But what I recall most about that morning is that only moments after the attacks, I was already thinking about how I was going to talk to the public.

I had gotten the news that the towers had been hit when I was at the breakfast meeting and rushed down to the site. Just before ten o'clock, with both buildings in flames, my emergency team and I left the fire department command post, heading for the police department command post, where we planned to hold a press conference. I had asked fire officials a couple of minutes before, "What do you want me to tell people? I want to give them the best advice on how to be safe." Pete Ganci, our highest-ranking fire chief, gave me five or six points that he wanted me to make on television—careful instructions, mostly, on how to get out of buildings as quickly as possible.

Looking back, Pete's concern was prescient. I remember he was worried about the tops of the buildings coming down. People were already getting injured by falling debris and from the bodies of those who had jumped, and Pete wanted to prevent as many casualties as possible.

Tragically, Pete himself would die later that day. He was only fifty-four years old.

We headed to the police department command post, but were stopped in our tracks when the first tower began to fall. We sprinted into a building to take cover and were trapped inside for about twenty minutes by the debris and smoke, choking on dust. The sound of the collapsing tower was thunderous, and for a moment we didn't know if we would make it out alive. Ultimately, we groped our way back out to daylight, only to be greeted by the most shocking scene of destruction I'd ever witnessed: crushed concrete and tangled steel, all of it barely visible through the thick gray dust that filled the air.

As we hurried up the street to the press conference, I suddenly remembered what Mrs. Gorumba had told me: On any given day, we may experience both the best and worst of life, and it is important—crucial, in fact—to embrace the beautiful even as we shoulder the terrible.

This, of course, begs the question: What on earth could be even remotely beautiful about September 11, 2001?

The answer I gave to the public that day, and in countless speeches and interviews and eulogies in the weeks and months that followed, is this:

We survived.

Even with the horror of that day's events—the pain inflicted, the devastation wrought—I instantly knew that the outcome could have been worse. Thousands of people died on September 11, but the death toll could have been even higher. Americans were more terrified than they had ever been before, but there was no runaway panic. Our nation was brutally and unconscionably attacked, but we did not capitulate.

We survived.

The more I thought about the words spoken by Mrs. Gorumba on the night of her son's death, the more they applied to the events of September 11.

When the towers fell, our fire department command was

killed instantly. This devastated me. These men were not only colleagues, but some were dear friends. Yet I immediately began focusing on the fortuitousness of the direction in which the buildings fell. The city's top command was only a block and a half away, and had the towers collapsed in our direction, New York government would have been wiped out. We would have had no mayor, no police commissioner, no fire commissioner, no communications director, no Office of Emergency Management director, no health commissioner—a man who would ultimately bring the city through the anthrax crisis—and dozens of others. However horrible that day's toll, New York City had survived.

We can also be thankful for the acts of heroism that transpired that day—deeds of bravery and compassion that spoke so eloquently to the lives lived by those who perished. One of the things that got us through the turbulent aftermath of September 11 was the telling and retelling of these great acts of heroism by our lost firefighters and police officers and ordinary citizens, not to mention the hundreds of inspiring rescue and survival stories. All of this could be embraced. The human spirit had survived.

And, of course, we can be grateful for the indomitable patriotism that swept through the country in response to this callous act. The first time I saw the now famous photograph of the firefighters putting up the American flag at Ground Zero, I knew instantly that we were on the road to recovery. Not since Pearl Harbor had this nation been so brutally assaulted, and yet people across the land immediately began to take comfort in the indestructibility of our national heritage.

Just like the day of the attack itself, the week that followed September 11 left little time for reflection. Tuesday, Wednesday,

Thursday, Friday—they all passed, and I know I slept at some point, but I can't for the life of me remember when. I do recall that the first time I sat down for dinner—an actual meal where you sit at a table and eat—was on Friday night. But throughout it all, I kept remembering Mrs. Gorumba's words. I even repeated them at press conferences. Soon reporters began to ask me if I would still be participating in the wedding.

"Absolutely," I said. "It now means more to me than ever."

I'm not very good at estimating crowds, but there must have been more than one thousand well-wishers lined up outside the church on the wedding day, waving and applauding and filling the street with a sense of hope and optimism and, yes, cheer.

When I walked Mrs. Gorumba's daughter down the aisle—something I had never done before because my own daughter is only twelve years old—I remember feeling that this moment was not only important for the bride and her family, but for the community as well. And, frankly, it was especially wonderful for me. In the space of a week, I had seen the worst that life can offer, this grim national calamity, but with God's good grace, I then lived to see the best part of life, a beautiful young couple so much in love, looking forward to a life together.

Mrs. Gorumba was right—it was something to celebrate.

Whoopi Goldberg

Actress

I grew up in Chelsea, New York, a mixed working-class neighborhood. I hung out with people from other parts of the city too. It was the hippie era and I was wearing bell-bottoms and Afros, and painting my face.

My appearance led to all kinds of commentary from the peanut gallery. People questioned the way I looked and who I hung out with. Those kinds of judgments used to bother me a lot because I didn't understand why my preferences in people and style should be questioned; and the critics were actually people I liked, so the pressure to conform was strong.

I remember one night I was getting ready to go to the movies with a friend from my neighborhood, and I was dressed in torn overalls, a tie-dyed shirt and I had a big old Afro. My friend looked, well . . . normal. My friend took one look at me. "I don't want to go anywhere with you looking like that," she said. "You should change your clothes."

"What?" I said.

"Change your clothes," she said. I didn't like that.

So I said, "You change."

Then she said, "If you're going to go looking like that then you're not going with me."

"Okay," I said.

And she split.

I looked at my mother who happened to be standing there when the discussion began. And she said, "Well, you can change your clothes and go ahead and be like everybody else. But if it's not what you want and you're strong enough to take other people's ridicule, then stand by your convictions. You need to know, however, that criticism is what's coming. It's not ever going to be easy because being different never is."

That was a shock to me. I understood then that people were not necessarily going to encourage or even support me as I explored other ways of being. But I didn't want to be limited by other people's ideas. When my friend said, "You have to go change," the dilemma became, if I change for you this time, how many times am I going to have to change in the future? And I guess what my mom realized was, in saying "no," I might be opening myself up to a lot more of these kinds of conversations in the future. People would always make judgments about what people are on the outside—what they're wearing, or how they look—instead of trying to understand the person inside. If you wanted to be an individual, you had to be tough enough to take the criticism. My friend's comment had been the first instance where I had to face the challenge directly. My mother's words assured me that I wouldn't be making a mistake by refusing to change, but she was also warning me of the tough road ahead if I refused to conform. Expecting difficulties made them easier to take.

This issue of conformity has run through my whole life. Nobody looked like me when I got famous. Nobody had dreds. Now lots of folks do. People would say, "Why doesn't she wear high heels to these functions instead of yellow-and-red Reebok sneakers. "Why doesn't she wear dresses? Why isn't she changing? Why isn't she like us?" In the end, the very thing that brought people to me was that I wasn't like everybody else.

You have to believe in yourself in spite of what other people believe. That self-confidence is what brought me through everything in my life, and that wisdom came from my mom. It is tough to remain an individual when we're all asked to be sheep. It is not easy being green.

Whoopi Goldberg

William Goldman

Novelist and Screenwriter

I t all started when Miss McMartin caught me cheating.

Math, junior year of high school, a surprise quiz. I finished in a blink and was staring out the window, which happened to be in the direction of the desk of the brightest girl in class.

Miss McMartin signaled me to the front, said simply that she had seen me copying, asked for my test, which I gave her, and said she would talk to me about this after school.

If this sounds humiliating, you should know that the way my life was going, we are talking about one of the good days. I was fifteen, totally a nerd, with few friends (none of them female), a father growing increasingly out of control hiding upstairs at home, and a deaf mother who had no successful means of coping with his madness.

School, which had once been a haven, was, in its own way, worse. I had suddenly, shockingly, become stupid. A's had once come running. Now I was praying for C's. The horrible thing for me was I didn't know when my brains had gone away, never dreamed that I was hiding from the world in mediocrity.

I wasn't cheating, in fact, was stunned when Miss McMartin thought I was. She was a tall Scottish lady, very smart, the head of the math department, and scary. At least if you were as bad at math as I was.

After school we met and she apologized. She said she was

wrong. "Obviously, if you had been cheating, you would have done much better than this." She handed me back my test. I think I had gotten a solid D.

We talked a little. I don't know what I said that might have interested her, but after a while she walked me down the hall to where Mr. Hamill's office was.

Mr. Hamill is the hero of this story.

As short as she was tall, hefty as she was thin, a southern gentleman, funny and fine, he taught me literature. They were friends and she mentioned the cheating incident, how she had gotten it wrong, then left us alone.

It was the start of me popping in regularly after school to see Mr. Hamill and spitball about stuff, nothing serious—books, sports, events of the day. I had never done that with a teacher before and sometimes other students would be there, or sometimes it would be just me.

We never got into the subject of my troubles at home, not specifics, but clearly he must have sensed I was slipping dangerously down the iceberg.

"Goldman," he said one day, out of some wondrous blue. "Who has it made?"

I didn't understand.

"In all the junior class, who do you most want to be?" he asked again.

Easy answer to that baby. "Jack Clark," I said. We shared homeroom, sat next to each other in chemistry class. He was always nice to me, knew my name—a big deal for me then—and dated Nancy Blessing, whom I dreamed of at night. He was also president of the junior class, an Eagle Scout, and captain of the football team.

Not to mention handsome and probably thrifty, brave, clean, and reverent.

"Thought you'd say Clark," Mr. Hamill said. And then his voice got soft, conspiring. "Want you to do something for me, Goldman."

I nodded, with no idea on planet Earth where he was heading.

"Spy on him," Mr. Hamill said.

I didn't get it.

"I want you to spy on brother Clark. Check him out. Follow him around. Report back to me in a couple of days."

Totally confused, I set off on my mission.

I walked behind Jack Clark from one class to another. No big deal. Everyone said hello to him; girls went out of their way to get his attention, boys too.

In homeroom, there was nothing to report. In chemistry class the same. At least the first day. The second day homeroom was a snooze.

It was later, in chemistry on the second day that the earth began to move.

I was sitting next to him and the teacher was going along our row, snapping out questions, getting answers.

Closer and closer he came to us. I was pretty relaxed during the wait, because there was no way I was going to get the answer right, didn't matter what the question was.

It was then that I realized that something terrible was going on with truly wonderful Jack Clark. . . .

As his time to answer came nearer, his hands began perspiring. All out of control. He wiped his palms over and over on the inside of his trousers, trying to get them dry.

But the panic had him and would not let go.

I continued to stare at his wet trembling hands.

"He couldn't stop," I said to Mr. Hamill that afternoon. "It was so stupid. A stupid chemistry question was all. And he was so embarrassed."

"Why was he so upset, do you think?"

I didn't say anything.

"Goldman, listen to me, I need for you to concentrate now. I really need for you to do that. What could it be?"

I wish I could tell you I had some brilliant zippy answer. But I don't think I did, not right then. But later that day, or maybe later that week, I must have realized this: *It isn't easy for anybody.*

I went back to Mr. Hamill with that thought, waited for his wisdom.

"It isn't easy for anybody?" he repeated.

I nodded. He looked at me a moment before talking. "You remember the question I asked you at the beginning? 'Who has it made?' Now tell me the answer."

"Nobody."

I wanted a smile from him. I got it. I still remember his face at that moment, and what he said. "Goldman," Mr. Hamill told me. "Head of the class."

Doris Kearns Goodwin

Historian

I was twenty-four years old and actually saying no to the president of the United States.

It was January of 1969, and Lyndon Johnson's term was ending and with it my year-long internship. A few weeks before leaving office, the president approached me about the possibility of my going to Texas to live on his ranch and help with his memoirs. The job, he said, would be full-time.

I was reluctant. My plan was to go back to Harvard to begin my teaching career, so I turned it down. Johnson, in his typical fashion, began offering me everything he thought would convince me to make the move.

"Is it money you want?" he began. "Don't worry. I'll give you tons of money. You want boyfriends? I'll import a millionaire every weekend. You want to be a writer? I'll give you a cabin on the lake—Lake Lyndon Johnson—so you can have a blue sky and a quiet place to work.

"Your field is the presidency!" he concluded, incredulously. "How could you possibly not take this option?"

But being young, and looking forward to joining back up with my friends in Cambridge, I held my ground. Would it be possible to do the job part-time, perhaps on weekends? I asked. "No," said Johnson, it was all or nothing.

"What's the matter with you?" he argued. "What twenty-four-year-old girl in her right mind would not want to work for a former president?"

For a moment I thought, "What *is* the matter with me? Why *don't* I want to do this?" But when you're young, you're not thinking clearly about historic experiences; you just want to be with your friends. I said no again.

On the second to last day of his presidency, Johnson called me into his office. Workers had already begun dismantling the West Wing in preparation for Richard Nixon's arrival, and the only room still intact was the Oval Office. I walked through the door, and Johnson looked up.

"All right," he said without preface, "part-time."

So over the next four years, I traveled to Texas on weekends and holidays. The ranch was extraordinary. There was a swimming pool with floating desks and notepads; a movie theater built into an old airplane hangar, playing first-run features. There was a speedboat, a sailboat, and a small fleet of cars, each one outfitted with a bar. An army of servants and Secret Service agents scurried around Johnson, attending to his every whim.

Given this overwhelming luxury, one would imagine that President Johnson was a contented man, grateful for a career that culminated in the most powerful job in the world. Now he was blessed with the time and resources to pursue any leisure activity he wanted.

And yet the Johnson I saw at the ranch was anything but content. Psychically and emotionally hobbled by the turmoil over the

Vietnam War and obsessed with the fear that his legacy had been destroyed by it, Johnson spent his days lost in anxiety, unable to commit himself to a lifestyle in which work wasn't his central activity. He didn't enjoy sports, so he rarely went to baseball or football games. Pleasure reading was foreign to him—throughout his life, his nightstand was a place for memos and legislation. Even the movies delivered to the ranch held little interest. He became especially restless when a film was fictional, instead of a documentary he could learn from.

Johnson spent his days re-creating his lifelong office rituals that gave him satisfaction before retirement. He held morning meetings with his field hands to determine which tractors would be used that day. He requested nighttime reports of the day's accomplishments— how many eggs were collected, or how many people had gone to his library, as opposed to the Kennedy library.

Our time together at the ranch was productive, but I couldn't shake the sadness of seeing what had become of this once vibrant, vital person. We completed our work on the first volume in three years, after which I stopped going to the ranch as regularly.

Around this time I became familiar with the works of Harvard psychologist Erik Erikson, who studied how history, politics, and culture can influence social psychology as well as individual identity. After I returned to Harvard, I told Erikson I wanted someday to write a book about Lyndon Johnson and he invited me to his home to talk about the psychology of the man.

Erikson shared one idea that profoundly affected my life, though not immediately. He said that the richest lives attain an inner balance comprised of work, play, and love in equal order; to pursue one at the expense of others is to open oneself to sadness in older age. Conversely, he said, pursuing all three with like dedication ensured a later life graced with serenity and fulfillment.

When I first heard Erikson speak these words, I found them interesting, though not particularly applicable to my life. At that time, I was still young and full of energy and ambition. The sphere of work mattered far more to me than the spheres of play or love.

But then a strange thing happened.

In late 1972, Lyndon Johnson attended a ceremony at his library in Texas in which his civil rights papers were being presented. I spoke to him on the phone the night before, and he made two comments I'll never forget: He said that his greatest hope was that, if indeed he was remembered by history, it would be by black Americans who had benefited from his civil rights legislation. Then he told me that, of late, he had been reading Carl Sandburg's biography on Abraham Lincoln, and trying, unsuccessfully, to conjure Lincoln to life. If he couldn't bring Lincoln to life, he said sadly, it was hard to imagine that anybody would be able to do the same for him one day. Therefore, he surmised, perhaps he would have been better off spending more time with his children and grandchildren in his later years, leaving a different, perhaps more personally fulfilling, legacy for the world.

A few months later, Johnson had a heart attack while taking an afternoon nap on the ranch. By the time the Secret Service reached his bedside, he had died.

Although I didn't know it at the time, one could argue that the confluence of these events—Erikson's words, and Johnson's tragic example in his final days—rapidly reshaped my outlook. The same year that Johnson died, I met the man who eventually became my husband. We married three years later, shortly after which we had two children fifteen months apart. It was then that I made the most eventful decision of my career. Aware that I couldn't teach, write, and be a mother at the same time, I gave up my teaching and set up a home office to write.

Losing my identity as a professor was not easy, nor was the slower pace I adapted for my work—indeed, my next book took ten years to write. I remember being at a cocktail party and overhearing someone say, "Whatever happened to Doris Kearns, anyway?" almost as if I had died, simply because I hadn't produced anything.

But I knew I was making the right choice. While it clearly didn't matter to the world when my next book would come out, I like to believe it mattered very much to my children that their mother was nearby. After all, one's goal in life should not be the perfection of work alone but, rather, the perfection of that life.

Doris Kearns Goodwin

Matt Groening

Animator

I'll never forget the first Boy Scout meeting I walked into in 1966. Bright-eyed and excited, my pals and I walked down the basement stairs of the First Methodist Church, just off Canyon Road, below the Suicide Bridge, in Portland, Oregon. We'd been reading *Boy's Life* magazine and we were ready for some fun and adventure and knot tying!

We were so new to the Boy Scouts that we didn't have uniforms yet—just our troop neckerchiefs, which we held around our necks with rubber bands, much to the disgust of the older Scouts, who made fun at our expense. They'd call us names and poke us in the ribs, and when we were distracted, they'd sneak up behind us and suddenly grab us by the balls.

This was called "roaching." It was painful.

Or they'd call us names and tweak our noses, and when we were distracted, they'd sneak up behind us and suddenly reach down the back of our pants and pull up our underpants as hard as they could.

This was called "snuggies." It was painful.

Thus began life in Troop 1. It was run like a precision military unit, with a lot of standing at attention, flag saluting, leader saluting, uniform inspecting, marching around in rectangular patterns, and moments of silence while we bowed our heads.

We shouted out the twelve Scout Laws so fast and so often—
"A Scout is trustworthyloyalhelpfulfriendlycourteouskindobedient-
cheerfulthriftybravecleanreverent"—that some thirty-five years later
I sometimes wake up in a sweat, babbling those laws.

My buddy Richard and I were placed in the Beaver Patrol,
which was run by a couple of freckle-faced tough guys named Bob,
who immediately shoved us in a corner and snarled:

"If you two don't shape up, we're gonna take you out in the
woods and we're gonna *deal with you.*"

We didn't know exactly what this meant, but we shaped up
anyway.

Richard and I immediately tried to form a new patrol—the
Slug Patrol—and we even got as far as designing a patrol flag, but the
leaders said it was against tradition to have a patrol called the Slug
Patrol. They confiscated the patrol flag, the Scoutmaster snapped the
bamboo flagpole in half over his knee, and we shouted out the
twelve Scout Laws in unison till we were hoarse.

We did our best to be good Boy Scouts, but it just wasn't as
much fun as *Boy's Life* made it out to be. We kept getting in trouble
for not standing at attention rigidly enough, for not marching single
file, for not saying "Yes, sir!" We failed uniform inspection regularly.
And they had their eyes on us at all times because of the Slug Patrol
incident, and because I had demonstrated how to tie a hangman's
noose during a knot-tying drill.

And then one Sunday night I got into even deeper trouble with
the two Bobs of the Beaver Patrol. I'd walked into the men's room at
the First Methodist Church and discovered Bob and Bob fiddling
around with the soap dispensers by the sinks. They were chuckling
like Batman villains until they saw me, then they clammed up and

looked guilty and zipped up their zippers and grabbed me and wouldn't let me leave.

I suddenly realized that they had unscrewed the soap dispensers, poured out all the liquid soap, and peed into the containers, so as to fool unsuspecting Methodists into lathering up their hands with pee.

And I had seen them do it. The two Bobs were nervous, because they had just received the esteemed God and Country Award the week before, and if I squealed everything would be wrecked.

They told me if I told anyone what I'd seen I would be dead meat. And one of them punched me in the stomach for emphasis.

I staggered out and the Scoutmaster grabbed me. "It's about time you and I had a special talk," he said.

We went into his office and the Scoutmaster started talking to me about the twelve Scout Laws. I was getting nervous.

"Matt, what is the most important of the twelve Scout Laws?" the Scoutmaster asked.

"That would be Reverent, sir," I answered.

He nodded with his eyes closed, and said, "Go get your Bible."

Uh oh. My Bible.

What could I do? I did have a Bible, but-but-but-I'd decorated it. With little doodles of monsters, weirdos, tough guys, Peanuts characters, and the precursors of Bart Simpson.

Not only that, I'd gone through the Bible with a yellow highlighting pen, underlining passages that I had found most confusing, sexy, or just plain odd. Like most of the Song of Solomon, various strange Proverbs, and such unusual stories as the one where Jesus sent the demons into the herd of pigs and then the pigs ran off the edge of the cliff.

We'd been instructed to bring our Bibles to every Scout meeting, but no one had ever mentioned them once we got there. And now I sat there trying to shield my defaced Bible and praying that the Scoutmaster wouldn't look inside.

First I was told to kneel by the Scoutmaster's chair while he took my Bible and perched it on his knee. The Scoutmaster told me if I accepted Jesus into my heart I could have anything I wanted.

I just kept watching the Bible nervously.

Then the Scoutmaster had me pray. I asked Jesus for good grades, a new bike, Converse tennis shoes, and so on.

When I was finished, the Scoutmaster reminded me that I had forgotten to accept Jesus into my heart.

He opened my Bible and began frowning.

"Did you do this?" he asked, pointing to a drawing of Frankenstein.

"No," I lied.

The Scoutmaster began flipping through the pages, stopping to read the passages I had underlined. He got to Isaiah 36:12 and got very quiet. That's the one that goes, *But Rab-shah-keh said, Hath my master sent me to thy master and to thee to speak these words? Hath he not sent me to the men that sit upon the wall, that they may eat their own dung, and drink their own piss with you?*

The Scoutmaster shut the Bible and was silent for a long time.

"Tell me where you got this Bible," he finally said.

I didn't know what to say. Was this a trick question?

"I got it from Disneyland," I stammered. "On vacation. With my family, last summer. We stayed in this motel. There was this Bible there, in the drawer. It was free."

The Scoutmaster just shook his head. "Matt," he said sternly, "you know and I know, and most of all God knows, that *you stole the Bible from the Gideons!*"

I gasped. I stole the Bible? I didn't know. I thought they were free!

The Scoutmaster stood up. "You," he sneered, "are the worst Boy Scout in the history of Scouting."

I too stood up. I felt like folding up, like bawling my eyes out, like falling to his feet and begging his forgiveness.

But instead I looked him in the eye and said, "Well, somebody's got to be the worst."

And instead of the earth opening up and swallowing me, instead of the church pillars crashing down on my head, instead of the flames of hell fire licking at my knees—nothing happened.

And I was free.

MATT GROENING

Uta Hagen

Actress and Teacher

The proudest moment of my life was being able to invite my parents to my Broadway debut. I even paid for the tickets. I was eighteen years old.

It was 1937, and the play was Chekhov's *The Seagull*, starring Lynn Fontanne. Just two years earlier, I had done my very first play in Cape Cod, a summer theater production of *Hamlet* starring Eva Le Gallienne. I played Ophelia and Miss Le Gallienne was my Hamlet. After the production closed, Miss Le Gallienne formed a company, which I joined. This nicely prepared me for my Broadway debut in *The Seagull*. Miss Fontanne would be playing Arkadina, and I was cast as Nina.

Opening night arrived and we were well received. A few performances later, my parents came to see the play. I had gotten them good orchestra seats, but not in the first row. I would never do that to them or me. It's very hard to play with someone you love that close.

The performance that night went well and, directly following it, my parents came backstage to see me. We were in the middle of a conversation when in walks the star herself, Lynn Fontanne.

Striking a somewhat haughty pose, and speaking in a tone that I can only describe as a bit too sweet and somewhat patronizing, Miss

Fontanne looked directly at my mother and said, "Aren't you proud of your little girl?"

Instead of gushing back in like manner, my mother politely smiled and said, "I'm very proud. She has so much to learn."

Miss Fontanne flinched. Obviously, she had been expecting my mother to respond, "Why, yes, wasn't my little girl wonderful?"—complete with the appropriate *oohs* and *ahs*. Instead, my mother's comment—"She has so much to learn"—clearly surprised Miss Fontanne, who suddenly grew silent. She left the room shortly afterward.

Watching all of this, I couldn't have been more thrilled. Strange as it may seem, my mother's words were exactly what I needed to hear at that important moment in my life. As I would later write in my book, *A Challenge for the Actor,* no work of art is ever finished, nothing is ever static, no performance is for keeps.

For her part, my mother was a wonderful artist herself, an opera singer and a teacher who was as humble as she was gifted. She knew better than anyone that good art is a process, not a destination. During her career, whenever she got rave reviews—and she got a lot of them—she'd say, "Oh, but I'm just starting."

Even with the successes I would have over the course of my career, I never fooled myself into thinking I was perfect, nor that I'd figured it all out. I always believed I had much, much further to go.

This idea—that an actor's work is never really done—would again be clear to me four years later, when I received what would ultimately become the best review of my career. I was performing in a Broadway play called *The Happiest Days,* by Mark Connelly.

By then I had been on Broadway five times, and though I wasn't a big star, I had begun to establish myself in the theater community. The play was a present-day drama in which I portrayed a young girl from Brooklyn who falls in love with a young boy. The two lovers have an affair, after which she gets pregnant. In those days, of course, this was the kiss of death to a girl's family, to her neighborhood, to her life.

So the boy and the girl make a suicide pact. But when the fatal night comes, he can't go through with shooting her as planned, and instead shoots himself. Hopelessly distraught, she kills herself, as well.

It was a little like *Romeo and Juliet,* but then, isn't every love story like *Romeo and Juliet?*

In any case, the week of our opening, I flipped through *The New Yorker* and came upon Alexander Woollcott's review. He was known for being a tough critic. The review bore the headline, DUSE IN BROOKLYN. Woollcott was referring, of course, to Eleonora Duse, who, along with Sarah Bernhardt, was probably the greatest actress who ever lived. He then went on to rave about my performance.

Although I was grateful to read such praise, I wasn't at all giddy. In fact, I was more relieved than anything. This was a contemporary drama, after all, and because I had such a personal fondness for beautiful classical plays and more experience in doing them, I had been concerned about how I would fare in a modern commercial production. Would I be able to deliver a performance as truthful as any I had done in a play by Shakespeare, for instance? Would I be able to give credibility to a work that didn't have the immediate cachet of a Greek tragedy?

Think about it: Most actresses would be elated to receive such a glowing review for a performance. Instead, I was simply thankful that I'd been able to adapt my craft. It's a subtle difference, I know, but looking back, I now see that I was lucky enough to grasp my mother's words and ultimately turn them into a philosophy that I would carry with me for the rest of my career: that an artist's greatest successes are not found in a single rave performance, but, instead, in the way he or she uses that experience to keep moving forward—to evolve, to learn, to work.

Six years later, I met a man named Herbert Berghof, a brilliant director and teacher with whom I would spend the next forty-three years of my life—as friend, colleague, spouse and cofounder of our acting school, the HB Studio in New York. From the start, Herbert picked up where my mother left off, constantly reminding me that an artist's journey is unending. Whenever I got lazy, for example, and decided I liked cooking better than acting, Herbert would be right there with the same sobering words:

"If a person has a gift," he would say, "it is her *obligation* to work."

Herbert was the miracle of my life. And absent those tragic Shakespearean elements, ours was a relationship not unlike Romeo and Juliet's. But then, isn't every love story?

Scott Hamilton

Athlete

My mother Dorothy had a profound influence on my life. I was adopted and it just so happened that I resembled her. She would tell me that people tend to resemble those who love them. I have always thought that was a really wonderful way of explaining things and it has provided me with a priceless foundation.

I lost my mom to cancer in 1977. She had philosophies about that battle that have often come into play in my own life. "You're only given so many minutes," she would say. "From the day you are born you're given so many minutes to live and you must take advantage of those minutes. Some people are given more minutes than others. The important thing is that you make the most of the time you are given."

In my mom's case, it was more than just words; it was how she lived her life. She was a second-grade teacher who ultimately became an associate professor of marriage and family relations at Bowling Green University and would share that outlook with her students. She was a living example of making the most of the time you are given and her life will always remain a source of inspiration to me.

I have been so fortunate to have people throughout my life

who have offered their wisdom and support to me, helping to shape the person I am today. I remember a time early in my career when I was in need of financial support to be able to continue skating. A family I had met graciously offered to sponsor my training, asking for nothing in return. Frank McLoraine was an amazing man who could always be counted on to come up with a great line when it mattered most. I was competing at the Midwestern Sectional Championships in Chicago and staying at his house. I was a bundle of nerves and he sat me down one day and said, very simply, "Skate the ice." Those three words have stuck with me for many years, and I have applied them to many different situations. What he was telling me was to take what is given to you. Always do the best you can with what you have. I took those words to heart.

I was the only skater at the time executing a difficult triple lutz in the compulsory short program, a risky move because there are mandatory deductions for mistakes. With Mr. McLoraine's words ringing in my ears I nailed the jump and thought to myself, *Okay, this works*. I was prepared. I had done my homework and it was either going to be great or not so great. I had done everything I could so I just had to let it happen. I had to "skate the ice."

My coach used to call that way of thinking "refined indifference." Refined indifference is a sports psychology precept: Train like there's no tomorrow and then accept whatever happens. Once you step on the ice realize that whatever is meant to be is meant to be. This can be applied to facets of our everyday lives as well. The way you prepare is going to dictate what you get in return.

People look at an event like the Olympics and think that the Gold Medal is the ultimate goal, but it's not. The process of getting there is far more important. The further removed I am from that time in my life, the more I know it to be true. Don't get me wrong. I am very proud of what I was able to accomplish, but I now realize that the greater results were achieved by what it took to get to that place of having the chance to succeed. It's about showing up and training with all you've got every day. It's about doing that run-through when you aren't feeling well, or dragging yourself to the rink when you didn't get much sleep the night before and giving the same effort as when you're feeling your best. There were those days when it was hard to put one foot in front of the other, but those are the days when champions are created. It's about making the most of the minutes you are given.

This was never more apparent to me than when I was diagnosed with testicular cancer in 1997. Initially, I looked at my situation as a terrible curse, but as I progressed with my treatment, I realized I was given a blessing. I learned that cancer is beatable, and I have tried to provide hope through the lessons I have learned to those people who are battling the disease.

I have recently founded an organization called The Fourth Angel, which provides a mentorship program for cancer treatment centers so survivors can share their experiences with current cancer patients. The Fourth Angel also provides practical information about the disease in terms that are understandable for people who are not in the medical profession.

There will always be adversity in life. It's the degree and how you deal with it that makes the difference. Do you know the old cliché about how some people see the glass as being half-full and others see it as being half-empty? Sure, that half glass is there but right beside it is a full glass. And that glass is the important one. As long as you are alive and kicking, as long as you have another day, you have a full glass. We are all in this race and we all have the choice of what to do with the minutes we have been given. Like my mother, I always try to make the most of mine.

Mia Hamm

Athlete

Talking with your coach about your athletic goals is a little bit like meeting with your dad to discuss your career plans—minus the unconditional love. It's very intense.

My soccer coach at the University of North Carolina, Anson Dorrance, was also the coach for the U.S. national team. We were a competitive group of women there; many of us played on both teams, and an essential part of performing in that environment was to have clearly outlined goals. Each semester we had to report to his office and tell him what we were shooting for. We came up with the goals, and Coach Dorrance helped us plan to achieve them.

Those meetings always made me nervous. I wanted to say the right thing. I hoped my goals would be ambitious enough to be challenging, but realistic enough to be attainable. It wasn't just an exercise for me. I took it seriously and I knew that the coach took it seriously too.

Anson Dorrance is a great coach. He's supportive, encouraging, and motivating. He's also direct and no-nonsense. He knows when you're faking it. I had gone through a couple of these meetings with him. I had played for the Tar Heels for a year and for the national team for a few years. I certainly understood the sport, but for some reason, in my sophomore year, I couldn't identify what I wanted to do next. Against my better judgment, I went into the meeting unprepared. It scared the heck out of me.

We sat for a minute—me on one side of his cluttered desk, he on the other—and he waited for me to speak. So I did. I filibustered, expressed uncertainty, danced around the topic. He listened patiently, nodded occasionally and waited for me to stop rambling. When I did, he leaned forward, looked at me, and said, "What do you want?"

Much to my surprise, I blurted, "To be the best."

I couldn't believe I had said it. It seemed totally absurd. "This semester, one of my goals is to be the best."

But it was true too. I sat there in shocked silence and waited for him to tell me that I needed to get serious. Instead, he said, "Do you know what the best is?"

I spent a minute thinking about it. "The Best." It was a fantasy thing, something I had thought about only in the abstract. When put to the test, I realized I didn't know what it meant. I started to sweat. I avoided eye contact. I fiddled with the upholstery on my chair.

Finally, he stood up and walked around the desk to the light switch on the wall behind me. He turned the light off. For one second we were in darkness. Then he switched the light back on. "It's just a decision," he said. "But you have to make it every day." He was telling me I had to choose between mediocrity and excellence every time I woke up, and if I reached for the best, then I had to work that hard to catch up to my dreams.

Over the past ten years, I've come to know how true those words are. Being the best is a simple decision, like flipping a light switch. It's not glamorous. It's not about glory or God-given talent. It's about commitment, plain and simple. But saying you want to be at the very top of your field and doing it are two different things. Saying it is exhilarating and a little bit scary because you are making a choice to stand out from the crowd; doing it is incredibly hard work. You can't ever live with "good enough." Sometimes deciding to be the best feels great. Sometimes it's discouraging, and almost always it's exhausting. The bottom line is, if I don't go into it every day consistently committed, I won't get results.

What my coach was telling me was that he would help set up the right environment for me to be the best, but I had to want it enough to actually do the work. He was giving me responsibility and also saying he had faith I could achieve my goal. By bringing it down to commitment, he turned "being the best" from an abstract fantasy into something possible—a larger commitment made up of a series of small efforts. So on days when it's tough, and my playing is off, I concentrate on one or two things—balance or making a specific goal—instead of trying to get everything right. The other things fall into place. No matter what I'm doing, I make the decision every day.

Mia

Dr. David Ho

Director of the Aaron Diamond AIDS Research Center

Hope was a theme throughout my childhood. Until I was twelve years old, I lived in Taiwan with my mother and younger brother. My father was an engineer and my uncle was a chemist. They could have stayed in Taiwan and pursued careers through the bureaucratic network, but they dreamed of greater intellectual and professional challenges. They went to the United States to pursue graduate degrees, to create a better future for our families, and we— my mother, brother, and I—understood that hope and waited patiently for our reunion.

For eight years, I didn't see my father. When we finally joined him in California, everything in my life became different. My name was changed from Ho Da-i to David Ho. At home in Taiwan, we had bicycles, not cars; a radio, but no television. I didn't speak English when we first arrived in the United States, but my brother and I were young and we learned fast. I ended up going to the Massachusetts Institute of Technology, then to Caltech, majoring in physics and biology. I continued my education at Harvard Medical School. This was the American Dream come true, my father's hope rewarded.

But then came a time in my life when hope seemed remote.

In 1978, I returned to Los Angeles to be a medical resident at Cedars-Sinai Medical Center. There, in 1981 while serving as the chief medical resident, I came up against the remorseless virus that turned out to be the cause of AIDS.

We were seeing patients with infections so severe, it was clear their immune systems had been knocked out. For a scientist, the new disease was a fascinating medical puzzle. But as I became more involved, I saw too many tragedies, too many deaths. I was deeply, emotionally affected. Patients would die, one after another, and our interventions would glance off without impact. For a decade and a half, we faced an enemy that consistently beat us.

HIV constantly churns and replicates. Over a typical ten-year course of infection, there may be a total production of nearly 10 trillion virions. What makes HIV so lethal and difficult to combat is that the virus incorporates itself into the person's chromosomes and becomes part of the infected person. In addition, the virus mutates so extensively that "monotherapy"—treatment with a single drug such as AZT—is doomed to fail. When we realized that fact, we looked at the problem differently.

We began to test combinations of potent antiretroviral agents, now sometimes referred to as a "cocktail." We first gave the protease inhibitors together with reverse transcriptase inhibitors to patients in 1995. When we saw the results, we were overwhelmed . . . to see the astonishment, the joy our patients felt when we told them that the amount of virus in their blood had dropped so precipitously, we could no longer measure it. We didn't know how long the effects would last, but by 1996, we started to see the "Lazarus Syndrome." People who were near death became functional and are still functional today. Since 1996, not one of the people whom we have followed in our clinical trials has died.

But with all the remarkable statistics, nothing touched me

more than something a patient said to me one day. We had been discussing the incredible readings we had just received on her HIV levels. "I'm going to buy a house," she said to me. "I'd given up on that. I'm planning to finish school now. I had been preparing to die, now I'm prepared to live."

That was the moment I realized that hope could not be lost forever. All of the research that had been conducted, all of the millions of dollars spent on combating this illness, had resulted in that extraordinary statement, a beautiful testament of life emerging out of what had seemed utter despair. I realized I was wrong to ever doubt hope's resilience. And I began to hear the sentiments that my patient expressed from more and more of the people under our treatment.

In 1996, when *Time* magazine so surprisingly named me "Man of the Year," what got the public's attention was the possibility that we might be able to do something against a tough foe, that hope had emerged from the disaster. Not that we've finished our job. In the United States and Western Europe, the death rate is one-fifth of what it used to be. Unfortunately, our work is not useful to 95 percent of the infected world because they lack the funding to buy the treatment. That's tragic, and the problem has caused us to make a substantial investment in vaccine development.

I have hope we will win that battle too.

Arianna Huffington

Author and Pundit

The journey toward self-discovery is life's greatest adventure. My grand adventure began in earnest when I was twenty-four. I was in the midst of a worldwide tour promoting my first book, *The Female Woman*. Up until that time, money—specifically, the lack of it—had always played a prominent role in my life. I had never been quite sure where the money would come from to pay my college tuition or my rent. Would my father be able to send me what I needed this month? Or would I have to ask, once again, my mother's brothers for help?

Then, with head-spinning rapidity, I was the author of a best-seller, which had brought me, at the very beginning of my career, things I thought would take a lifetime to achieve: financial independence, and offers to lecture, to write other books, to appear on talk shows. Courage, it has been said, is the knowledge of what is not to be feared. That knowledge had always sustained me, but in my early twenties my courage was based, almost exclusively, on naiveté. What you don't know, they say, won't hurt you. In my case, it might even have helped.

Yet behind all my apparent confidence, there grew a cloud of confusion, the result of an inner struggle between secular seductions and spiritual yearnings, between hopes for the ephemeral and glimpses of the eternal. I remember the moment when the struggle gave way to insight—and then resolve—as if it were yesterday.

I was sitting in my room in some anonymous European hotel during a stop on my book tour. The room was a beautifully arranged still life. There were yellow roses on the desk, Swiss chocolates by my bed and French champagne on ice. The only noise in the room was the crackling of the ice as it slowly melted.

The voice in my head was much louder. It was coming from me, but it sounded just like Peggy Lee. "Is that all there is?" sang Peggy over and over like a broken record. "Is that all there is?" The musical question kept echoing in my brain, robbing me of the joy I had expected to find in the unexpected success. "Is this *really* all there is?" I wanted to know, and I wanted to know now. If this is "living," then what is life? Can life's goal really be money and recognition, followed by the struggle for more money and even greater fame?

From deep within me came a resounding "No," a life-altering reply that turned me away from lucrative offers to speak and write, again and again, on the same subject I had covered in my first book and started me, instead, on the first step with which the journey of a thousand miles begins.

On the career front, I veered away from the easy money of writing more books on the same subject and instead locked myself up and wrote my first political book, *After Reason*. It was definitely the tougher road, and the book was rejected by thirty-six publishers before it was finally published, but it started me on my adventures in politics, which continue to this day. On the personal front, I made a firm commitment to following more closely my inner drummer, even when that wasn't always the easiest choice to make.

The goal of life is not to see what we can make of it, but what it can make of us. And I'll always be grateful to Peggy Lee for reminding me of that fact.

Arianna Huffington

James Jeffords

United States Senator

When I was a young man, my father was the chief justice of Vermont. I was basically reared on the notion that laws were everything. Human beings might be frail and emotional, but laws were clean in their logic and should override any nonsense that humans might decide as individuals.

Through my father, I met many men of strong feelings and deep courage in my youth. The first was a gentleman—in the most traditional sense of the word—named Leonard Wing. He was a law partner of my father, but he also served in the Vermont National Guard. When World War II began, the guard was mobilized to the Pacific, and Wing became a major general. Throughout the war, he wrote my father often, always enclosing a small note for me. Even at the tender age of seven, I was really impressed by him and his strength of character, and he became a hero to me. When he returned from the war, there was a huge celebration. Boy Scouts had the main responsibilities in the parade's color guard, and though I was only a Cub Scout, I was allowed to carry the American flag because of my special relationship with Major General Wing. When I passed by him in the review stand holding the flag, he leaned over and said, "Hi, Jimmy." That simple hello was a proud moment in my life because I knew he was a true hero.

While Major General Wing left a strong imprint of patriotism and courage on me, the man who carried through on the idea of what it means to be a true patriot was Ernest Gibson. He was a plain-talking World War II hero, who served in the U.S. Senate and served as governor of Vermont in 1946. As a radical outsider critical of the incumbent, he famously derided his opponent as "a study in still life." In 1950, he resigned to become a Federal District Court judge, and I met him when I was twelve years old. Every time my father went to the courthouse to see Judge Gibson, he would take me along and I would listen to the strong-minded judge expound on a variety of issues.

I went to Harvard Law School and right after graduation got hired as a clerk for Gibson. In that year working for him, I began to see that there were moments when even law-loving people could question the wisdom of the rules inscribed in the dusty library books. The law is often impractical and Judge Gibson was a very practical man, so the two were often at loggerheads. He believed that sometimes justice may not quite square with all the facts, so on those occasions, you need to consider common sense, not just a rigid legal point of view to achieve true justice. One time, Judge Gibson was issuing a decision on a strange tort case involving skiing. To my surprise, he blatantly and completely ignored the law. He defended the decision by saying, "Never let the law get in the way of justice; justice is what counts."

That phrase—"justice is what counts"—hit me hard. As the son of a judge, with years of legal education under my belt, and a future as a state's attorney general in front of me, there was nothing more jarring than hearing that declaration. Here was a man I had an unbelievable amount of respect for ignoring the law.

The more I thought about it, the more I realized he was right. I tucked that thought into the back of my mind and from then on, and in my work as a U.S. senator, I used it on all my tough legislative decisions. Strangely enough, those words relating to a skiing case became the basis of my decision in 2001 to switch political parties, which historically tipped the balance of power in the U.S. Senate from Republican to Democrat.

In the early days of President George W. Bush's administration, I worked extremely hard with Senator Harkin to put together a $450 billion educational package as part of the first budget. The money would go to public schools, with the largest part going to children with learning disabilities. In March 2001, the budget passed in the Senate and then went to what is called conference committee. There the leaders of the House and Senate get together and, with the White House's input, reconcile the spending bills passed in each house of Congress. Four conservative Republicans, including Senators Trent Lott and Pete Domenici, represented the Senate.

When the budget bill came out of conference committee, the $450 billion in education spending came back as zero. Those conservative Republicans totally ignored us moderates, and I was shocked. None of the money could be put back into the budget because votes on postconference budget resolutions are yea or nay. We didn't have enough senators to vote down the entire U.S. budget just to restore this education spending.

This happened at a most unusual moment in the history of American government. For the first time since the 1950s, the Republicans controlled the White House, the House of Representatives and the Senate. The Senate was actually 50–50 with Vice President Dick Cheney holding the tie-breaking vote. (The Senate had not been equally divided along party lines since 1853.) The net effect gave the Republicans—and particularly the conservative leadership that sat in conference committee—control over the final version of bills without debate. Moderate Republicans, of which I was one, were not only being marginalized but eradicated.

My conscience dictated my actions, and it was telling me that if you know something is wrong, then you must do the right thing or live with the consequences for the rest of your life. The words of Ernest Gibson echoed in my head in the weeks that I wrestled with what to do. If I switched parties from Republican to Independent, the Senate would tip to a Democrat majority, and they could balance the power of conservative Republicans.

The path was not easy. When I made up my mind, I had to tell my colleagues. Senator John Warner asked me to meet with a group of ten moderate Republicans, and they pleaded with me to change my mind. Emotionally, it was tough because we had all been through so much together. Chuck Grassley, one of my best friends since our days in the House, broke down in tears, and when I saw that, I had tears too. But I had to switch. If I didn't, I would have been miserable because I would have let justice get away, and I could have saved it.

Jim Jeffords

Philip Johnson

Architect

W hen I initially heard about this project, my first thought was: *I'm ninety-five, an old man. Why do they want to talk to me? My work is over, thank God. I don't give a damn.* And then I thought: *That's it.* Although less than poetic, the words that have inspired me throughout my life are that simple. I don't give a damn.

I think if one is an artist, that's the only way you can be. You have to trust yourself and your instincts. Creativity is an intuitive process, and you have to learn to trust that intuition. Luckily through architecture, I was able to find a means of expressing myself. But it wasn't my first pursuit.

When I began Harvard back in 1924, I wanted to study the highest intellectual pursuit I knew, and for me, that was philosophy. Fortunately, I had a professor at Harvard who saw things otherwise. His name was Alfred North Whitehead, and along with Bertrand Russell, he had written an obscenely thick book called *Principia Mathematica*, the principles of mathematics. I remember Professor Whitehead said to me, "I have two types of students, Philip: A students and B students." The A students were those who understood and could synthesize the nuances and complexities of philosophical logic. Then there were those students who couldn't do that, and those were the B students. I remember Professor Whitehead said, "Philip, you're a B student."

Thank God for that. I was a bad philosopher. Well, I didn't give a damn. I certainly wanted to be good at what I pursued but there wasn't really much room for artistic expression in philosophy anyway. So I was fortunate at that juncture to recognize that my future lay elsewhere.

I remember, at age thirteen, my mother took me to Europe. I distinctly remember seeing the Parthenon and it bringing tears to my eyes. It sent shivers down my spine. Harkening back to that event, I realized that I wanted to pursue an area of expertise that sent shivers down my spine. To me, that is architecture. The shift from philosophy to architecture made perfect sense as a kind of fusion of the mathematical mind with the artistic, and so I eventually found my life's pursuit.

To have the words "I don't give a damn" as your guiding philosophy, you need to be a person who trusts himself and I always have felt that way. Everyone comes to the world with a different perception of life and one needs to understand that and nourish that uniqueness. For example, I like to spend some of my year at a house at Big Sur, overlooking the ocean and rolling hills. From the deck, I see in the low-lying vegetation three hills away a golden cross form. When I try to point it out to some of my guests, they don't see it. And you know something? I don't give a damn.

That's not said in a spirit of hostility, but rather, in the spirit of recognition that we all see the world differently. And thank God for that. Otherwise, what a boring world this would be.

Philip Johnson

Robert Johnson

Founder of Black Entertainment Television

The idea of whether or not I would go to college wasn't an issue for me because no one in my family went to college. Both my father and mother were factory workers, and I was the ninth of ten children. That meant my parents were in no position to pay tuitions.

Grades were not the issue for me. I was on my way to graduating with honors. The problem was I simply couldn't afford college so I hadn't even considered it. My destiny was set, I thought. I was going to follow my older brother into the air force. I wanted to become a fighter pilot.

We lived in Freeport, Illinois, a farming and light industry community about an hour and a half northwest of Chicago. Of the thirty thousand people living there, about 10 percent were black. Only one-third of the high school graduates—white, black, Hispanic, Asian or whatever—went to college, which translated into just three or four black students a year. I knew for certain that I was not going to be one of those three or four black students. I had no designs on college whatsoever. But then one day, I got boxed in by a seemingly innocent question.

It happened in advanced English class my senior year. Our teacher was standing at the front of the class, leaning against his desk. "How many of you are going to college?" he suddenly asked.

Hands shot up all around me. Pretty soon, I realized that all of the kids had their hands in the air, everyone except me. I was the only black kid in the class, so down every row were these white hands raised high in expectation of the bright future that awaited them. I scanned the room and noticed that everyone was looking at me. I felt completely embarrassed. The only kid not going to college. The only black student in the room.

I didn't want to be singled out, so I raised my hand.

I didn't think too much of the possible consequences. I figured the teacher was just doing a casual survey and would forget about the whole issue by tomorrow. But a month later, he brought up the college issue again. He said that since we had all raised our hands a few weeks back, he assumed we had all made appointments with a guidance counselor and begun filling out applications. He asked for a show of hands from those who had begun the process. All the white hands shot up again.

Now for the second time, I reluctantly raised my hand. At that point, I realized the teacher's hounding was never going to end. If I didn't want to be squirming every few weeks I would at least have to go through the motions of applying to a school. Solely on the basis of that teacher asking who was going to college and his follow-up question about the application process, this member of the Johnson family was forced to consider another option for his life.

My only lead in choosing a school was a friend named Preston Pearson, who graduated a year ahead of me. Preston, who later played in the NFL for the Dallas Cowboys and the Pittsburgh Steelers, was the school's star athlete. He had gone on to attend the University of Illinois at Champaign-Urbana on a basketball scholarship. I visited Preston, and he showed me around campus.

I applied to the school and was accepted, but that wasn't a complete surprise to me, since my grades were strong. I knew the harder part was figuring out a way to pay for this opportunity.

The tuition at the University of Illinois was $224 a semester for in-state students, which wasn't a deal breaker. But room and board and books added up. I was just a teenager, but I started putting the financing together myself. I applied for a National Defense Student Loan, which lent money at low interest to anyone who would get a degree in education. I also went out and got a job cleaning a microbiology lab.

The toughest part for me was actually dealing with the money itself. When I cashed my first loan check, I put the money in a toothpaste box in my dresser drawer. One day I forgot the cash was in there and threw the box away. Luckily, I retrieved the box before the trash got emptied. That afternoon, I opened my first bank account.

Going to college changed everything for me. Not only did I love learning and socializing, but college opened my eyes to the limitless opportunities available to someone willing to look for them. During my junior year, the U.S. State Department and the Ford Foundation started a program to attract minorities to Foreign Service. If you successfully completed a Foreign Service program, the Ford Foundation would pay for graduate school. I ended up going to the Woodrow Wilson School at Princeton University and earning a master's degree in international affairs.

Looking back, it occurs to me that coming up with the $224 to finance college was my first multipart deal. My most recent deal was selling BET Holdings, the parent of Black Entertainment Television, to Viacom for nearly $3 billion. And it all started because a teacher asked one question. And wouldn't let it go.

Quincy Jones

Musician

As a black man, you get attuned to racism when you're, like, two years old. The antenna for it starts working when you're real young. That's why you've got to come up with some way to deal with it early. First, you've got to understand what you're up against, and then you've got to come up with some way to keep yourself sane.

I was born in Chicago during the Depression, in one of the biggest black ghettos in America. I didn't really run into too much racism there—we were too busy fighting gangs from street to street. But when I was ten years old, my father took my brother and me away. We got on a Trailways bus to go to Seattle, and on our way, we stopped in Idaho to get something to eat.

They wouldn't even let us in the diner.

I'd been to places like Louisville and St. Louis when I was little, but I had never been exposed to anything that severe.

Later, when I became a musician, I was exposed to racism all the time. I was touring with Lionel Hampton in the 1950s, and the hotels weren't integrated *at all* then. So we usually stayed with the Brown Skin Girls, who were dancers like the Cotton Club girls. They were all over—Oklahoma, Texas, everywhere. They would always have a room they could rent to you for seven, eight dollars, and you would get a meal.

But sometimes they wouldn't be around, and you would have to find some other place to sleep. I remember one night, singer Jimmy Scott and I had to sleep in a funeral parlor, next to all the caskets.

But that was all part of it, in those days. Black bands had to have white bus drivers, so that they could eat. It was the only way to do it in the South: The drivers would go in the restaurant and get the food. We stopped one night in Texas at about 1:30 in the morning, and everybody was hungry. But fat chance that we were going to get to eat. At that hour, we couldn't find a restaurant that even our *driver* could go in.

Then dawn came, and it was about 6:00 A.M. We get to the next stop, an affluent town in Texas, and we were *hungry as hell.* The bus drives past the biggest church in town, and hanging off the steeple from a rope was an effigy of a black dummy. Which, to us, meant: DON'T STOP HERE. So we kept driving.

It was that way for a lot of black entertainers, back then. In the 1950s, Nat King Cole became the first African American to live in Hancock Park in Los Angeles. He had become his own industry—he was that big—and they *still* burned crosses on his lawn. And in Las Vegas, people like Lena Horne, Harry Belafonte, and Sammy Davis Jr. would be starring in the big rooms, and then have to eat in the kitchen and live across town. It was ridiculous. I have to give Frank Sinatra credit. He broke down that tradition almost single-handedly. When Count Basie and I played with him at the Sands in 1964, Frank hired seventeen bodyguards to protect us. He called for a meeting and said, "If anybody even looks at the band funny, break both of their legs."

About a year later, another friend of mine, Henry Mancini,

helped me out. I wasn't that well known, but I was set to appear as a conductor in my first Hollywood picture, *The Mirage,* with Gregory Peck and Walter Matthau. The producer didn't know I was black, and he freaked when he saw me. Then he collected himself and said, "Wait here just a minute, I'll be right back." Fortunately, he called Henry, and Henry says, "Get into the twentieth century, man! This man studied with Nadia Boulanger," who was a very well reputed music teacher. Henry made it clear to the producer that that sort of stereotypical thinking—like lumping all black people into one category—was completely off base.

Nobody knows how to get over that sort of racism, but the best advice I got in terms of coping with it came from the wise musicians I had the pleasure of befriending when I was just starting out. Count Basie, Nat Cole, Ben Webster, and Clark Terry were like big brothers to me. They told me to try to develop a spiritual center so that I wouldn't allow any external elements define who I was. When you get down to it, racism is about people not being impressed enough with themselves—trying to make themselves feel like giants by making everybody else feel like a midget, having someone to look down on so they can feel better about themselves.

And it's a terrible feeling for the person being looked down on, knowing that somebody seeing you from two blocks away already has a blanket indictment of who you are as a human being. So it's essential that you don't let anybody define who you are. You *have* to define yourself. Develop your own inner strength, so that you're not reacting defensively when those external forces try to undermine you. Nat Cole and Count Basie and the brothers taught me just what to say when we walked into a restaurant hungry as hell from hours on the road.

We'd walk in and the restaurant owner would say, "Sorry, we don't serve niggers here."

"Well, that's fine," we would say. "We don't eat 'em."

Andrea Jung

CEO of Avon

Igrew up in a traditional Asian family, where the belief in equal opportunity for women was novel. But my mother made a world for me within the culture, a universe without limits.

She was extraordinary herself and she wanted me to be too. She was born in Shanghai and attended a missionary school in China. Because she demonstrated real gifts in science and mathematics, the people she met through the missionary school arranged for her to attend boarding school in Toronto. After her studies, she stayed in Canada to pursue an advanced degree and became the only female chemical engineer in her class at the University of Toronto. My father also achieved great things, even as a young man. He studied architecture at the Massachusetts Institute of Technology, and when I was growing up, he ran a successful practice. They expected my brother and me to do well too and rewarded us when we achieved. I remember in the fourth grade coveting a set of sixty-four colored pencils that came in a velvet box. My parents bought them for me when I got all A's.

When I was little, I certainly didn't dream of being a female CEO, but my mom's words showed me I had the potential to become anything I wanted to be. "Andrea," she would say, "girls can do absolutely anything that boys can do. A woman can reach any height in any discipline if she works hard enough."

That stayed with me. Because I cared most about making my parents proud, it didn't really matter what other people might think I could or couldn't do. My parents understood how much my brother and I had internalized their encouragement. But they also knew that when we went out into the world, we would need strength to carry us through other people's doubts. My mother particularly knew how difficult it could be for a woman to break through barriers.

As I've climbed the corporate ladder of success, I've encountered a few stumbling blocks (such as not being taken seriously because of my young age and gender), but what has always gotten me through is calling on my mother's deep confidence in herself, in me, and in women in general. I feel blessed that I have such a rich family heritage. My parents taught me to this day not to take anything for granted and to realize that every little thing you do counts. I knew that my coming to this country was a gift and I should work hard and never be lazy. Because my parents set a high bar for me, I set an even higher bar for myself. I'm tougher on myself than anyone else could be. I hope that if I set my own expectations high, if I fall, perhaps I will still have overachieved other people's expectations of me.

My best friend in life is still my mom. Even though I'm now in my forties, my mother still pushes me. She's my biggest supporter, my biggest critic, and I talk to her every day.

Now I have a twelve-year-old daughter and the advice my mother gave me I am passing on to her. I truly believe that she can be anything she wants to be and I want her to believe that also. But she, too, will have to work hard. There are still only six female CEOs of Fortune 500 companies.

I feel the next ten years are going to be defining ones for

women. Soon a female head of a corporation won't be much of a story anymore; it will just be a fact. Hopefully everyone will realize that professional and personal satisfaction is knowing that it's not just earnings per share that matter, but ensuring that you are also giving something back to people and making a difference in their lives. Because of the tragedy of September 11, I think my daughter's generation is going to be kinder, gentler, and far more community-oriented. And because of women like my mother, who were willing to break the barriers, this generation will be strengthened by the talents of both men and women, pulling together to make a better world.

David E. Kelley
Television Writer

Sometimes it isn't words at all.

In the 1970s, Bobby Orr was indisputably the best hockey player in the world. Soft-spoken, he was a man of very few words, in fact, who always chose to let his actions speak.

Like any young boy growing up in Boston at the time, I wanted to be Bobby Orr. So much so that one summer, at age eleven, I ventured to Orillia, Ontario, for two weeks to attend his hockey camp. Somewhat to my disappointment, but not total surprise, Bobby was not actually there much. But I did meet him. I had the very brief joy of talking to him, skating with him . . . having my shin pads tapped by his stick . . . being touched by his kindness.

The two weeks went by quickly, and when it came time to leave, I vowed to come say hello at a Bruins game in Boston and he graciously encouraged me. "Do that," he said, as I'm sure he did to so many other starry-eyed kids.

Well, three months later, I got my ticket and set off to that Bruins game. I was sure to get there early, so I could secure a position on the runway between the Bruins locker room and the ice surface. I waited there for well over an hour, sandwiched among hundreds of other fans, all there for the very same reason: to get an up-close look at the best hockey player in the world.

Game time finally arrived, the locker room doors opened, and out came the Boston Bruins. Immediately, of course, everyone was screaming one man's name. I did my best to join in, but to little avail. You see, at game time, Bobby Orr's focus was singular, and it didn't include hysterical people yelling for his attention. All that mattered now was the contest before him, and Bobby Orr marched forward, head down, making it clear that he and I would not be exchanging pleasantries today.

But it wasn't a loss. Because, up close, I got to see something else: the game face of Bobby Orr. I got to see the work ethic in his eyes, the intensity, the total concentration . . . the mental fierceness that helped him achieve such greatness. In one glance I saw the competitor, the warrior, and I was mesmerized, so much so I even stopped calling his name. I just stood there in awe, watching this legend pass.

At first I didn't even notice the oncoming hockey glove. I did see the multitude of hands reaching out to take hold of it. But the glove, containing Bobby Orr's hand, had only one destination. Me. I don't know how he saw or heard me in that mass of people, particularly since I was partially blocked and his head was down, but as he passed, he grabbed my hand and squeezed it before stepping onto the ice. It all happened in a second. That squeeze of a hand said "hello." It said, "I remember you." It said, "good to see you again." But what it mostly said to me in that moment . . . was who and what Bobby Orr was. The greatest hockey player in the world had touched me once again with kindness. With one gentle squeeze, he taught me it is not what you say in life, nor what you do, but rather . . . how you "be."

That squeeze occurred over thirty years ago but I can still feel it. Today, I am a father of young children, and like any parent, I have dreams for them. But mainly, I hope they grow up to be like Bobby Orr, whether or not they choose to play hockey.

Billie Jean King

Athlete

My parents were always big on character, not reputation, so I've been clear on the distinction since I was a child. Reputation is what others think about you. What's far more important is character, because that is what you think about yourself.

This became very clear to me when I got into tennis. Many people think I'm an extrovert, but actually I've always been incredibly shy. In elementary school I was so afraid to give oral book reports, I was in danger of flunking fifth grade. My teacher, Mr. Bamrick, talked to my parents about the problem and then put me on a schedule of regular informal presentations in front of the class until I overcame my performance anxiety.

That same year I took my first tennis lesson and the minute I hit the ball I knew tennis would be my destiny. I still remember that day perfectly. The sky was bright blue, the eucalyptus trees shaded the court, and when my mom picked me up in her green DeSoto Fluid Drive, I jumped in the car and told her I knew what I wanted to do with my life. I started saving money from odd jobs around the neighborhood to pay for lessons and equipment, and when I bought my first purple and white Wilson racquet for $9.28 I loved it so much, I took it to bed with me at night.

But the most significant learning experience came when I

finally made the front page of the sports section of my hometown newspaper, the *Long Beach Press Telegram*. At fourteen years old, every match mattered enormously to me. That's why it hurt so much to see the front page that day, to read the article about how I lost 6-0, 6-0. I hadn't even won one game. I was devastated.

My dad took me aside and told me something I have never forgotten. He told me he didn't think reading press clippings was a great idea and he didn't think I should read mine. He warned me of the distortions and exaggerations I would encounter. The danger, he said, was not so much that I would hear or read something bad about me, but that I might tend to believe my glowing articles too much. He didn't want me to get a bighead. Then he said something that really rang true to me. He said that reading about your results was reading about yesterday. As an athlete, you are only as good as today's match. You need to live now to shape your future.

Living in the moment was something my father did his whole life. As a physical trainer in the navy, he had guts and determination. He was a firefighter for over thirty years, and though he didn't dwell on the dangers of his job, in the back of our minds we knew that one day he might not come home. From him, I learned the importance of valuing each moment, of carrying on and doing your best no matter what the difficulties. To overcome challenges, you need an unwavering sense of self, and if you listen to what everyone else says about you, you won't gain that personal insight. That's why I don't read my press clippings.

But five years ago, I finally did look at some of my media coverage. It was the tape of my "Battle of the Sexes" match with Bobby Riggs in 1973. I needed to review the tape, so I could answer questions for interviewers. What struck me as I watched it were the comments made by Howard Cosell as I was brought out on that Egyptian litter. He said if I took my glasses off and let my hair grow, I could be in the movies. Excuse me? I had won a few titles in my life, thank you, and I was the first female athlete to ever make over $100,000, and he didn't talk about me as an athlete, only about my looks. Do you know how outraged I was?

The match was fun and entertaining and I understood the value of that. But I also knew the match would be an incredible watershed for women in sports and an instrument for social change. That's why I played Bobby. People believed then that a woman would choke before a man did, and that women couldn't walk and chew gum at the same time. There wasn't one female sportswriter covering the match.

But the day after I won, I went to Philadelphia to promote the Philadelphia Freedoms franchise of World Team Tennis and saw firsthand what that match meant. A group of women who worked for the *Philadelphia Bulletin* approached me and told me that for the past ten years they had been too afraid to ask their boss for a raise, but after watching the match, they asked for one. And they got it.

That's why I understand now that the most important reviews of my actions, I will hear firsthand. I didn't need to read press clippings to understand how that match against Bobby Riggs helped women. I didn't need Howard Cosell to tell me. I just needed to look around and see how the victory had changed real women's lives.

Ted Koppel

Broadcast Journalist

When you're in a war zone, and you've got a Jeep engine that has just quit on you, the person who can fix it is the smartest person in the world. When basic resources are scarce, it doesn't matter what you've learned in school if you don't know how to find food and water. In this country, we place a premium on education—"perform well in high school, then go to college"—but different kinds of knowledge are important, each in its own way.

Will Rogers once said, "Everybody is ignorant, only on different subjects." That concept, and its natural counterpart, that we are all experts on something, has been an invaluable tool for me. We all have something to learn and we all have some kind of expertise, and when we acknowledge that, it affects not only the way we take in information, but also the way we disseminate it.

One of the best examples of this philosophy at work is ABC's *Wide World of Sports*. In 1961, ABC was the fourth network in a three-network race. We had few, if any, major sports contracts and we were fighting to stay afloat. To compete, Roone Arledge, then president of ABC Sports, decided to take a completely different approach with the program. *Wide World of Sports* would become the "everything else" show.

Arledge knew that there were sporting events taking place all over the world—cycling, luge, soccer, curling—dozens of sports that people in the United States knew nothing about. He also recognized the connection between knowledge and interest. People wouldn't watch something completely unfamiliar, because they wouldn't care about it. So he created "Up Close and Personal," a two- to three-minute segment that featured a particular athlete and told his story. He introduced viewers to the subject matter through a personal anecdote so that they'd have a vested interest in the sports coverage that followed.

We used a similar format during coverage of the 444 days Americans were held hostage in Iran, which ran from November 1979 until January 1981. Initially, on a program that was called *America Held Hostage*, we would begin the broadcasts by giving people a combination of news updates and background sketches of Iran and the people who were holding the American prisoners. That process and that program evolved and, on March 24, 1980, became *Nightline*.

As a general guide we began by assuming that people would be unfamiliar with what we were presenting. For the show to be successful, we would then have to deliver information in a way that would be appropriate for every viewer, from the novice to the expert, without alienating anyone.

We decided that each show would begin with a four- to six-minute piece explaining the story, followed by a series of guests. The quick summary at the beginning would educate the novice viewer and update the expert viewer, so that anyone could turn on *Nightline*, quickly learn about that evening's topic, and then enjoy the expert commentary that followed. The assumption that our viewers were unfamiliar with the subject matter made it possible for us to present information in a way that was inclusive and universal.

It's an effective way to tell a story, and it has made an impact. I'll give one of my favorite examples: In 1995, I had the opportunity to meet and interview Morrie Schwartz, who would later be immortalized in the bestseller *Tuesdays with Morrie.*

Morrie was a retired sociology professor from Brandeis University, and a victim of ALS, or Lou Gehrig's disease. Unlike many of our *Nightline* guests, Morrie was neither famous nor was he infamous. He was a man, however, who agreed to come on *Nightline* to talk about an issue of universal interest: death and dying.

I began the first of three programs by asking the simple question: "Who is Morrie Schwartz, and why, by the end of the night, are so many of you going to care about him?" I gave my brief introduction, and then Morrie and I talked. He spoke with passion, warmth and great candor. The consummate teacher, he had powerful life lessons to share and gave us a firsthand account of what it's like to face one's own death. He moved us, and by the end of the three programs, people cared about Morrie Schwartz. They also knew more, and maybe cared more, about ALS. We've had more requests for copies of "Lessons on Living," the title of the series, than we've had for any other *Nightline* broadcast.

In 2000, *Nightline* celebrated its twentieth anniversary. Thousands of programs later, I still refer to Will Rogers's words. It's humbling to acknowledge the truth of them: "We are all ignorant about something." But recognizing that allows us to do more than give information inclusively. It also opens the door to receiving information. If we're able to identify our own ignorance, we can then identify someone else's expertise. We learn how to listen to each other. And that is the foundation of human understanding.

Ralph Lauren

Designer

As a kid growing up in the Bronx, my heroes were guys like Mickey Mantle and Joe DiMaggio, but the person who inspired me the most throughout my life was Frank Sinatra. It wasn't his face or persona or even the clothes he wore that impressed me, but his music and inner drive. Sinatra was a guy who had it all, then seemed to lose it, and then, with integrity and dedicated resolve, got it back again.

The Frank Sinatra I remember in my youth was down and out. Here was a guy who had once been adored by his bobby-soxer fans and now, all of a sudden, was yesterday's news. No one played him on the radio. I read how he had lost his voice and was having emotional problems over his marriage to Ava Gardner. I didn't know what exactly had happened to him, but it did seem that nobody cared about him anymore. This big star had all of a sudden become a big zero and now he couldn't even get a job.

As a kid, I loved Sinatra and was listening to him when other people my age were into rock and roll. When he sang a swinging song I felt like I was filled with confidence, and when I heard him sing one of his lonely ballads, I felt sad, as if my girlfriend had just walked out on me. When Frank Sinatra sang he really got into you and he became part of your life.

The great thing about Sinatra's comeback was that he didn't sell out. Instead of trying to become someone else, he stayed the course, he never lost belief in his own vocal tastes, and he was always true to himself. The words from his most famous song, "My Way," said it all: "I did what I had to do and saw it through without exemption." That's how Frank lived, and at the beginning of my career his belief in himself was a great inspiration to me.

I can still remember the day in 1967 when I took samples from my first collection—men's ties—to Bloomingdale's. I wore a bomber jacket and jeans that day, and I was excited to show my wide ties to the store's buyer.

The buyer spent some time looking them over, then said to me, "Ralph, these are nice, but we'd like you to make them a little narrower and take your name off them so we can sell them on the Bloomingdale's label." I knew narrow ties where "in" at the time, but I wasn't interested in doing what everyone else was doing. I really believed in my designs. Even though I was dying to have my ties in Bloomingdale's—knowing what a huge break that might make in my career—I said no thanks. I closed up my bags and left. I believed in myself and what I was doing enough that I didn't give in to the moment.

Six months later I got a call from the same buyer saying Bloomingdale's would like to sell my wide ties under my own label.

I've always tried to stay true to myself and hold to my own course in this business. Like Sinatra, I don't change with each new trend. Change is the nature of the fashion business, and though there are always hot new designers and pressures to create the new hot look, those things don't mean anything to me. Consistency and integrity of product are far more important to me than following the pack.

Success isn't based on "look what I can do!" but more on an inner sense of self and believing you have something to say in your own consistent way. And I think we all have to fight to maintain our own unique style and taste in a world that would have us conform.

Ralph Lauren

Ang Lee

Director

My words are not from anybody's mouth. My words are the title of a book: *Sense and Sensibility.*

I became aware of these words for the first time when I was given the book by a producer, Lindsay Doran, who was making it into a film. She had a script written by Emma Thompson, and she was thinking of me as the right person to direct it.

Until that time, I had made no English-language films. I had just done three Chinese-language films. They were family dramas—because basically I am a domestic person—about the tensions between the world of social obligations and the world of personal freedom. It was the world I grew up in, a society where there was always a struggle between the rigid Chinese classic traditions and the liberal social ideas (particularly regarding women) that came when the Communists took over China. This great clash of traditions can be troubling. And now, it is even more so because China is moving toward the West and changing even more.

So I was thinking about how you maintain your own culture during that kind of clash of traditions. This is not life, but the subcurrent of life. It is what forms life's texture in my country and for people everywhere as well. So I was making films about this clash and some aspect of this idea was present in all the work I was doing.

But the strange thing was that, at that time, I could not say exactly what my work was about. Perhaps I was too close to the work, but I could not explain the theme that now seems so clear, even to myself.

But suddenly, just reading the title *Sense and Sensibility,* I realized what I had been doing. I was sorting out the difference between the way we act because we are told to by society and the way we act because we want to. I realized that my work was about the tug-of-war between personal desires and cultural obligations. So that was quite enlightening to me, and it clarified the essence of my struggle.

The words of this English lady gave me another important understanding. They showed me that in some ways "sense" and "sensibility" are the two ways I have of seeing the world. To an Asian director like me the thing that stood out about them was that they are words that express a duality. Most people, I think, know of the yin and yang that is so much a part of Eastern life. Jane Austen's words showed me that in the West you also see duality. And that tells me that—East or West—duality is essential to life. It is the source of our struggling. It is deep in our nature. This cleared up a lot of things for me.

At first I thought of the word "sense" as meaning rationality and the word "sensibility" as meaning emotion. Those are very different concepts. Yet when I was making the film *Sense and Sensibility,* I saw that the words describe far more than that. Yes, they are very different ideas but they are not opposing ideas. They are deeply related to each other; in this way, they have a sophistication to them. The word "sensibility" actually derives from the word "sense." And in the book, sensibility is depicted as more than emotion. The book is really about the sensible discovery of sensibility.

Jane Austen put it so well. Her words have such a strong meaning centuries after she wrote them. Many things change, but many others do not. It's quite natural for a Chinese man of this century, like me, who must confront the battle of cultures all the time, to have so strong a feeling about the words she wrote so long ago.

John Leguizamo

Actor and Comedian

I was a nerd in junior high. A really bad nerd. Originally, my father put my brother and me in Catholic school; but he split when I was thirteen years old, and we were too poor to keep going there. So my mom decided to send us to public school. I couldn't wait to get there.

Once I did, though, I knew right away I was seriously out of touch, especially the way I dressed. When you're a poor kid at a poor school, you worry a lot about how you look all the time, how much money you're spending on clothes and all that. I had problems, man. I wore high waters. And my shoes? Forget about it. I had fake sneakers—you know, the kind your mother finds in those big wire bins.

"Hey, John, here's one I like! Go find the one that matches!"

"I found it, Ma, but it's only a three and a half."

"Don't worry. We'll cut out the toes."

So there I am, pants too high, sneakers too tight, underwear without leg holes. I was the Quasimodo of Jackson Heights. Then it hits me: This is no way to get girls. So I had my mission then: Become cool.

I totally changed. I hung out with the gangsters. Cut class. Smoked weed. Started getting laid at thirteen—everything. By the time I got to high school, I was getting in trouble all the time.

By then, I was going to a place called The Murray Bergtraum

High School for Business Careers in downtown Manhattan. It was a vocational school. The best kids from all the ghettos got to go there. At first the school didn't want to take me because I had been so bad in junior high. But my mom wrote tons of letters to them and finally they let me in. My brother had gone to Bergtraum and gotten incredible grades, so I guess they assumed I might be worth something, too.

Big mistake. I was just as bad as I was in junior high—locking teachers out of the room; organizing mass student walkouts in the middle of the day; rigging the water fountains to shoot across the hallway. I was even worse out of school. My friend and I once broke into an empty subway conductor's compartment and did a comedy routine about sex over the PA. We thought we were a riot. The cops didn't.

But what I loved most was cracking jokes in school. I liked keeping the kids laughing. Even the teachers laughed sometimes, which was the best part. See, I was still so out of it in a way—too cool to hang with the nerds, not cool enough to be with the *real* cool guys—I figured my only value was to be funny. I enjoyed people enjoying me.

Anyway, one day during my junior year, I was walking down the hallway, making jokes as usual, when Mr. Zufa, my math teacher, pulled me aside. I got collared by the teachers all the time, so I didn't think much about it. Mr. Zufa looked at me and started talking.

"Listen," he says, "instead of being so obnoxious all the time—instead of wasting all that energy in class—why don't you rechannel your hostility and humor into something productive? Have you ever thought about being a comedian?"

I didn't make a smart-ass comment back to Mr. Zufa like I usually would have. I was quiet. I probably said something like, "Yeah, cool, man," but for the rest of the day, I couldn't get what he said out of my head.

It's not like Mr. Zufa was telling me something I didn't already know. I mean, all the other kids at school had started making plans about their futures, and I was realizing I had none. I was working at Kentucky Fried Chicken and having nightmares that this was my destiny. You know, I'm 102 years old and still croaking out, "Would you like it crispy? How 'bout some extra barbecue sauce?"

It started to hit me, like, "Wow, I'm going to be a loser all my life." And I really didn't want to be a loser. I wanted to be somebody.

But that one moment Mr. Zufa collared me was the turning point in my life. Everything kind of converged, you know? The planets aligned.

The big change didn't happen overnight. I knew I'd have to go to acting school, but it took me almost a month to figure how to get there. I didn't know anything about drama classes and didn't have anybody to talk to about it. Finally, I just took out the Yellow Pages. I looked up THEATER and came across the name, "Sylvia Leigh's Showcase Theatre." I picked that one because of the word "showcase." It sounded kind of snazzy.

So I got into Sylvia's class and she turned out to be very strange. She thought she was Vivien Leigh, or something. Maybe she thought she was Blanche DuBois. In any case, over the next two years, we all worked on our scenes, did performances, and got to invite real audiences to watch our stuff.

Outside of class, I did lots of children's theater and loved it— the most fun I ever had. We'd go up to Spanish Harlem—and regular Harlem—and do crazy, funny stuff with the kids. Three Stooges skits. Jerry Lewis impressions. We went nuts, and the kids ate it up.

Eventually, I got into New York University, where I did student films. One of the movies won a Spielberg Focus Award, and suddenly my life changed. I got an agent and wound up as a guest villain on *Miami Vice.* That started my career.

I've run into Mr. Zufa a bunch of times since high school and told him how his advice turned my life around. And I'm not just saying that. Here's a guy who was able to look beneath all the stuff I pulled in class and find some kind of merit in it, something worth pursuing. How cool is that?

Jay Leno

Talk Show Host

The words that affected me weren't words I heard. They were words in the first book I ever read, *Mike Mulligan and His Steam Shovel*. I was five or six at the time, and the words in this book cleared something up for me; they gave me a way to understand myself.

When I was a kid, my favorite thing to do was go to the supermarket. I would run away. One of the managers would find me and ask if I was lost. "I can't find my mother," I would tell them. And they would get on the loudspeaker. "MRS. LENO . . . MRS. LENO . . . ," this big voice would boom. "MRS. LENO . . ."

My mother would be dying. Hearing her name being called was the single most embarrassing thing she could go through. To hear her name announced in public?! Nothing could be more humiliating than being singled out in a crowd, having her name resounding through the market. She comes from Scotland. And to a person from Scotland there is nothing more embarrassing than having everyone paying attention to you. That's why it's *The Tonight Show with Jay Leno,* not *starring* Jay Leno.

Of course to me, it was the best. She would come down the aisle after me like a little tank.

It's not like I wanted to be bad. I couldn't help it. I kept doing things like that, and I never understood why. Because when you're a kid you want to obey your mom. But I was a very outgoing, happy kid. I suppose I was also an annoying kid because I was always trying to be funny. I was a show-off, especially when relatives were around. The relatives encourage you. They want you to try to be funny all the time. For my mother, there never seemed to be a good time. She was always saying, "Not now. Stop that!"

So then I read this book. A normal kid would just sit on the couch and read it, but not me. I made a ceremony out of it. I read it in our neighbor's basement. I know this is dating me, but we had a neighbor with a coal furnace. The coal truck came once a week and poured coal down the chute, and there would be a big pile of these hard little black chips in the basement. There was something romantic about it. It was an old-fashioned thing. Like all kids, I guess, I liked stuff that had a pioneer, Davy Crockett feel to it.

So I took my book and sat on a pile of coal and read these words that explained me to me. The book is about a little steam shovel in New York City. I don't know if you remember, but back when I was a little kid, contractors would construct a wooden fence around a site where they were building a skyscraper. There were a lot of little holes in the fence and if you wanted to see what they were doing, you found a hole and looked through.

In the book, all these people are watching Mike Mulligan and Mary Ann the steam shovel. And the more people watched, the faster Mike and Mary Ann dug; the more people peered in, the harder they would work. And the better at it they got. And I thought, you know, that's the way I am. Because the more people watch, the better I do.

For instance, I wasn't a very good student. If I did something by myself, I didn't do a very good job. But if I thought people were watching me, or had an interest in seeing me accomplish a particular task, I would be able to accomplish that task much better. After reading the words in that children's book, I understood why I was that way, with a kind of kid logic, you know, where you don't process things consciously, but you *get* them.

I hadn't thought about *Mike Mulligan and His Steam Shovel* for a long time, and then I was at a book fair where someone was selling an old copy. I thought, *I'm going to read it again.* Even all those years later, I could see why the words in that book had such an effect on me. And it seems amazing to me now that I first understood myself and my place in the world sitting on the heap of coal in my neighbor's basement, reading about Mike Mulligan. I obviously didn't know then I would have a nightly television show that is viewed by many millions around the world. But I knew that, like Mike Mulligan and Mary Ann, I would always do better if people were watching.

Maya Lin

Artist and Architect

I was raised to always think that exploration, observation and perception were crucial to living a full intellectual and artistic life. My mother and father were my mentors, not so much in what they said, but in how they lived their lives and looked at the world. We lived in Ohio, where both of my parents taught at a small-town university, Ohio University. My mother was a literature professor and my father was the dean of fine arts. Their talents represented the left side and right side of the brain, academic and artistic.

We were the only Chinese Americans in the community, and for that reason, I had a very insulated childhood. My parents and my brother really were the great mentoring influence in my life. I think the image that shaped me most as an artist was the memory of my father in his ceramics studio. Every day after school my brother and I would go to watch as he created his ceramics. His skill was incredible. He could pull a pot up as long as his arm and then, at the perfect moment, touch the rim in a certain way, and the whole thing would open up into a platter or other form. The spontaneity of his creative process has been a great influence on my work.

The only pressure my parents ever put on my brother and me was to find something in life that made us happy, and inherent in that was the idea that we would use our minds. There was no discussion about *how* to go about finding this thing. We intuited it, my brother and I. But my parents did give us some tools to choose our path: We learned from them to never assume anything, to ask questions, to open ourselves up to what we were seeing. We learned to have a critical eye.

I was still an undergraduate when my design for the Vietnam War Memorial in Washington was selected in a national competition and built. After completing that project, I returned to Yale to continue my architectural studies.

Architecture, as a discipline, requires a process that no other art form does. You must access the creative process—which is always mysterious—while combining it with a rational explanation of the path taken. I found this procedure problematic. A painter is never asked to dissect his or her work, to trace the path of each choice, to justify every point of composition. The inspiration—and the end result—is enough. If you analyzed a painting at the level that architecture is scrutinized during a charette, the formal critique, you would kill the art.

My professors could not understand why my process was so "irrational." At one point, a professor told me, "I don't know how to respond to it. It's too intuitive." She thought I was deliberately rebelling. I remember her coming to my studio one day and sitting me down. "Well, Maya," she said, "you can't be both. You've got to make a choice. Are you going to be an architect or an artist?" I didn't have any idea how to make that choice.

A little while later, one of my favorite professors came to me. "Maya," he said, "there's a word you use when you're talking about your architecture and you shouldn't use it." That word was "play."

My professor considered architecture too serious for the idea of play. That really bothered me.

My professors weren't trying to hurt me by saying what they said. Ironically, they were trying to help me. They thought that I had the most incredible beginning for any architect, and that I was ruining it. I started to think about why I was so disturbed by what my professor said, and I realized it was because "play" was central to how I worked.

I struggled for a long time to figure out my relationship to art and architecture. In art there is more emphasis on personal seeking and identity. Architecture, on the other hand, steps into a functional world. It's about problem solving. I only learned to balance the two about ten years ago. The book that assisted me most was Lawrence Weschler's study of the artist Robert Irwin, *Seeing Is Forgetting the Name of the Thing One Sees.* Weschler describes one artist's creative process—how he makes things and, even before that, how he views the world. An artist needs to see things like a child, without the baggage of emotions and predisposition. I remember reading that book two or three times, practically in tears.

It makes much more sense for me to occupy the space between art and design, to mix the artistic and the academic, like the reflection of my mother's academic side and my father's artistic side in me. I'm much happier now as an artist who happens to build buildings.

That image of my father pulling pots affected me not just because I often use a claylike material in my work now, or because as an artist, my work is integrally connected to the earth and land, but because it reminds me that sometimes art needs to be intuitive and spontaneous. There I am with the material, trying to figure out what it is, and it's trying to tell me what it is. I never assume anything until I've played with it and let it become what it wants to become.

MSL

David Mamet

Writer

I had a dance teacher in college named Mark Ryder. He had been a member of Martha Graham's original company in New York and so was the real thing. He was, into the bargain, the first example of the real thing I had ever encountered, and he was a very nice man.

I wrote my first play—a collection of sketches, really—and passed it to him, as my only connection to show business.

He read it and said it was great.

"But, I'm not sure it's a play," I said.

"Don't worry if it's a play," he said. "It's great." Then he said it was as good as *27 Wagons Full of Cotton.*

Well, there I was, an accomplished failure and ne'er-do-well, and a respected member of the profession had just compared my work to that of Tennessee Williams. I could not completely assimilate and credit the praise, yet neither could I discount it. I just had to live with it; and so I left the meeting very much having been charged with the responsibility of making the endorsement true.

The second set of words came in my personal life. I was working in the theater in London. A play of mine was being staged and a young actress was performing in it.

Our various situations precluded more than a respectful professional relationship between us, so I suffered philosophically, deranged by my immediate, impossible love for her.

The play opened, and I saw her, briefly, at the cast party. I told her how much I had enjoyed working with her and hoped we could do so again. There was a pause and she said, "I don't seem to be able to leave." I apologized and moved aside for her, only to find that I had mistaken her meaning quite completely.

Wilma Mankiller

Former Principal Chief of the Cherokee Nation

The Mohawk have a saying I particularly like: "It is hard to see the future with tears in your eyes." I have had many occasions to call on this wisdom in my life.

In 1978, while in graduate school, I was involved in a horrendous head-on auto collision. The driver of the other car was coincidentally my best friend, Sherry Morris. She was killed and I was badly injured. I spent months in the hospital, in a wheelchair and with casts on both legs, mourning my cherished friend's death. I was told I might never walk again.

Despite the loss of my friend, and my own serious injuries, I made an effort to find something good about the situation. My life was spared and so I felt a special responsibility to go live the rest of my days fully, authentically. To do that, I realized there was much I needed to learn. I had always wanted to read classical literature, so I spent the year of my confinement reading the classics and writing to old friends. This period of study and reflection was an important foundation for my personal development.

Before the accident, I had been active in the Native American rights movement. Now I brought the lessons I gathered during my time of contemplation to bear on my political work. Four years after the awful day of the accident, I won the election as the first female deputy principal chief of the Cherokee Nation. Four years after that, I was elected to the first of two terms as first female principal chief. I now look back on that terrible accident and period of recovery as a gift: a time of growth and preparation for leadership.

Those campaigns were extremely difficult. But I remained relentlessly positive despite considerable opposition because I am female. If I had focused only on the negative aspects of the campaign, my energy would have been siphoned off into nonsensical arguments about whether women should be in leadership positions. I probably would have lost the election through the sheer distraction. Instead, I prayed to have a good clear mind, to remain positive, and I even prayed for my political foes. By remaining positive in the midst of the most hurtful periods of my political campaigns, I was able to stay focused on the issues that concerned Cherokee people—and their future—and ultimately win the elections.

Then in 1996, after having served three elective terms at the Cherokee Nation, I became a Montgomery Fellow at Dartmouth College. I suffered another trial there. One day I started to feel ill and soon was diagnosed with systemic non-Hodgkin's lymphoma, already in its second stage. Since I had a compromised immune system due to an earlier kidney transplant, treatment options for the lymphoma were narrow. I had to move to Boston for medical treatment, far away from my family and friends.

During that care, I used my mind to get through a staggering set of physical and personal problems. I never let myself fall into depression or allow dark thoughts to permeate my being. I knew getting into a negative state of mind was a slippery downward slope. I tried to keep images of strength and wellness in my head. I surrounded myself with flowers and color. I sang, played guitar, and even danced. Once I was shocked when I caught a glimpse of myself in the mirror as I cavorted by—pale, completely bald, and slightly nauseated. My appearance did not match my spirit, which was soaring.

Illness continued to test my strength, my will. I have a favorite Cherokee prayer that begins, "First, let us remove all negative thoughts from our minds so we can come together as one. . . ." This simple prayer has helped me fully understand that I can control my mind and the way I respond, but I can't always control what happens in my life or even to my body. This prayer has helped me find value in even the most difficult situations.

Recognizing the good, not just in one's own personal circumstances, but in the world, makes anything possible. When I am asked about the important characteristics of leadership, being of good, positive mind is at the top of my list. If a leader can focus on the meritorious characteristics of other people and try to play to their strengths, as well as find value in even the most difficult situation, she can inspire hope and faith in others and motivate them to move forward. Few people of good will are inspired to follow negative, pessimistic people. People with clear minds are like magnets.

While it is important to acknowledge and deal with historic or contemporary problems, it is equally important not to let them become so overwhelming that one can't see the future. With dry eyes and the faith, hope and optimism that have sustained our people since time immemorial, I eagerly anticipate the future.

Mary Matalin

Political Adviser

My husband James Carville and I have been known, on occasion, to get slightly emotional or irrational. So he has adopted two rules that apply to fights within a marriage, yet have universal application outside the home. One of them is: "You think like you think; you need to think like *they* think"—his point being that you can't get to the core of a problem until you understand what's going through the other person's mind. He also says, "It doesn't matter if everything you say is right and everything I say is wrong. The fact is, I still *feel* this way, so it counts." More than once, this brilliant bit of logic has stopped a fight in its tracks. It's a perfectly Jamesean thing to say.

Over the years, a lot of people have voiced their opinions to me for better or worse and at a variety of volumes. My father, for example, used to remind me constantly that only one thing separates successful and unsuccessful people. "It isn't money or brains," he would say. "It's confidence. And what creates confidence is three things: being prepared, having experience, and never giving up."

I remember one time in particular when these words had an enormous impact on me. It was the late seventies and I had just gotten out of college. My first job was in the steel mills—everybody in south Chicago worked in the steel mills at some point—and because it was still a man's world, I was the only woman in the company's training program. The experience was daunting and emotionally eviscerating. I felt completely isolated. But once again my father advised me, "The only difference between them and you is that they've been doing it longer. Work hard, be conscientious, and I promise you, you'll kick their ass."

It was like a slap across the face. A good one.

My mother, meanwhile, was a paragon of persistence and ever-present love, which, at the end of the day, is more important than anything else. Despite her having been a working mom (when moms didn't really work), she always told me, "No matter what you're doing or where you are—whether you're making bread or heading off to college—there's nothing more important than the family." I can remember being very little when she first told me this, perhaps seven or eight years old. And yet it would take me nearly thirty years, when I finally had a family of my own, to fully grasp what she was talking about.

The workplace has also provided me with precious bits of wisdom. My first important political job was working on a Senate race in 1980. It was rare at the time to have a woman as the campaign manager, but Maxene Fernstrom ran the show with grace and wisdom. After a pretty good start—we won the primary—something stupid happened and the campaign took a nosedive. Everyone was cranky and bummed out. Maxene told us something that was even more of a life lesson than a campaign strategy. "You become the way you behave," she said. She meant that if we acted like losers, we would eventually lose. She was right. We did lose. A passing failure transformed us into precisely what we didn't want to become.

So now every time I get cranky or dispirited, I think of Maxene's words and try to break the downward cycle, remembering all the while that success begets success. It's not an easy thing to do, but it's vital.

Twelve years later I would once again be moved by simple, valuable words, but this time they were spoken by no less than the president of the United States. It was during the 1992 campaign, and I was on *Air Force One* with President Bush. We were talking about something unpleasant that had just happened on the campaign trail, and I asked him, "How can you put up with this? Why do you do it?" And the president just looked at me and said, "Duty, honor, country." Now, he often said this in speeches, but this wasn't a speech; nor was it one of those "now go spin this" comments that he expected me to run off and repeat to media. On the contrary, it was a genuine, personal remark that reflected his real sense of patriotism and civic responsibility.

"Duty, honor, country." I know it sounds cornball, but to me it was—and remains—a daily guidepost.

But it was James's mother who coined a phrase that will stick with me forever. James comes from a big Catholic family. His mom had eight children—James is the oldest. Throughout her life, she told something to her daughters, who passed it on to James, who then passed it on to me after we had our own kids. She said: "Once you have children, you'll never think of yourself first again. Ever."

Nothing could be truer in my life. Since becoming a mother, there has not been one day when my girls weren't my first thought in the morning and last at night. Never was this life-changing concept more tangible to me than on September 11, 2001, when in the early moments of the attack on America, we were hustled down to PEOC (Presidential Emergency Operations Center) in the White House. Once we were secure in the bomb shelter, everyone began working.

But I could not focus entirely on the tasks at hand until I located my daughters. Even after I found out they were safe, the same thoughts kept running through my head all day long: "Where are the kids? How are the kids? Are the kids okay?" It was just as James's mother had said it would be.

Which reminds me of another favorite quote. In 1990, First Lady Barbara Bush made a speech at Wellesley College in which she uttered the now famous line: "At the end of your life, you will never regret not having passed one more test, not winning one more verdict or not closing one more deal. You will regret time not spent with a husband, a child, a friend or a parent."

The comment caused quite a stir, especially among members of my generation, which is full of feminist wackos. It was the early nineties, remember, and at the time nobody wanted to be married, nobody wanted to have kids, least of all me.

And yet Mrs. Bush's remark was like an epiphany for me. I wasn't even tracking her speeches at the time, but when I read the quote in the paper, it hit me hard.

By the end of the decade, I was living by her words.

Dave Matthews

Musician

By the time I was seven or eight years old, I had a stash of Beatles albums and paraphernalia that would put a collector to shame. I was, and still am, obsessed with music. But it wasn't until a particular family dinner and some parental wisdom from my father that I thought about music as something I could do rather than something I should appreciate.

We were sitting at the dinner table—my two sisters, my brother, my parents and I—and I was singing off-key on purpose. Dinner was sacred at our house. No matter where we were or what we were doing, we always sat down together for dinner. On that particular night, I was deliberately disrupting the meal, goofing off and annoying everyone in the process. Instead of scolding me or telling me to put a lid on it, my father looked across the table at my mother and said, "Look, he sings so well he can sing *off*-key."

What a clever compliment: one part praise and one part admonition. I was a kid, so I latched on to the praise part. No one had ever told me that I could sing well and I was filled with pride. Consequently, I shut up.

My father lifted me and humbled me at the same time. It was as if he were saying, "You have a great talent, now knock it off." I stopped singing off-key and dinner resumed peacefully, but for me, everything was different. I'd been given a very important piece of information: I could sing.

Not long after that, my father died, and those words took on new importance. They weren't profound, but they had come from him, and because so much of him had faded for me, I treasured them.

Years later, I started to think about playing music in places other than my mother's living room and a big part of me was saying, "Who do you think you are to try to get up in front of people?" I was overwhelmed by doubt. I had stage fright. I wondered if writing music was ridiculous and self-indulgent, but I let my dad's words push me along. They got me thinking: *Maybe music isn't just something I like. Maybe it's what I am.*

Just like I did when I was a kid, I held on to the praise in my father's words. It sounds silly now, "My dad says I can sing," but in the beginning of my career, those words offered exactly the encouragement I needed.

Today, the admonition part of my father's comment is equally profound. I use the "knock it off" part to keep me focused and grounded. I'm lucky to have a talent that I've discovered, but it's just one thing, not the only thing. When I need a boost, I remember the first part of what my dad said, and when I need a reminder that family dinners are more important than record deals, I remember the second.

John McCain

United States Senator

Nothing crushes your spirit more effectively than solitary confinement. Having no one else to rely on, to share confidences with, to seek counsel from, you begin to doubt your judgment and your courage. The loneliness robs you of everything—everything but time. When you are in solitary confinement you have nothing to think about other than time and just making it through another day. So needless to say, keeping track of the date is not difficult for a man held at length in solitary confinement.

In the five and a half years I was a prisoner of war in Vietnam, Christmas was always the most difficult time of year for me. I distinctly remember Christmas Eve 1969. I had been a POW for more than two years already, most of which was spent alone in my cell. Like many other cells in the Hanoi Hilton, mine was a small, empty room, roughly seven feet by ten feet with a concrete slab on the floor, which served as my bed. The walls were eighteen inches thick and the windows of each cell were boarded up so that the POWs could not communicate with each other. I remember there being a single, naked lightbulb dangling on a cord in the center of the ceiling and a small loudspeaker in the corner on which the Vietnamese would play various propaganda pieces.

It was about eight o'clock on Christmas Eve 1969. I was in

pretty bad shape, having received some severe beatings from the North Vietnamese. On top of that, I had still not recovered from the injuries I received when I was shot down two years earlier. I was cold. I was injured. And as I lay there in my cell listening to Hanoi Hanna report on "the latest heroic victory over the American imperialists," I had some real serious doubts of my chances for survival.

Then the prison guards began to play a series of Christmas songs over the camp's public address system, the last of which was Dinah Shore singing "I'll Be Home for Christmas." As I lay there listening to that particular song, my spirits dropped to the lowest possible point. I was not sure if I would survive another night, let alone ever return home for another Christmas with my family.

It was then that I heard the tapping on my wall.

Despite the strict rules against it, the POWs communicated to each other by rapping on the walls of our cells. The secretive tap code was a simple system. We divided the alphabet into five columns of five letters each. The letter K was dropped. A, F, L, Q, and V were the key letters. Simply tap once for the five letters in the A column, twice for F, three times for L, and so on. After indicating the column, pause for a beat, then tap one to five times to indicate the right letter. For example, the letter C is sent as: *tap . . . tap tap tap.*

We became so proficient at the tap code that in time the whole prison system became a complex information network. With each new addition to our population, word quickly passed from cell to cell about every POW's circumstances and information from home. The tap code was my sanity's saving grace. That daily personal contact through the drumming on my wall made my isolation more bearable. It affirmed my humanity and kept me alive.

The cell on one side of me was empty but in the other adjacent room was a guy named Ernie Brace. Ernie was a decorated former marine who had flown more than one hundred combat missions in the Korean War. He had volunteered as a civilian pilot to fly missions to secretly supply CIA-supported military units in the Laotian jungle. During one such operation in 1965, he was captured and handed over to the North Vietnamese. He was brutally tortured and kept in solitary confinement for three years at a remote outpost near Dien Bien Phu before he was even brought to the Hanoi Hilton in 1968.

As soon as I heard the tapping that Christmas Eve, I knew it was Ernie. I got up and pressed my ear against the cold stone wall of my cell. At first it was difficult to make out the faint tapping of my neighbor. But it soon became very clear.

"We'll all be home for Christmas," Ernie tapped. "God Bless America."

With that I began to cry.

When you are imprisoned, the enemy can take almost everything from you but they cannot take your spirit. Those unspoken words coming from Ernie—who, due to his work with the CIA, had the least chance of getting out of the camp alive— were a poignant affirmation that as Americans, we possessed a divine spark that our enemies could not extinguish—hope.

"We'll all be home for Christmas. God Bless America."

That simple message, in my darkest hour, strengthened my will to live. Ernie helped me realize that we would get home when we got home. Until then, we had to manage our hardships as best we could.

Without his strength, I doubt I would have survived solitary confinement with my mind and self-respect intact.

It was long ago and far away. But around the holidays, when I hear "I'll Be Home for Christmas," I am always reminded of that time, that place, and the words of my friend Ernie Brace. He kept me going and lifted my spirits when they were in their greatest need of lifting. When I hear that song I think about Ernie. I think about my friends that never made it home for another Christmas. And I think of what a blessing it is to be an American.

John McCain

Paul McCartney

Musician

I was going through a really difficult time around the autumn of 1968. It was late in the Beatles' career and we had begun making a new album, a follow-up to the *White Album*. As a group we were starting to have problems. I think I was sensing that the Beatles were breaking up, so I was staying up too late at night, drinking, doing drugs, clubbing, the way a lot of people were at the time. I was really living and playing hard.

The other guys were all living out in the country with their partners, but I was still a bachelor in London with my own house in St. John's Wood. And that was kind of at the back of my mind also, that maybe it was about time I found someone, because it was before I got together with Linda.

So, I was exhausted! Some nights I'd go to bed and my head would just flop on the pillow; and when I'd wake up I'd have difficulty pulling it off, thinking, "Good job I woke up just then or I might have suffocated."

Then one night, somewhere between deep sleep and insomnia, I had the most comforting dream about my mother, who died when I was only fourteen. She had been a nurse, my mum, and very hardworking, because she wanted the best for us. We weren't a well-off family—we didn't have a car, we just about had a television—so both of my parents went out to work, and Mum contributed a good half to the family income. At night when she came home, she would cook, so we didn't have a lot of time with each other. But she was just a very comforting presence in my life. And when she died, one of the difficulties I had, as the years went by, was that I couldn't recall her face so easily. That's how it is for everyone, I think. As each day goes by, you just can't bring their faces into your mind; you have to use photographs and reminders like that.

So in this dream twelve years later, my mother appeared, and there was her face, completely clear, particularly her eyes; and she said to me very gently, very reassuringly, "Let it be."

It was lovely. I woke up with a great feeling. It was really like she had visited me at this very difficult point in my life and gave me this message: Be gentle, don't fight things, just try and go with the flow and it will all work out.

So, being a musician, I went right over to the piano and started writing a song: "When I find myself in times of trouble, Mother Mary comes to me" . . . Mary was my mother's name . . . "Speaking words of wisdom, let it be. There will be an answer, let it be." It didn't take long. I wrote the main body of it in one go, and then the subsequent verses developed from there: "When all the broken-hearted people living in the world agree, there will be an answer, let it be."

I thought it was special, so I played it to the guys and 'round a lot of people, and later it also became the title of the album, because it had so much value to me, and because it just seemed definitive, those three little syllables. Plus, when something happens like that, as if by magic, I think it has a resonance that other people notice too.

Not very long after the dream, I got together with Linda, which was the saving of me. And it was as if my mum had sent her, you could almost say. The song is also one of the first things Linda and I ever did together musically. We went over to Abbey Road Studios one day, where the recording sessions were in place. I lived nearby and often used to just drop in when I knew an engineer would be there and do little bits on my own. And I just thought, "Oh, it would be good to try harmony on this." But I had a high harmony in mind, too high for me, and although Linda wasn't a professional singer, I'd heard her sing around the house and knew she could hold a note and sing that high. So she tried it, and it worked and it stayed on the record. You can hear it to this day.

These days, the song has become almost like a hymn. We sang it at Linda's memorial service. And after September 11, the radio played it a lot, which made it the obvious choice for me to sing when I did the benefit concert in New York City. Even before September 11, people used to lean out of cars and trucks and say, "Yo, Paul, let it be."

So those words are really very special to me, because not only did my mum come to me in a dream and reassure me with them at a very difficult time in my life—and sure enough, things did get better after that—but also, in putting them into a song and recording it with the Beatles, it became a reassuring, healing statement for other people too.

Paul McCartney

Dennis Miller

Comedian

When I was a fledgling comedian I used to regularly MC at a comedy club in Pittsburgh. Many of the headliners who rolled through town were hail-fellows-well-met, but they lacked a certain, shall we say, direction. And then Jay Leno came to town. Leno always functioned as a patriarchal figure to the younger comics and was very expansive in his advice. Some of it I found unusable because like everyone else in the world my work ethic was not akin to Jay's. He's like Peter Benchley's Great White: a perfect comedy machine. But I remember one particular admonition that always stuck with me: "Just stay on the road." Leno knew that peers would spin out left and right and eventually the convoy would thin itself out. That stuck with me. And like my friend Jay I've tried to "stay on the road" where I often see Leno who is, much to my consternation, usually driving a nicer car. Thanks, Jay.

Dennis Miller

Toni Morrison

Writer

The best news was the two dollars and fifty cents. Each Friday She would give me, a twelve-year-old, enough money to see sixteen movies or buy fifty Baby Ruth candy bars. And all I had to do for it was clean Her house for a few hours after school. A beautiful house, too, with plastic-covered sofa and chairs, wall-to-wall blue and white carpeting, a white enamel stove, automatic washing machine—things common in Her neighborhood, rare in mine. In the middle of the war, She had butter, sugar, steaks and seam-up-the-back hose. Around the house, Her grass was mowed and Her bushes were clipped to balls the size of balloons. Amazed and happy, I fairly skipped down sidewalks too new for hopscotch to my first job.

I wasn't very good at it. I knew how to scrub floors on my knees but not with a mop and I'd never encountered a Hoover or used an iron that was not heated by fire. So I understood Her impatience, Her nagging, Her sigh of despair. And I tried harder each day to be worth the heap of Friday coins She left on the counter by the back door. My pride in earning money that I could squander, if I chose to, was increased by the fact that half of it my mother took. That is, part of my wages was used for real things: an insurance policy payment maybe or the milkman. Pleasure, at that age, at being necessary to my parents was profound. I was not like the children in folk tales—a burdensome mouth to feed, a problem to be solved, a nuisance to be corrected. I had the status that routine chores at home did not provide—a slow smile, an approving nod from an adult. All suggestions that a place for me among them was imminent.

I got better at cleaning Her house; so good, I was given more to do, much more. I remember being asked to move a piano from one side of the room to another and once to carry bookcases upstairs. My arms and legs hurt and I wanted to complain, but other than my sister, there was no one to go to. If I refused Her I would be fired. If I told my mother she would make me quit. Either way my finances and my family standing would be lost. It was being slowly eroded anyway because She began to offer me her clothes—for a price. And impressed by these worn things that looked simply gorgeous to a little girl with two dresses for school, I eagerly bought them. Until my mother asked me if I really wanted to work for castoffs. So I learned to say "No thank you" to a faded sweater offered for half a week's pay. Still I had trouble summoning the courage to discuss or object to the increasing demands made on me.

One day, alone in the kitchen with my father, I let drop a few whines about my job. I know I gave him details, examples, but while he listened intently, I saw no sympathy in his eyes. No "Oh, you poor little thing." Perhaps he understood I wanted a solution to work, not an escape from it. In any case, he put down his cup of coffee finally and said, "Listen. You don't live there. You live here. At home, with your people. Just go to work; get your money and come on home."

That is what he said. This is what I heard:

1. Whatever the work, do it well, not for the boss but for yourself.

2. You make the job; it doesn't make you.
3. Your real life is with us, your family.
4. You are not the work you do; you are the person you are.

I have worked for all sorts of people since then, geniuses and morons, quick-witted and dull, wide-hearted and narrow, and had many kinds of jobs, but from that moment on, I never considered the level of labor to be the measure of self—or placed the security of a job above the value of home.

Ralph Nader

Activist

I remember the teasing started in class early that afternoon. The boys in my fourth-grade class started picking on me for the way I was dressed. At that age, kids are a pack of conformity. Any kind of difference is bound to be bait. And there I was, the only boy in class still wearing short pants.

It was early fall 1941, and at that time it was popular for little boys in the first, second, and third grades to wear short pants. The fourth grade was a different story. By the fourth grade all the boys in my school were wearing long pants. The difference between short and long pants was much more than a couple of inches. Wearing long pants meant that you were a big boy, that you were growing up. But if you continued to wear short pants in the fourth grade you were considered a little boy, a sissy even.

As I left the big red schoolhouse that afternoon, I knew that I only had to put up with the humiliation for another ten minutes. Everything in my hometown of Winsted, Connecticut—the library, the grocery, the fire station, and the school—was within a ten-minute walk from my house. But on that afternoon the boys in my class were merciless with their teasing. The ten-minute walk felt like it took hours.

Needless to say, I was pretty upset when I arrived home.

I can remember walking through the front door and sitting down at the kitchen table with my mother. Life at our house revolved around the kitchen. Both my parents emigrated to the United States from Lebanon, and they instilled in all their children from an early age the importance of the family eating together. Food, my mother likes to say, is not just sustenance but a means of communicating, of teaching. We loved to laugh and tell stories in our family and the kitchen was where it all happened. It is also where I learned one of the most valuable lessons of my life.

So there I was, sitting at the kitchen table, my eyes on the verge of tears, telling my mother how all the other boys in the fourth grade were wearing long pants. "Why can't I? The boys are laughing at me," I said.

My mother had strong views on raising children and she believed—and still believes to this day—that even though I was in the fourth grade I was still too young for long pants. "Tell me why you want to wear long pants?" I remember her asking gently.

I thought for a moment, then answered, "Because all the other boys are wearing long pants."

That obviously was not the answer my mother wanted to hear. She stood up from the kitchen table. "Ralph, are you going to grow up to be a leader or a follower?" she asked and walked out of the kitchen before I could say another word.

I sat there in silence thinking about what she said. I was pretty savvy for my age and understood what she was getting at. She wanted me to think independently, to be myself. Night after night, around the dinner table, my mother extolled responsibility and independence. She had brought up my brother, sisters, and me to march to our own drummer, to stand tall and go our own way.

I knew what she was trying to say, asking me if I was going to be a leader or a follower. And I so much wanted to be a leader. I just wanted to be a leader wearing long pants.

The very next morning I got up and put on my dark blue shorts and went to school. While some of the boys in my class continued to tease me I tried not to let it bother me. But it still hurt.

That afternoon, on the playground behind the school a group of boys was having races to see who was the fastest in the class. I lined up for the race to the chagrin of some of the boys. They were all in their long pants but I was wearing my short pants.

Ready . . . Set . . . GO!

Full of adrenaline, I ran as fast as I could. I just ran and ran and ran. I had a distinct advantage in my short pants over the boys who wore the long pants. At first the only sound I heard was that of my heart pounding. Then the sounds of labored breathing as the other boys closed in behind me, and then the yelling and cheering of the little crowd that had amassed on the side of the field.

Guess who won?

That was a turning point in my life. Winning the race persuaded me that my mother was on to something. I felt self-confident and began to see that being different could be a source of strength.

Here I was, nine years old, trying hard to be a leader, not a follower. Striving to be a leader made me more assertive in class. I took initiatives most pupils would not take. I began to see that it was often weak to conform.

Through the years I have contemplated my mother's advice from time to time, and I have always tried to live up to her wisdom.

She helped me understand that a leader need not care about being mocked for his or her unique views, and that one person can make a difference. If you want to change the world, or just your community, you need to be the kind of person who is willing to run life's race in short pants.

Ralph Nader

Willie Nelson

Musician

I grew up in a town in Texas called Abbott. It's a small, country town. The incomes around there were all farm-related. You either owned a farm or you worked on one, manning cotton gins and stuff. No one had any money, but everybody raised his own food in a garden behind the house, where he also had some chickens and a couple of hogs.

As I grew older and ran into other people from other places, they said, "Man, that must've been pretty tough." But life wasn't tough in Abbott. In fact, it was a great place to grow up. The population was only three hundred. (It's still that, or less.) The school was small, and there weren't a lot of kids in the classes. So you got more attention from the teachers and had more opportunity to learn. Whether we did or not, though, was entirely up to us.

School was okay, but I liked church better. As far back as I can remember, I was singing in a gospel choir on Sundays. "Amazing Grace" was a song we sang every week. It's one of the first melodies I ever heard. Later in life, the preacher from that church told me it was the first song he ever remembered hearing me sing. There I was, six or seven years old, walking through the streets of Abbott singing "Amazing Grace." Even at such a young age, there was never a doubt in my mind about what those words meant:

Amazing grace,
How sweet the sound
That saved a wretch like me.
I once was lost
But now I'm found,
Was blind but now I see.

They're all about faith and positive thinking. Which, to me, are the same things.

It's a pretty daily occurrence how "Amazing Grace" seems to rescue me at just the right time. See, I live and breathe around negativity. It's all around me and always has been since I decided to become a musician. I had been writing poems since I was five. I had been playing guitar since I was six. But no matter how much I loved music, I still prepared a backup by studying law at Baylor University because I thought I would need something to fall back on, in case the music thing didn't work out. It didn't take long for me to realize that writing, performing and singing songs was what I was meant to do, but what other people thought was an entirely different issue.

If I had to break it down, I'd say about 99 percent of the people in my life were telling me I wasn't going to make it. All that adversity and lack of faith ended up just strengthening my own convictions. All that negativity really helped me in the end, because there's no better inspiration for doing something than having somebody say that you can't do it. Between that and the positive message of "Amazing Grace"—which was so much a part of me, like DNA—I felt like I had something to prove and the power to prove it.

And it's still that way. No matter how much success I've had, I still have to prove myself all the time. Maybe it's to the people who are always coming up with different ideas for my CDs or the songs I write. Or maybe it's against all the unfortunate circumstances I've faced, be they financial problems or failed marriages. In that sense, it's a good thing that I'm able to sing "Amazing Grace" onstage every night. That song has rescued me many, many times. It helps me believe that everything's going to be all right. The more I believe that, the better chance I have of getting through the troubles. If you start *acting* like you feel good—whether you believe it or not—that's the first step. Just act like you believe it for a while, and something good will come along.

I'm not the only one who responds to that song; those lyrics send a universal message. *Everybody* knows the chorus to "Amazing Grace." All the musicians I know love that song, and nobody has ever resisted it at one of my shows. I've performed it all over the world, in places where people don't even speak English, and they still feel the power of "Amazing Grace."

There's a reason for that that maybe we can't completely explain. It strikes a tone, hits a chord that cuts right through the BS of the day and goes right to the bone. The words and the melody have a healing quality. It brings people peace, lets them know there are other people in the world who are going through the same thing.

A lot of times when I perform that song, people start singing along just like we used to at church. And everyone benefits from that churchlike atmosphere, whether they go to church or not. You don't have to be sitting in a pew to feel that sense of spirituality. We're all living in our own churches; our bodies are our temples. At least that's what they told me when I was growing up. "Amazing Grace" makes you feel the hope of church wherever you are. I try to catch some feel of that hymn in all of my songs, some sort of light at the end of the tunnel. None of my songs are entirely hopeless. That's been entirely intentional. I'm always trying to find a path to get us through the hard times.

Paul Newman

Actor and Philanthropist

Iwas having dinner one evening during the filming of *Butch Cassidy and the Sundance Kid* with the director George Roy Hill. I told him that "luck" had been the most significant factor in the birth and propulsion of my career. "Garbage," said George. "Luck is an art. Luck marches right past most people. Their brains are too cross-eyed to notice."

I let the comment simmer for twenty years or so while luck, for the most part, favored me, especially with the improbable success of my Newman's Own food company. That good fortune seemed, according to George, a bit of luck that I had uncrossed my eyes long enough to notice.

So when the first profits started rolling in, it seemed right somehow that the money should help children whose luck had been simply brutal—children with life-threatening diseases, cancer, blood conditions, tumors, the kind of luck that the children might not have a lifetime to correct. We couldn't change their luck, but it occurred to me that maybe we could lighten the load.

So we came up with the idea of a camp for sick children. We had no credentials to build or run it, and there were several false starts. We looked at the wrong places, at the wrong people. The most important bit of luck came when we found Dr. Howard Pearson of

Yale, a pediatric oncologist, to oversee the place. Without the credentials that he brought to our undertaking, we couldn't have gotten off the ground.

But once off the ground, few parents were inclined to trust us with their children, most of whom had not been away from home and hospital care. That first session we were half full. I stood in the driveway waiting for the buses, but traffic was light. Parents were not about to release their sick children to an untested, untried place. For me, it was like being ready for a party and hardly anyone showing up.

We did fill up the camp by the end of the summer, though; because word spread that this camp was special, indeed—a safe and caring place. Now, of course, as I look back, if we had been full that first session, it would have been a disaster. We had the sheer luck of under-occupancy, which gave us a chance to work the wrinkles out.

I had visited other camps for children who were ill and couldn't see the difference between the look of a camp and the look of a hospital. Both of them had a lot of steel and glass—chilly, to say the least. So I tried to create a place that would have a sense of romance, adventure, and humor for kids. The Hole in the Wall Gang is from *Butch Cassidy;* the look is a turn-of-the-century Western town.

We have a counselor for every two campers, which allows us to give children who would not be able to attend a traditional camp a place where they aren't any different from the other kids, and where they can behave badly and raise a little hell. Over the years, our medical staff has grown, which increases our ability to deal with chemotherapy and other treatments. There are no mandatory activities. Children can choose anything from handicrafts to theater to fishing. We have a gymnasium, rope climbs, and horses. Any kid who wants to, regardless of his condition, can participate. They are a loud and raucous bunch most of the time. What could be better?

Nothing, except—

You hope you have created a sanctuary where children are the beneficiaries, but as "luck" would have it, you find out that the staff is getting back as much as it gives, maybe more, because the kids give back as much as they get—a reciprocal trade agreement, so to speak, people in the service of others, which is, of course, the best part of this country in which we live.

As it turns out, it is possible to mess with luck, slow it down, hassle it, and maybe even overtake it. Fourteen years ago, only 30 percent of the children who attended our first camp session would survive. Today that number has been reversed: Seventy percent of our campers will now overcome cancer and go on to have normal lives, thanks to medical advances, which is not luck, it's perseverance. But then some say the quality of perseverance is genetic, which is luck of the genes, got it? Which is what I said from the very beginning.

Mike Nichols

Director

When I attended the college of the University of Chicago in the fifties, you didn't have to attend class or take any exams till the end of the year, when there was one comprehensive exam, which you passed or failed. Obviously, there were classes and quizzes and quarterly marks, but none of this was compulsory. You got to choose what to do. This approach had been originated by the great educator Robert Maynard Hutchins, who was chancellor of the university, leaving after my first year. He had famously disbanded the football team saying he considered it a distraction from learning.

It had also turned out that in the greatest secrecy the atom bomb had been developed in a commandeered squash court under the grandstands of the university's Stagg Field. Enrico Fermi and his colleagues on December 2, 1942, had achieved the first self-sustaining controlled release of nuclear energy. By the beginning of the fifties there was a plaque on the stadium, which apprised us of this.

All this was heady stuff, and although I started out going to my classes and doing the reading suggested, after a while I stopped going to class. I preferred to sleep, hang out in the co-op where I lived, and talk to my friends.

There was one class that I did attend because I loved it so much. It was called *Humanities 3,* which is the kind of name classes had in those days. It followed *Humanities 2*, which some people had taken the year before. There was no *Humanities 4*. Nowadays classes have names like *Global Women Filmmakers in the Independent Cinema Movement*, or *Imagining the American Empire: Race, Gender, and Nation in the Discourses of Imperialism and Anti-Imperialism*. But for us it was *Humanities 3*, which we called Hume 3. Our teacher was Mr. Rosenheim. Ned Rosenheim. I loved him. He was very funny and was teaching us Aristotle's *Poetics*, an analysis of the elements of drama.

I didn't yet know that I would work in the theater and movies, but the pull of the ideas was very strong. Without my being aware of it, the theater was what held my interest above all else. I was very excited about reading Dostoyevsky and E. M. Forster, T. S. Eliot, and Ezra Pound, and my new friends and I talked about all this, sometimes all night, driving the waiters in the restaurants of Chicago's South Side crazy as we stayed till 5 A.M., ordering no more than a cup of coffee. I was different from most of my friends in that I read plays a lot too. Unaccountably, when I was fourteen, I had read every word written by Eugene O'Neill, something I could not do now any more than I could climb Everest. Still I had no real sense that I would end up doing some of the things that so fascinated me.

But Ned Rosenheim was my hero. During the course of his taking us through the *Poetics* his examples were like burrs that stuck in the mind, in some cases forever. He was truly Socratic in that he got your mind working and providing the answer to his and your own questions. When we were in the stage of discussing the structure of a play, Aristotle's definition of beginning, middle, and end, he presented us with what he called "Rosenheim's *Othello*." He said, "Here's my *Othello*. In the first act Othello discovers that his wife is cheating on him and he kills her. For the next three acts he regrets it. All right, what's wrong with it?"

When we got to the definition of tragedy and comedy he said, "OK. According to Aristotle, tragedy is the fall of someone greater than us. Comedy is also a fall, the fall of the dignified without serious harm. Here," he said, "is an example: A very elegant man in a silk top hat slips on a banana peel and falls. This is very funny." We stared at him unsmiling. "But," he said, "imagine," and he doddered before the class, speaking with a thin quavery voice, "a dear little old lady . . . ." As Noël Coward liked to say, we laughed like drains. Rosenheim stared at us, shocked. "You people are monsters!" he said. Like I said, I loved him.

Somewhere in the unconscious of people in a certain generation there is the idea of student and teacher as seen in the play and movie of *The Corn Is Green* in which a spinster schoolteacher in Wales—Bette Davis, of course, in the movie—coaches a boy who is a miner, and he gets into Oxford and becomes an important writer. This was the actual story of the playwright who wrote it, Emlyn Williams. When he got to Oxford his roommate was Richard Burton, also Welsh, as we know, and the rest is Camelot, if not history.

So anyway, there I was, loving college, which to me meant the people I knew and was coming to love, and our running conversation, and rapt in the one class I was taking, Hume 3. There were occasional quizzes for the people who wanted marks at the end of the quarter, but they were not compulsory, so I didn't take them.

One day I waited for Professor Rosenheim after class because I had a question. When he left the class I fell in step with him and I asked my question. I have forgotten what it was. I remember his answer and always will. He said, "You're very clever, Nichols, and very charming, but I'm sorry, I owe my time to the people who do the work." Then he walked on.

Two or three times in my life I have read or heard something that seemed in a moment to change me so palpably that I actually heard or felt a click, a sound, tumblers falling into place, what have you. Whatever it's called it was a physical sensation. Freud calls it an *Ahah Erlebnis*, an "ah-hah" experience. It is neither pleasant nor unpleasant; it is simply the experience of becoming somebody slightly different, somebody new, the next you. That is what Ned Rosenheim caused to happen to me by telling the truth.

That was the beginning of my understanding that, whether you have good study habits or not, the only way to get to do the things that excite you is to find out everything you possibly can about them. That was the beginning of my working life. The present that Rosenheim gave me had a value that is incalculable: a change to myself.

There are, of course, other things that have changed me and other people who have told me the truth and made it a gift, but Professor Rosenheim was the first and maybe made the most profound change. It is at least partly because of him that I love the truth. Horrible as it sometimes is, beautiful as it can be, and all the degrees in between, it is still the only truth and thus the best thing we have. Thanks, Professor. *The Corn Is Green* has nothing on us.

Jack Nicholson

Actor

Lots of folks like to give advice. I tend to listen when I know the person isn't the advice-giving type.

My sister Lorraine was the quiet one in my family. But she was kind of fiery. We lived in Neptune City in New Jersey, what we call The Shore. I was sixteen and I'd skipped a grade so I was already done with high school. I didn't know what to do with my life. I wasn't sure about college and I didn't exactly feel like working a straight job. I'd been hoping to be a professional athlete, probably a ballplayer, second base, but maybe in the back of my mind I knew that wouldn't pan out. So then, I thought, maybe a sportswriter. That's when my sister Lorraine said, "Look, Jack, you're gifted, but if you stay around here you'll always just be Jack Nicholson. Everybody will know everything about you and no matter how good you are you'll be a big fish in a little pond. But if you take a shot and get out of town, you might feel differently. You could at least be a fish in a big pond." This was Lorraine, so I listened. I went to California to see what it was like. I figured I'd be back soon enough.

Looking back, it was kind of crazy. I was an adolescent with no visible means of support. I applied at MGM but while I waited, I made some money at the racetrack and playing pool at night. It wasn't really working out. But the day I was thinking of going home

I got a call about a job in the cartoon department at MGM. I did everything there—mail boy, production, punching and stacking the papers, keeping the cartoonists happy with supplies. One day I was in the elevator with a guy named Joe Pasternak. He asked me if I'd ever thought of being an actor. I actually had by then, but for some reason I said, "No." I went back to work and all of a sudden my boss Bill Hanna of Hanna-Barbera called me into his office and said, "Did Joe Pasternak ask you if you wanted to be an actor?" I said, "Yeah." He said, "Well, what did you say?" I told him I'd said, "No." "Well, Jack," he said, "let me ask you a question. Do you want to be a goddamn office boy all your life?" I think that was the first quality professional advice I ever received.

Thing was, I hadn't gone out to L.A. to be a movie star. I'd come to see movie stars. Right from the very beginning, movies had a lot to do with me. I was a big fan of *Thunderhead* and *My Friend Flicka,* and those propaganda films of World War II. I even remember the movies I never saw, but heard about from other kids, like *Thirty Seconds Over Tokyo.* All I had to hear was that they cut off a guy's hands with his black gloves on and that image stuck with me forever. My last two years of high school I assistant-managed a movie theater. To this day if I really wanted to know how a movie would do in advance I would take it to a small theater somewhere. When a theater manager tells you, "Oh, this movie is going to do well," you can bank on it. You see the people going in and you see them coming out. You don't need a pollster.

I've had a fortunate career from the beginning, though it took me a long time to really get started. There were definitely some people who said the right thing along the way. I took a class at the Players Ring Theater with Joe Flynn, a wonderful character actor. One day he pulled me aside and said, "Look, we're at the end of this class here. There's not much I can teach you with the time we have left. But I want to say one thing to you, Jack, that's very important. Everyone you meet in this business is going to try to get you to take voice lessons. Don't do it." That's the only advice he gave me and I took it. Of course, everybody did try to get me to change my weird voice.

Sometimes it's not the advice directly that's important so much as being called on something and having to explain yourself. I had one of the best acting teachers in the business, Jeff Corey. A lot of the people I'll know for the rest of my life I met in Jeff's class. We worked at night, and we worked constantly. One night he got mad and said, "Jocko, there's absolutely nothing happening. What are you doing? Why are you in class? You're not doing anything. I don't see any work." I looked over at him and said, "Well, Jeff, let me ask you something. Do you think it's possible that I'm doing something and you're not seeing it?" He tells that story, too. What I was trying to figure out was how much can you show and what becomes indicated and what's really being. You never stop trying to suss that out for yourself.

That's why I appreciated working with John Huston. We did *Prizzi's Honor* together, and he had the lightest hand of any director I've worked with. It reminded me of what Truffaut always told his editor: "Remember, better is the enemy of good." When John thought he had it good enough, that was it. I had complete confidence in him, and confidence is crucial. You might disagree with a director, but you've got to believe he has his reasons.

I used to have trouble with directors because I talk slow. Whether they were right or not, I didn't want that to be what I was thinking about. When I did *Chinatown* with Roman Polanski, he said, "Jack, can you do this faster?" He was a friend, and I said, "Roman, why? Why are you telling me to do this faster? Give me a chance here." And he said, "I'll tell you why. We've got a hundred-something-page screenplay here. It's a detective picture and we have to get all the facts in. If you talk at this pace, the movie will be three hours long." It was the first time I'd heard a legitimate piece of direction about how fast an actor should talk.

Some of the advice I've gotten is basic, essential stuff. The actor Peter Lorre told me that if you want to last in this business, you'd better be frugal. I still live in the first house I ever bought. Some advice is ageless. When we were making *The Border* the director Tony Richardson said, "Remember, in life it's the things that you don't do that you regret, not the things you do." That's a pretty damn good one. I guess it's what Lorraine was telling me all those years ago.

Jack Nicholson

Conan O'Brien

Talk Show Host

I'm not one to brag, but I just might be the smartest person who ever lived. I was multilingual in the womb, and my brain, when submerged in a saline solution, displaces over eight liters. By comparison, Einstein's brain displaces only six liters and has a weird smell. Like Uri Geller, I can bend steel simply with my thoughts and, also like Uri Geller, my fame peaked in the late seventies.

Although none of the above is true, it is a fact that my strength has always been my mind. It's not that I'm inordinately bright, it's just that my complete lack of physical skills and my quaint "chimney sweep" fashion sense have, by process of elimination, made my mental ability my main asset. I was always thought of as kind of "quick" and this quality saw me through four years at an accredited college and a career in comedy second only to Gerald Ford's. In short, if the first twenty-two years of my life taught me anything, it was that my meal ticket in life was going to be my mind.

Maybe that's why I was taken aback when I was first told to "Stop thinking so much."

These were the words of an improvisation instructor I met in 1985. I had just arrived in Los Angeles to take a job as a comedy writer and I was interested in doing some performing. So, I signed up for a class taught by a wise and charismatic woman named Cynthia Szigeti. Her words added an entirely new dimension to my life and, I believe, ultimately made a big difference in my career. Were it not for her, I would be driving a bus somewhere and earning just about what I make today. (I really need to speak to my agent. . . .)

Honestly, though, Cynthia opened a door for me. When I entered her class I was determined to blow everyone away with my wit and verbal agility. When asked to get up onstage and spontaneously create a scene with another actor, I was going to "write" everything in my head and, thus, reveal my innate genius. I was going to use this advantage to spare myself any humiliation.

But there I was, scheming away, and she barked out, "Stop thinking so much," from somewhere on the sidelines. I didn't know what to do. I didn't even know how to get off the stage without writing my exit.

Cynthia could see that writing was a crutch for me. Real performing is much more fluid than the measured, carefully crafted job of composing. Writers draft outlines and plot plots. They write and rewrite. It's exactly as you see it in movies and on television: We furrow our brows, crumple up pages, order Chinese food, and sexually satisfy women in a way that no one else can. But this kind of overthinking in your brain is anathema to the process of thinking on your feet. Which is what performing is all about.

Eastern philosophy teaches that our strength is our weakness and our weakness is our strength. My mental ability was stopping me from reacting in the moment. Instead of thinking onstage

I needed to *be* onstage. To really perform, you have to give yourself over to the fact that you don't know what you're creating until you are done. If this all sounds too Zen, well—I am at peace with that.

On the show now, I sometimes find myself doing something odd when a guest is speaking: I shut up and listen. While once my instinct would have been to mentally race ahead to find a funny place, I instead listen to a guest and find the funny moment there. Or not. Unfortunately, we have a lot of archival footage of Conan O'Brien failing to say something funny. But my favorite moments on the show are when a joke dies an ugly death, because the recovery afterward makes the moment memorable. These recoveries don't always work, but when they do, the moment is so sweet that all mistakes tend to be forgiven.

"Stop thinking so much" proved to be the mantra of my subsequent weird career. People ask me all the time how I wound up with my own talk show or how I managed to make it last nine years. The truth is I don't know. It's like asking someone, "So how did you get hit by a meteor?" My *Late Night* career has largely been the result of reacting honestly and spontaneously to people and problems around me. I don't know how I got here and I certainly don't know where I'm going. This is the essence of my philosophy, and, coincidentally, the words to most Jimmy Buffet songs.

Which finally reminds me of one last piece of wisdom I heard a running back say about football. He said that, despite the best planning and blocking, "The hole is never where it's supposed to be." What this man was saying is that real life is about reacting quickly to the opportunity at hand, not the opportunity you envisioned. Not thinking and scheming the future, but letting it happen and reacting. In this way life is a lot like football, right down to the part where you pat the ass of the man next to you.

"Stop thinking so much." I still think about that today—in fact, I think I think about it too much. Which means I've learned nothing. Which isn't what I planned. So, I guess, that's okay.

Rosie O'Donnell

Talk Show Host

I spent years searching for the words to make sense of the tragedy that changed my life at age ten. Words that conveyed painful emotions were not welcome in my father's house, and my search was lonely, even furtive. But that suppressive environment also impressed upon me the power of words—to hurt and to heal.

I was playing at my friend Jackie's house that late winter's day in 1973 when the phone call came. Jackie's mom went into the other room so I couldn't see her face, and then came back and told me to go home. I knew something was wrong, because she never told me to go home before. When I got to my house, there were all these unfamiliar cars in our driveway. I went inside and joined my four siblings at the kitchen table. My father came in and told us our mom had passed away. His words jarred. I remember thinking that I didn't know what that meant, "passed away."

But my father was a man of few words and still is to this day. So that was all he said.

Then people started to cry. I remember going outside and playing hockey. I kept looking at the sun and the trees and thinking that something is going to be different. But I was left alone to figure it all out.

At school they put up a memorial plaque to my mother, who had been president of the PTA. ROSEANNE O'DONNELL, it read. WHAT

WE ARE GIVEN WE SHALL KEEP. I always thought the plaque should have read, "What has been taken away we shall pretend never was." Because after her death, everyone around me seemed to act as if she'd never existed.

I wanted to talk about losing her. To cry about it and paint about it and dance about it and sculpt about it. But I was not encouraged to express my feelings at home, and that turned me inward. I found solace in writing, filling countless journals. And I began to notice that when emotions are turned into words written down on white paper, they gain a power that can make them challenging, even threatening.

But it took the words of others to unleash my grief.

I saw *Les Miserables* the day it opened on Broadway, six years after my mother died. Valjean sings: "And must my name until I die, be no more than an alibi? Must I lie? How can I ever face my fellow men? How can I ever face myself again? My soul belongs to God, I know I made that bargain long ago. He gave me hope when hope was gone. He gave me strength to journey on."

For all the denial and pain I had known, here was a simple message: Be true to yourself, to who you are and what you want and care about and need. It simply blew me away and left me a blubbering mess.

After that, I became mildly obsessive about musical theater because it expressed in broad strokes and grandiose gestures the emotions I had been suppressing all my life. In theater, and also literature, I have found words that sent shivers up my spine and inspired me at key moments in my life.

If my mother's death had drained the color from my world, my son Parker's birth in 1995 restored it. Amid the torrent of emotions that raged in me as I held him in those first days of his life, I remembered a line from one of Anne Rice's books about a slave who, despite the degradation of his captivity, "moved with the grace and dignity that could only come from having once been cherished." My goal as a parent is to fill my children with enough of the feeling of being cherished, important, loved and nurtured that they will move through their lives with grace and dignity.

And it was Parker himself who offered the words to carry me through the third defining event of my life—the devastating tragedy of September 11. That event etched itself onto my spirit like a tattoo. And it made me realize that for all my efforts to protect my children, I can't control their world. So I can't live in the fear; I have to let go and live in the love. Parker helped me understand that. He insisted I take him to a fire station, even though I feared he was too young to deal with all the pain there. But he said, "Mommy, I need to go." So eventually I took him. And there were these shell-shocked firemen in dress blues, on their way to another funeral, and grieving for fifteen of their firehouse brothers who had died in the World Trade Center. I saw my son walk over to a very big fireman and tug on his coat. The fireman stooped close, and Parker said, "Sorry your friends died trying to save us. But they're with God now." And my son started to cry. And the fireman started to cry. Then I started to cry, and everyone else who had heard. I had been trying to protect my son, thinking it would be too much for him. And he ended up saving me as he has done ever since he arrived.

Shaquille O'Neal

Athlete

I was about seventeen when my mother said the words that changed my life. It was the summer before my senior year in high school, and I was playing basketball at Cole High School in San Antonio, Texas. My game was pretty good for a kid my age. My picture was always in the papers. I was a high school all-star, a child superstar I guess you could say.

Basketball was more than a game to me. Before I became a player, other kids were always picking on me, always joking about how big I was. There was no question I was different: I was six feet four by the time I was eleven. Kids always called me names, nasty names like Shaquilla the Gorilla. When I started playing basketball everything changed. They were able to admire me instead of laughing at me. Basketball saved my life. So it wasn't just that I wanted to play. I needed to play. And things were going real well for me.

But that summer, I went to basketball camp. That's where guys go when they're looking to the NBA. And once I got there I started doubting myself. I didn't know whether I was going to be able to make it in basketball, whether I had what it takes.

Camp is real competitive. You've got all the best high school players from everywhere in the country. At Cole High, I was always ranked first, but at camp, I saw other guys being put ahead of me. I was always put behind guys like Alonzo Mourning and Jimmy Jackson. Those guys got more attention, more individual coaching, the best shorts. It seemed like people were more excited about them than about me. It was a great shock. My first instinct was to think, *Maybe I'm not as good as I thought I was. I don't think this is going to do it for me.*

Whenever I had a problem I went to my parents for whatever information I needed. I had older friends but they were knuckleheads, and you can't go to knuckleheads for life lessons. So when I needed guidance I looked to my mother or my father. They always had the words that put me back on the right course.

They both had very different ways of saying these words. My father was brash. He told me: "Don't walk around with your head down." He meant: Don't give up; don't be embarrassed about yourself; stand up and fight.

My mother had a different way. She was strong, like my father, but she was gentle too. She said, "You must fulfill your dreams while there's still room for you to do so. Attack them with a full head of steam. There's no opportunity like now. This is the time you can show people."

I didn't feel like I could stand out among those players. I tried to brush her off, saying, "I can't do that right now. Maybe later."

Then my mother said the words that changed everything for me. She said, "Later doesn't always come to everybody."

That got to me. Those words snapped me into reality and gave me a plan. You work hard now. You don't wait. If you're lazy or you sit back and you don't want to excel, you'll get nothing. If you work hard enough, you'll be given what you deserve. Everything got easier for me after that.

For the rest of that summer I had a focus. I worked really hard and by the end of that camp no one could tell me anything different than what I already knew: I was the best. And when Jimmy Jackson and Alonzo Mourning and I were in the 1992 NBA draft, Jackson was the fourth pick. Mourning was the number two pick. I was the number one pick.

I wasn't going to wait for later.

Al Pacino

Actor

It's 1977. My throat's dry, my body is jumping. There's too much going on. Too many new people coming at me from every direction. Too much business, too many contracts, too many projects, too many requests, too many tempting beautiful women everywhere. I can't go anywhere without being recognized. Everything's happened very fast. I'm overwhelmed. Agents want to promote me, managers want to handle me, reporters want to quote me on everything from Mao's death to who I was with last night. This spotlight.

I'm over my head.

It feels like only yesterday I was living in a basement with a sink as my bathtub and a toilet in the rooming house hall shared by a tenement full of waywards rehearsing a Shakespearean monologue for some obscure theater group in the bowels of Brooklyn. What happened?

Now there are plays I can do, movies I can make. It's all there, all of it in front of me; I can see it but not clearly, taste it, feel it. But what I want, what I *really need now,* is a drink. The drink that will help take the edge off. The drink that will get me through all this another day. The drink that will dull my senses and make it palatable for a moment—only a moment.

It wasn't long ago I was helping my friend Charlie up from

an alcoholic blackout in a doorway, where he had decided to take a rest. Where was that? When was that? I can't remember. Was it a year ago? A year since he had decided to become sober, to give up what we had shared for so many drunken crazy years. Charlie, my acting teacher. Charlie, my mentor. Charlie, who walks across the Manhattan Bridge with me in the wee hours of those freezing February nights, broke and undaunted, as we quote everything from Villon to Shakespeare. Charlie, always my best interests at heart. Charlie, who sees something in me I don't see myself. He'd stopped drinking a year ago. I can't believe it. I am abandoned. What will I do?

I call him. We meet. We sit down in the Lion's Head Café, in Greenwich Village. I will never forget the moment. We sat across from each other at a wooden table, where I had my vodka and lemon peel backed by a good strong stout on the side. Charlie just sat on the other side empty-handed, a glass of cola somewhere in his vicinity. He looked at me in a way that I have never seen him look for all the years I've known him. He smiled. There was a sadness in his smile. He watched me sort of swaying in the chair. He leaned over and said, "Al, please. Just be aware of what you're doing." Somehow those words rang. I don't know why to this day. I don't know why. "Be aware that you're taking that glass, you're lifting it to your lips, you're sipping it. You're swaying in your chair. And this is what you're doing," Charlie said. "You continue to do it. If you wish. But be aware that's what you're doing. It's not something everybody does. It's not breathing in and out. It's an action. Don't take it for granted. Just give it some thought. Please, Al." Those words could sound, I guess, preachy or whatever had they not been delivered with such compassion. And such a sense of love and fear. Even though I thought I was in control, I knew what I was doing. I still took heed somehow. I hear him.

I down the glass and look into Charlie's eyes. My friend's really talking to me. He is concerned. I've made five movies now. He wants to see five more. Maybe ten. Maybe fifty.

I look at the empty glass. At the half-filled bottle. How is it possible a person can do something and be so naturally oblivious, so utterly unaware of the very *act* of doing it? It took me a few months but finally I got it. I saw to what degree this thing had taken over my life. How it occupied me, owned me. I capped the bottle. I became conscious. I was aware. It was time.

Ten years later. It's 1987. I'm in the audience at Carnegie Hall waiting for Sinatra to come out and sing. It's early. Buddy Rich comes on first to open the show. He's sixty-five years old. He gets behind his drums and my mind begins to wander. I'm thinking about all the drinks and drugs I haven't had since that day Charlie made me aware. Not a day goes by . . . but I know this: I'm still here. I may not have been otherwise. Listening now to Rich play the drums while I wait for Sinatra. My eyes are closed and my mind wanders. What am I hearing? It sounds like the ocean. Like there are two drummers. Does he have brothers playing with him? I look up to check it out. It's just Rich, moving so fast it seems like six sticks are hitting the drums. The drums are talking. Then the cowbell. Now he's slapping just his two sticks together. I've never heard or seen anything like it. Carnegie Hall is filled to capacity, and one lone drummer is holding us captive. Is anyone even breathing? Where is he going to go with this? Just how much can you do with two sticks? And then it happens—that transcendent moment. He lifts both sticks in the air way above his head and suddenly, swiftly, separates them. There is a visible inch between the tips. There is a total silence in the Hall. Then a roar. The approval is overwhelming. I'm standing with everyone else. Bravo! Bravo! Sinatra, the legend, has to follow this? And when he comes out he pauses, then looks at us and acknowledges our awe. For what we just heard from Buddy Rich. And he simply says, "There's something to say for keeping at a thing, isn't there?" That's all.

Sinatra is on the money.
There is something to be said.
For keeping at a thing.
For being aware.
Charlie was right.
Thank you, Charlie.

Gwyneth Paltrow

Actress

M̲ary has been my best friend since kindergarten. We met in Los
Angeles, where I was born, and attended the same grammar
school together, a little place called St. Augustine By the Sea. It was a
hippie-type school, actually—a place where, if they asked you,
"What is two plus two?" and you said, "Five," they would say, "Well,
if five *feels* good to you, then okay!"

Although I didn't grow a lot academically at St. Augustine, I
did learn everything I needed to know about friendships and feeling
good about myself. Most important, it's where I met Mary. She has
always been a soul sister to me and always tells me the truth.

Never was this more obvious than years ago when I was going
through a bad time with a boyfriend of mine. I always seemed to be
unhappy. Although I loved him, there was something about him that
made me believe I was never enough for him. Day after day, I picked
apart our troubled romance, all the while crowding my mind with
thoughts like if only I were smarter, or more beautiful, or wittier; if
only I were all those things, I could somehow get my boyfriend to
care for me the way I cared for him.

My mind works in a linear fashion. I certainly don't have
low self-esteem. And yet, for some reason, my relationship was
making me doubt myself and my instincts. Because these feelings

were so new, I couldn't let them go. I was driving myself crazy.

Around this time, Mary and I decided to attend a weekend workshop in yoga and meditation at a Japanese Zen Buddhist monastery up in the Catskills. We often did interesting things together, but this was a flight of fancy for us—we had never been on a retreat before. The schedule was, to say the least, unique: We would get up at five—to gongs—put on our robes, then meditate for forty-five minutes, without moving a muscle. After that we would have sessions in chanting and yoga, then eat lunch in silence; eye contact was not permitted. Admittedly, some of this was bizarre, and at moments it was really hard for Mary and me to keep from laughing; we had been friends since kindergarten, after all.

You would think that in this serene setting, I would shrug off the bad feelings I had been harboring about my boyfriend and enjoy myself, but instead, I felt the bottom drop out. Looking back, I suppose this was inevitable: When you're in an environment that is so still and pure—when you don't have all of that outside noise—the volume on your inner monologue turns way up, and along with it, whatever unfinished business you may have in your heart and soul.

So there we were, sitting by a beautiful lake after our morning activities and, once again, I was complaining, telling Mary how bad I felt, listing what to me was an unending stream of offenses—whether it was not calling me back when he said he would or not showing up when we had plans.

"This is so awful," I finally said to Mary. "Why am I doing this to myself? Why do I feel this way?"

Mary paused for a moment. "Gwyneth," she said, taking a breath, "you feel this way because you are not getting what you need."

"What do you mean?" I asked.

Mary simply and calmly repeated her words. "You're not getting what you need, Gwynnie."

Uncharacteristically, I didn't respond immediately. I remained silent for a long while. Maybe it was the setting, maybe it was the simple directness of Mary's strong, loving words. But suddenly, I realized that I was, in fact, a valuable person who, for some reason, had permitted an unhealthy relationship to provoke these awful feelings. Like a fog lifting, it instantly became clear that my boyfriend wasn't the problem—*I* was, by not allowing myself to get what I needed. In other words, I was taking care of him, not me.

As the day wore on I began to feel a little angry, resentful even. After all, if it was true that I wasn't getting what I needed, then the obvious conclusion was that this guy wasn't the right person for me. And I wasn't ready to accept the verdict.

For the rest of the weekend, Mary's words played in my head. I actually felt glad to leave the monastery and return home where I could clutter my days with distractions—shopping for groceries or returning e-mail or remembering to give my dog his monthly flea pill. In retrospect, I was clearly relieved to steep myself in activities that kept me from doing what needed to be done.

But, of course, it wasn't long before I acted on Mary's advice. I broke up with him and everything started to look brighter.

To this day, Mary's lakeside counsel continues to have a profound effect on me. Whenever I feel displaced or off balance, those simple words—"You're not getting what you need"—can still set me straight. I have chosen a profession in which demands, reasonable and otherwise, are frequently made of me, whether it's working overtime or making a public appearance after a thirteen-hour workday, when all I really want to do is sleep. And in these situations, when I find myself struggling to be a version of myself that would please somebody else but not me, I quietly ask myself, "Are you getting what you need? Are you drawing boundaries?" And if the answer is no, I immediately know what I need to do.

Self-esteem is a fragile thing, and I've learned that. In the end, it's within our power—it's our responsibility, actually—to take care of ourselves and nourish feelings of worthiness.

Gwyneth Paltrow

Sarah Jessica Parker

Actress

Ironically, the words that perhaps had the greatest impact on my life were words I never heard spoken.

I was eight years old and living in Ohio. My family didn't have a lot of money at the time, and for a brief period, we were dependent on the state for financial aid. This is not to say that our household was constantly running on a deficit, but, yes, there were occasions on which my parents would say, "There is not going to be Christmas this year." Naturally, this was a disappointment to us as kids, but looking back, I wouldn't trade my childhood for anything: I was never deprived of love, food or shelter.

It was around this time that my brother, Toby, who was eleven, and I decided that we wanted to audition for the Cincinnati Ballet, which was then among the most respected ballet companies in the country. Although my parents always had been supportive of our interest in the arts, they clearly didn't have the means to invest in our futures as dancers. Attendance at the school required up to six classes a week, sometimes two or three a day. In a million years, we never could have afforded that.

So my mother approached the head of the ballet company school, a man named David Blackburn, about getting a scholarship for Toby and me. There wasn't a big financial aid program at the

Cincinnati Ballet, but as my mother found out, Mr. Blackburn was a determined and resourceful man.

"We think Toby and Sarah Jessica have potential," Mr. Blackburn told our parents after our audition, "and could have a career in ballet. They're going to have to work very hard, of course, and maintain a decent grade-point average in school. But we believe it's worth the company's time and financial commitment to have them with us. They will get scholarships."

I wasn't present when Mr. Blackburn delivered this news, and to his enormous credit he never once mentioned the scholarship to me in the three years I danced with the company. Never did he imply to me, "You're here for free and have a lot to prove, so you better live up to it," nor did he make me feel beholden to him, or that I'd have to raise my hand to get my free lunch. He just let me be an equal among students.

Because Mr. Blackburn saw it in his heart to put out a hand to me, a whole new chapter began in my life. As the years passed, the program became more intense, and in the process, Mr. Blackburn taught me that dance was not simply about technique or the act of whipping your feet into various positions. Instead, it was about telling a story to an audience, with your face as well as your body. By enlightening me to this invaluable concept, Mr. Blackburn was unconsciously teaching me about acting, as well, which, of course, became the most important skill I would need in the vocation I eventually chose.

Mr. Blackburn's generosity didn't end when our family moved to New York three years later. He took care to see that Toby and I got into American Ballet Theatre, that our scholarships were in place and our transitions smooth. This was beyond the call of your typical ballet teacher, but Mr. Blackburn had an interest in our lives and our future, which was unusual and special.

Although I didn't understand it at the time, the older I got, the more I recognized what a great leap of faith Mr. Blackburn took with my brother and me. That single act of generosity taught me that someone could believe in you, regardless of where you come from or what you look like or what you may or may not have to offer in return. I learned that a person's real value is based not on their means but instead on who they are. Many people think the world is closed to those who don't have; Mr. Blackburn was sending precisely the opposite message.

If I could have one wish, it would be for children to know that doors aren't open only to the affluent in this country. Disadvantaged kids in the inner cities often think, *I can't be a dancer; I can't pursue the arts; I can't be a sculptor or make pottery or come to New York City and become an actor because I can't afford it. My lot in life will be the minimum wage.* This is simply not true, and I speak from my own experience.

There is free culture out there—libraries, scholarships, arts programs and theater in the park. And just because one is not of a certain pedigree—because he or she is perceived as a mutt of some variety who has been disenfranchised and marginalized—doesn't mean that one's innermost dreams still can't be realized.

When I became a working actor and had discretionary money of my own, I set up a scholarship at the Cincinnati Ballet in the name of David Blackburn, who has since retired from dance and now lives across the water in Kentucky. The scholarship is intended for another child who has the desire to study ballet but, perhaps, can't afford it. I set up this fund not out of a sense of indebtedness, but more as an expression of hope. It is my belief that two Mr. Blackburns could change a whole school, and from that school we could possibly have a movement—and after that, who knows, maybe a whole new way of thinking.

Although it has been nearly thirty years since that memorable time, I can say with all confidence that Mr. Blackburn's words—of support to my parents, of encouragement to me—provided a vital spark in my life. And as I have been blessed to learn, a little spark of belief goes a long way.

Sean Penn

Actor and Director

I'd been broke in California and broke in New York. Now I'd gotten lucky, found myself back in Hollywood with an acting job. I could feed and house myself. I had freedoms I hadn't known before. This was the beginning of the 1980s. I did *Taps* and *Fast Times at Ridgemont High* and *Bad Boys* and a few more roles. I knew I was getting a chance to explore a whole spectrum of characters. But at the same time I was starting to find the bottom-line atmosphere there disruptive to the creative process. I'm not a puritan about this, and I don't mean to say that economics is something you can completely divorce from art, whether it's the financial plight of the people in your story or the funds you need to realize that story. These things are to be accepted. But what became clear to me was that a lot of the people I'd known in hungrier days had become beaten down by demands to be "professional."

Most of them seemed more concerned with protecting the studio's investment or making sure they got hired again than taking any kind of artistic gamble. Everything was on an economic clock. Everything was becoming less and less inspired. I remember feeling overwhelmed by what I considered a sort of appropriated maturity in people whose nature was not to behave that way. Everybody wants to be liked so much that nobody likes anybody. Each person giving in one little bit adds up to a whole lot of whoring. This could explain the state of the American film today.

Then one depressed night, drinking large amounts of Wild Turkey and smoking an inordinate number of cigarettes, I stumbled across a cartoon. I started giggling like a kid. Here was this tiny man looking up at another man in a three-piece suit and bowler hat, saying to him, "Don't mature. Mature people do shit work." Now, maybe that resonated with me in a regressive way at first, a sort of refuge for those who don't want to quit their indulgences. But on a deeper level, I think, was the fact that nobody knows the secret to the universe, and short of that, our nature is to not be entirely evolved and mature. To represent that immature nature, we, as artists, have to be able to laugh about stuff, appreciate mystery, and not try to answer all the questions.

I don't know where this cartoon appeared or even when, precisely, I saw it, but I think of it often. I bring it up to actors as direction when I think they're playing it too safe. There's a lack of emotional ambition in my game. There's a lack of adventure. This is the problem with professionalism, with so-called maturity. The mainstream has become increasingly intolerant. It doesn't want to see imagination engaged outside of its boundaries. I look around at the actors, or the painters, or the writers and directors who have something to say, and they are appreciated less and less in our culture, marginalized, written off. Where once maybe their case was overstated with terms like "rebel," which is ultimately an adolescent idea, now they are simply dismissed as upstarts.

The notion of the individual, a notion this country was founded on, has in many ways been lost. Maybe it had already begun to fade when Brando came along. Maybe the disappearance goes back further. I do see artists who keep adventuring, who keep doing what they do for the same reason they did it in the first place. But I can't tell you how many people have been beaten down. I remember the conversations we had, the youthful idealism. Now they don't remember the conversations. They sit around and talk about the balance of art and commerce. What is that? Are you an artist or are you an art-and-commerce balancer?

It doesn't mean you shouldn't be responsible. When I make a film, I don't spend more than I say I'm going to spend. I like to work small so I can have freedom, so that no outside condition must be met at the cost of discovery. It's not just about art, though. I think this false idea about what maturity means runs through politics, life. Human beings are not perfect. We make mistakes, we're sloppy, and we're silly. We're immature. William Saroyan wrote, "Discover in all things that which shines and is beyond corruption. Encourage virtue in whatever heart it may have been driven into secrecy and sorrow by the shame and terror of the world." We all get blindsided by the shame and terror, and by compromise, but you have to monitor yourself. You have to make sure you don't wake up wearing the bowler hat. With glue.

Itzhak Perlman

Musician

O f the thousands of pieces of advice, inspiration and encouragement I've received over the years, the most powerful one—the
one that has played a central role in my life, both as a child and an
adult—boils down to a single word: practice.

I was three and a half years old when I first started playing the
violin. My parents listened to the radio a lot, and whenever I would
hear a violin solo, I would say, "I want to play that instrument." Plain
and simple, I liked the sound.

So my mother and father got me a little fiddle—a one-
sixteenth-size, which is maybe fifteen or sixteen inches long. But
such a tiny instrument can't possibly produce good music—even at
three I knew it didn't sound right—so when I turned five, I graduated to a one-quarter-size violin, which was a little bigger.

Next I needed lessons. One day, my parents heard this fellow
playing in a boardwalk café in Tel Aviv and approached him about
giving me instruction.

"Do you teach the violin?" they asked him.

"Oh, sure," he responded eagerly. "I'll do anything."

I began taking lessons from this man, but after a while it
became apparent that he wasn't a particularly good teacher. So

eventually I went to the conservatory in Tel Aviv, where I learned to play the violin properly, under the tutelage of a woman named Ryvka Goldgart. Mrs. Goldgart was Russian and taught me to play according to traditional methods. She was a wonderful teacher, and my only one for the thirteen years that I lived in Israel.

And yet the word "practice" entered into my universe almost from the beginning. Although my parents loved to listen to music of all kinds, they weren't professionally trained; therefore, they couldn't help me learn the mechanics of the violin, nor could they instruct me on such matters as speed or pitch or phrasing. What they could do, however, was monitor my commitment to the instrument by listening for the sound of music coming from my room. If they heard me playing, they knew I was hard at work. If they didn't hear me playing, it was, "Practice!"

Mrs. Goldgart, meanwhile, also invoked the P-word, only in her case, she adopted—as we say in music—a variation on the theme. For her, the commonly heard phrase was, "Did you practice?" For instance, if I came in and played a passage pretty well, she would immediately know that I had been doing my homework. If things didn't sound quite right, I was busted. Consequently, what I was taught in my lessons depended on how well I had prepared for them beforehand.

Like most children learning a musical instrument, I wasn't really fond of practicing. I did it, mind you, sometimes three or four hours a day. But I found it to be mostly drudgery. What I really wanted to do was play new pieces or be outside with other kids.

But because the discipline of practice was instilled in me at just the right time—when I first picked up the violin, to be exact—it has become an elemental part of my craft. Nowadays, practicing is second nature to me, a matter of habit, really. How often I practice depends on how well I have been playing. If I perform in a concert and afterward can say to myself, "Well, that sounded okay—but I'm just getting away with it," I know it's time to brush up. Sometimes this requires an hour of work, sometimes just five minutes. I call this: "practicing on an as-needed basis."

Over the years, I have passed on this little but crucial word of advice to my own students. Like Mrs. Goldgart, I have put my own spin on it: I remind young musicians that they need to practice slowly. Time and again students complain to me that, despite the hours they are putting into the violin, they are not getting any better. So I ask them to show me how they practice, and 90 percent of the time they are playing too fast.

The brain functions as a series of tiny sequences, and for it to process complex information—a complicated Paganini passage, for instance—that information has to be input in a clean and precise manner. If a violinist tries to practice that passage by racing through it, the brain simply can't absorb all the necessary data, and ultimately the fingers won't learn what they are supposed to learn. So practicing slowly is the key.

In the end, practicing is really just about commitment—to your craft and ultimately to yourself. If you want to be truly good at what interests you, whether it is music or math or even your backhand, for that matter, you have to be willing to put in the time to be the best you can be. After all, as the old saying goes, "Genius is one percent inspiration and ninety-nine percent perspiration." It was Thomas Edison who first said those words. Of course, Edison didn't play violin.

Now maybe if he had practiced . . .

Bob Pittman

President and CEO of AOL Time Warner

My teenage son was going through a particularly turbulent time, as teenage sons do. I was sharing the saga with my dad. I talked to him at least twice a week, and he commiserated with me. My dad was a great guy, a Methodist minister in Mississippi. He was a Southerner with a dry sense of humor, full of stories and always thinking things through. He was used to doling out counsel, but he was not judgmental. He didn't give me a whole lot of advice, so when he did, I listened.

I was worrying about my son's behavior. He was fourteen at that time and we were at odds. He would push the limits, and I would push back; I was confused over where to draw the line with him. I was afraid to be a pushover. I thought I had to let him know strict and inflexible limits.

It's difficult when you arrive at that time as a parent when your child stops adoring you. When he stops hanging on your every word and begins thinking that almost every idea you have is stupid; when he goes from thinking everything you say is right to being sure that most of what you say is off the wall. This is the time when parents usually freak out. You are tempted to come down hard, and if the child doesn't listen after the first three times, you tend to come down harder.

At that point, I just didn't know the answer to essential questions. How far do I let my son go? Where do I draw the line?

My father finally told me where. He said never draw the line at a point where the two of you can no longer talk. There's nothing he does that you should lose your line of communication over it, that you should ruin your relationship.

This made such an impact on me. I realized that this was the rule that my father had always followed with me. You know, preachers' kids come in two flavors: Perfect and Always Getting into Trouble. My brother was the first, and I was closer to the second. I was the kind of kid who hung around with the crowd that kicked out lights in the interstate highway system and hotwired bulldozers at night to knock down new construction. I wasn't a direct participant, but I tended to push the rules. I nearly got thrown out of school, I wouldn't participate in programs that I didn't see any sense to, I refused to cut my hair.

To my surprise, my dad agreed with me about the programs and the length of my hair. He went to bat for me in school. If I was right, he would stand up for me. And even more amazing, if I was wrong, he would stand up for me. He let me do all kinds of things. My dad understood.

My biggest surprise happened when I was fifteen years old, and he let me drive to Jacksonville, Florida, for the Gator Bowl with three guys and girls. We were there for a week—quite a bit of freedom for someone of that age.

After my father's advice, there was a major change in how I dealt with my son. I listened to him more carefully; I let him know that everything was open to discussion. I began giving him more responsibility; I asked him what he thought the punishment should be if he stayed out past his curfew, and he came up with the idea that his curfew should be reduced the next time by the amount of time that he was late. He determined how he should work his life—his allowance, his homework. If he got certain grades, he got more freedoms. I decided that there had to be a set of rules, and he would decide what they were. He never abused this responsibility. There was a marked difference in our relationship and it lowered my stress level considerably.

My dad helped me see that the more you clamp down, the angrier everyone gets. You have to figure out how to empower your kid. You have to anticipate events and settle things before they happen. Dad undoubtedly was smiling when I was going on about my son. He was a man attracted to irony. He never said a thing, but I know he must have been remembering me as a teenager, thinking to himself: *Well now, it's payback time.*

Sidney Poitier

Actor

I owe the City University of New York for my daughter's education. I owe the streets of New York City for mine—and the streets of Miami, Florida, and the streets of Nassau and Cat Island in the Bahamas. Those are the places where I was taught that *honor* comes with *responsibility*. Where one *pays* as one goes. Where an unpredictable mix of curiosity, risks and rewards—unto themselves—can very often determine survival.

I was on a street like that when I first heard the words that would set my course and keep me steady at the wheel. On that morning in the summer of 1945, I had no way of knowing that trial and error, and curiosity, risks and rewards were positioned for a life-altering impact on my existence. Let's pick it up a half hour before the moment arrived.

I was a dishwasher. That's how I survived my early years in New York City. Only minimal skills were required to be a dishwasher. The job provided a salary and three meals per day.

But I was in between job assignments, and my pockets were almost empty. So empty, in fact, that if no dishwashing position were available, I was ready to glom on to any kind of work that a black kid with no education might qualify for. I purchased a copy of the *Amsterdam News,* one of Harlem's leading newspapers, and started scanning the want-ad pages for dishwasher openings. The last page faced the theatrical page, which contained an article with a heading, ACTORS WANTED.

A troupe called "The American Negro Theatre" needed actors for its next production. My mind got to spinning. My eyes bounced back and forth between the want-ad page and the theatrical page. *What the hell,* I thought, *I've tried* DISHWASHERS WANTED, PORTERS WANTED *and* JANITORS WANTED . . . *why not try* ACTORS WANTED*?*

I figured I could do that. It didn't sound any more difficult than washing dishes or parking cars. But when I went in and auditioned, the man in charge quickly let me know, in no uncertain terms, that I was misguided in my assumptions. I had no actor's training. I could barely read! And to top it off I had a thick, singsong Bahamian accent.

He snatched the script from my hands, spun me around, grabbed me by the scruff of my neck and back of my pants and marched me on my tiptoes toward the door. He was seething. "You just get out of here and stop wasting people's time. Go get a job you could handle," he barked. "Get yourself a job as a dishwasher or something." That was the line he ended with, as he threw me out and slammed the door.

I have to tell you his words stung worse than any wasp on any sapodilla tree back in my childhood. I hadn't mentioned to him that I was a dishwasher. How did he know? If he didn't know, then what was it about me that seemed to have implied to this stranger that a dishwasher's profession would accurately sum up my whole life's worth?

Whatever it was, his comments made me realize that I had to change, or life was going to be mighty grim. And so I set out on a course of self-improvement. I worked nights and, on my evening lunch breaks, I sat in a quiet area of the restaurant where I was employed, reading the newspapers, trying to sound out each syllable of each unfamiliar word. An old Jewish waiter, noticing my efforts, took pity and offered to help. He became my tutor, as well as my guardian angel. Each night we sat in the same booth in that quiet area and he helped me to read better.

My immediate objective was to prove that I could be an actor if I wanted. Not that I had any real desire to go on the stage, not that I had ever given it a thought really. I simply needed to prove to that stranger that Sidney Poitier had a hell of a lot more to him than washing dishes.

And it worked. The second time around they let me in.

But it was still no slam dunk. In fact, I made the cut only because there were so few guys and they needed some male bodies to round out the incoming class. But not even that lucky break was enough to ease my forward progress. After a couple of months they were going to flunk me out, and once again I felt that vulnerability, as if I had fallen overboard into deep water. If I lose this, where am I? One more black kid, who can barely read, washing dishes on the island of Manhattan?

Not if I can help it, I thought. So in desperation I conjured a truly outrageous offer they couldn't refuse: I would become their janitor without pay, if they would let me continue to study. After some brief negotiations, it was so agreed.

Things began to improve, and maybe even I began to improve as an actor. But when it came time to cast the first big student production, in walked a new guy, another kid from the Caribbean, not a member of the group, but someone to whom the director had assigned the part *I* secretly hoped to get. After all of my studies, busting my butt trying to learn to act—not to mention busting my butt sweeping the walk and stoking the furnace—she cast him in the lead.

Well, I had to admit he was a pretty good-looking kid, and he had a good voice. (He could even sing a little.) I tried to find some consolation in the fact that they made me his understudy. But how could I know how events would unfold? On the night of the first major run-through, the one night an important director was coming to watch the show, the other Caribbean kid who had been cast for the lead—a kid named Harry Belafonte—couldn't make it. I had to go on for him. Then, son of a gun, the visiting director liked what I did and called me in to audition for a play he was planning to take to Broadway.

"I'm opening *Lysistrata* on Broadway," he said. "There might be a small part you could try out for . . . if you're available."

Are you kidding? I thought to myself.

Next thing you know, five weeks later, on opening night, I'm staring out from a Broadway stage, into a sea of white faces in a packed theater. They are all staring back at me. Scared beyond belief, I fumbled unsuccessfully for my lines.

The word "bad" cannot begin to accommodate my wretchedness. I was giving the wrong cues, jumbling the lines . . . and within an instant the audience was rolling in the aisles. The scene came to its torturous end, and it was time for this Caribbean kid to run for cover. The void was opening up once again to receive me. I didn't even go to the cast party, which meant that I wasn't around when the first reviews appeared. The critics trashed the show.

But oddly enough, they liked me. I was so god-awful they thought I was good. They said they admired my "fresh, comedic gift." (If you saw this in an old black-and-white movie on TV, would you believe it?) Someone was looking out for me, for sure.

My "triumph" in *Lysistrata* led immediately to an understudy's job in the touring company of *Anna Lucasta*. Then after a long, lean and frustrating period I found out, quite by accident, that 20th Century Fox was about to cast a movie called *No Way Out*. That, as it turned out, was my first motion picture job. Fifty years and fifty-six movies later, here I am recalling the year, the day, the resolve, and the words that forged a new and undreamed of beginning, that launched a journey more incredible than I could have imagined, to a destiny written in a time before I came, by hands other than my own.

Sidney Poitier

Vladimir Pozner

Journalist

In 1977, living in the Soviet Union, I found myself at a point where I could no longer endure the psychological pressure of living under confinement, both physical and mental. If the KGB had come to me and made another offer to coax me to their ranks, I don't know how I would have reacted. I am glad to say that final offer never came.

Allow me to set the stage. In 1952, my father moved our family from the United States, via Germany to Moscow. He decided on this path because first of all, he had been born in Russia and spent the first fourteen years of his life in Petrograd and, second, even though he emigrated with his parents, he grew up a staunch Communist and a Soviet supporter. From the age of eighteen, I grew up in the Soviet system. I received a biology degree from Moscow State University. I worked as a managing editor of *Soviet Life,* a monthly propaganda magazine circulated in the United States in exchange for *Amerika* being circulated in the U.S.S.R. After nine long years at the magazine, I moved to the Soviet version of *Voice of America.* Looking back on that time, I can now say that what I really wanted was to be accepted, fully accepted as "nash," a word that can loosely be translated as "one of ours." After having been moved from place to place in my youth, never setting down roots and being accepted as one of the boys, I wanted to merge with the crowd. Despite my loyal service to the Soviet media, I knew I had never officially been admitted.

The clear signal of my outsider status was that I was never allowed to leave the country. In the Soviet Union, every person who traveled abroad had to be vetted by the KGB, and that agency apparently regarded me in the same category as *refuseniks* and dissidents—people I certainly did not admire. I wanted to travel! How I yearned to go to America and look up my school buddies, walk my New York paper route again. How I wanted to enjoy travel—that supreme expression of my new country's faith and trust in me, a freedom I profoundly believed I deserved, being as I was, one of the most visible and effective proponents of the Soviet Union.

I never saw my KGB file, but I strongly suspect the primary reason I never got a visa was that I refused to cooperate with the KGB. For several years, they hotly courted me. The last time I met with a *ghebeshnik,* as those agents were called, I flatly told him to go to hell. "You will rue this day," he said to me. "I promise, you will never forget us." And he was right, I haven't.

My desire to travel went unanswered for many years. Imprisoned in my own country, I began to care less about things that had been most important to me, including my family. I began to drink. Strangely enough, by the time I was informed that I was being sent to Hungary as part of a Soviet delegation—clearly a test run for further travel—I felt neither joy nor relief. I no longer cared. I had given up, mostly on myself.

So there I was, walking down a street in Budapest, completely disinterested, when something caught my eye. On a movie theater marquee were the English words: ONE FLEW OVER THE CUCKOO'S NEST. JACK NICHOLSON. IN ENGLISH.

I had never heard of Jack Nicholson, let alone the movie. But the idea of watching a film in my native tongue appealed to me, so I bought a ticket.

I came out a changed man.

For those who have never seen the movie, Nicholson plays a somewhat violent man named McMurphy, who is committed to a mental institution. What he enters is in fact a small-scale model of totalitarian society. Some members of this society are indeed insane. Others have problems (who doesn't?) and have been committed either by relatives only too happy to get rid of them, or, fearing society and lacking self-confidence, have committed themselves. The institution is expensive, so the administrators try to keep them there. The less the patients believe in themselves, the greater they fear the outside and become dependent on the institution. If they give up, they'll stay until they die.

But McMurphy challenges the patients to rebel. One of his favorite tricks is to make bets that they are sure to win, thereby building their confidence. At one point, he bets that he can pick up a massive stone sink bolted to the bathroom floor. Watching the scene, I thought, *The guy's nuts. There is no way he's going to pick up that sink.* The bets are made. McMurphy bends down, grasps the washstand with both hands and pulls. And pulls. And pulls. The veins in his neck stand out like ropes. As he strains up and back, you feel he is going to bust a gut. You can almost see the blood beating in his temples. You stop breathing. The effort has you on the edge of your seat. You feel you are going to explode—and then with a whistling, hoarse sigh, he lets go. And the patients start laughing at him and pocketing the cigarettes (money is not allowed) he put up. And at that almost mystical moment in my life, Nicholson looks at them with the most haunted expression I'll ever see and says, "At least I tried."

And I wept.

All the way through the movie, the tears kept coursing down my face, up until the very end, when one of the patients, a huge Indian, rips that sink from the floor, bolts and all, hurls it through the barred windows of the institution and lopes off like some great graceful moose into the freedom of the velvety black night.

Only later, much later, did I realize that those were tears of joy, of recognition that, by the most unexplainable confluence of circumstances, I had been saved. That I would never again be tempted to give up, sell out, betray myself.

That no matter what, I would be able to say I tried.

Anna Quindlen

Writer

My mother only worked at a job long enough to entitle us to Social Security survivors' benefits after she was dead. As soon as she married and had children, she settled into the acceptable career for women of her era, that of wife and mother. As a result she had few possessions of note to parcel out when she realized that she was not going to live much past the age of forty. An Italian cameo brooch, a watch. I was given her engagement ring, a diamond slightly less than one carat set in white gold. Whoever broke into my apartment in lower Manhattan when I was twenty-four years old took it along with my stereo and television.

My mother left one item to all five of her children, who at the time of her death ranged in age from eight to nineteen. It was an ordinary lined index card, and on it she had copied out in her some-what angular script St. Paul's best-known letter to the Corinthians. The familiar words were written in pencil:

Though I speak with the tongues of men and of angels and have not love, I am sounding brass or a clanging cymbal. Though I have the gift of prophecy and know all things, though I have faith strong enough to move mountains, but am without love, I am nothing. Love is patient, love is kind, love is not jealous. Love is never boastful, conceited or rude; never selfish, not quick to take offence. Love is not vengeful; does not gloat over the sins of others but delights in the truth. Love bears all things, believes all things, hopes all things, endures all things. Love never fails.

I have gotten a good deal of advice in my life from women I have known and loved, about how to negotiate my salary, get a story onto page one, deal with a baby with colic or a toddler with chicken pox, make a teenager's curfew stick. My mother taught me a good deal, too, most of it by example: about speaking only when you truly have something to say, about unconditional love, about how to make a tasty meat loaf and great tomato sauce. But I think over the long haul no words she shared with me face-to-face made as great an impact as those words from the New Testament that she took the time to copy out and leave with the list of her possessions, words that came to me only after her death.

For many people those verses from St. Paul are familiar ones. You hear them read sometimes at weddings, occasionally at funerals. After my mother was gone, from time to time someone who knew what she had done would give me a plaque or poster with some part of St. Paul's letter on it.

But because of the circumstances, that passage became not so much a piece of advice but an atmosphere in which I went about the living of my life. When my mother left that card behind I was a smart and self-absorbed college student on compassionate leave, so anxious to get on with what I hoped would be a brilliant career that you could almost see the smoke rising from my heels. In retrospect, I see myself as one of those pieces of glass that carelessly wind up on the beach sometime that you pick up and throw into the wire-mesh trash can so that passersby won't cut themselves. I glittered, but my edges were sharp, and at some level I was broken.

But over time I learned that opening my arms to the world, to strangers and friends, to the family I had grown up with and the one I overcame my deepest fears to create, worked upon my jagged edges, until I was more like sea glass, with a softer patina and edges that were smooth and curved. And I think that happened because I came to believe, slowly but surely, that love never fails. Those words of St. Paul seemed so simple and so impossible, like a recipe for perfection. But I know that, in loving us better than she ever loved herself, our mother managed to embody them. Having them after she was gone was proof that she had once existed.

The fact that the passage is about love puts people off it, I think, but I'm not sure that's really what it is about at all. It has become fashionable, in the blessed face of feminism, to tell our daughters that they can do anything, that the terrain of their future can be boundless. But what we usually mean by that is that our girls can aspire to fulfilling roles in the world, to power and influence undreamt of by those who went before. I think my mother believed in another kind of power and another sort of terrain, the terrain of the human heart. And the real message of that passage is this: Our ability to understand, to embrace, to help, to know, to feel and to love is bounded only by our own emotional ambitions. The capacity to open ourselves up to one another is as huge as we dare to make it. There has always seemed to me something so poignant about the fact that my mother wrote her words in pencil; although it well may be that in our often chaotic and crowded household it was the only thing she could find, it has also occurred to me that, quiet and self-effacing as she was, she might have felt it would be presumptuous to use something as indelible as a pen. She probably never imagined that she was writing with something infinitely more powerful, and that the words would be carved into our hearts for the rest of our lives.

Anna Quindlen

Dr. Sally Ride

Astronaut

To this day I remember a simple line my father Dale Ride told me one afternoon when I came home from school, somewhat despondent. I hadn't said anything to him about my mood, but he sensed I was down. It was early on, during my years at Westlake High School in Los Angeles. Now, what he said may not seem earth-shattering; in fact, I'm sure it's a line everyone has heard, but somehow what he said to me that day not only bolstered my confidence then, it stays with me even now.

Like a lot of kids in high school, I was suffering through a loss of self-esteem; I had no confidence in myself whatsoever. I felt that all my friends were much smarter. This is not to say I was ever taunted. It was just a building sense of insecurity and anxiety that I'm sure a lot of kids go through.

So after school one day I came home and was obviously still in the down mood well into the evening. My father was one of my biggest supporters. He always tried to motivate me and, more important, get me to set my goals high. So, this one day, we just started having a casual conversation. Then in the middle of it, he just said, "You know, you've got to reach for the stars."

That instant, the phrase hit me. This was long before I had any aspirations to be an astronaut—I had no notion at all of NASA or anything related to space. Certainly, even at that age, I was really interested in science, but I was equally passionate about tennis and already had a place on the U.S. junior circuit. What that phrase clarified for me was that whatever you are doing you have to reach for the top.

Some years later I dropped out of college to pursue the dream of being a professional tennis player. I did well and worked hard but after a while I realized that I would never be a top-ranked player. I would never reach the stars by that path. So I returned to my other love—science—ultimately getting my Ph.D. in astrophysics and landing a spot in the space program.

It is of course possible that my father's phrase planted an idea in my subconscious. It may very well have helped shape my aspirations—and my becoming the first American woman to go into space. The words still have the power to stop me dead in my tracks and make me reevaluate my attitude toward myself and my abilities.

I try to pass on these words and the idea behind them, of never limiting your visions for yourself, and always recognizing that a person can reach the pinnacle of any profession or avocation she chooses, if she is willing to keep fighting for her vision. I like to especially emphasize to girls and young women growing up today the idea that there is a world of opportunities out there for them, but that it is ultimately up to them to establish their goals, to set their sights as high as they wish, as high as the stars, and then stay focused and determined and make them a reality.

Cal Ripken Jr.

Athlete

In 1981, I went to my first spring training for the Baltimore Orioles in Miami, Florida. I had just come off my best year in the minors with the Orioles' double-A club, earning myself a place on the team's protected roster and, as a result, an invitation to train with the big leaguers.

But this didn't guarantee me a lock on getting into the majors. At the time, the Orioles had a preset lineup, and there wasn't really an opening for me to come in and push someone else out. All the same, I thought if I played well enough and opened some eyes, maybe I could break through.

But it wasn't to be. Just before the end of spring training, Earl Weaver, the Orioles' manager, began making his cuts.

"Look," he said, after calling me into his office. "You really didn't have a chance to make the club this year, so I'm sending you back down to triple-A. Work hard, play well, and I hope to see you in the bigs this year."

To be honest, I was a little disappointed. I guess I had gotten a bit caught up in my first exposure to the big leagues. Once you get a taste of the majors, it's a little hard to let go.

Still, I went down to triple-A and had a terrific year. I got off to a fast start, putting up some great numbers. I was among the league leaders in batting average, RBIs, and home runs. (I never considered myself a home-run hitter, but that particular year I felt like the home-run guy.) Because I had jumped out as early as I did, I wound up making a statement, and halfway into August, I got the call I'd been waiting for: I was going to the majors.

Joining up with the team in Baltimore, I was really ready to play. Unfortunately, the Orioles were trying to make the playoffs, so they went with their tried-and-true players and I hardly got to take the field. Instead, I sat on the bench—which I couldn't stand—eating a lot of sunflower seeds, wishing for all the world that I could be out there playing.

One day, my father joined me in the dugout. Dad was a coach for the Orioles and had spent fourteen years in the minor league system. He knew everything there was to know about developing players, so I valued his advice not only as my dad, but as someone who'd been around the game a long time.

I was talking about my frustration over being so close—and yet so far—from the action, and my father said something that would take me not only through the season, but my entire baseball career.

"It's one thing to get to the big leagues," he said, "it's another thing to stay there."

My father didn't say this because he doubted my abilities. On the contrary, he had confidence in my talent. He knew I belonged on the club. He knew I played well. But because he'd personally seen players crash and burn in their first years due to overconfidence or self-satisfaction, he didn't want to see me make the same mistake.

What my dad was telling me was that although some players are happy just to get to the majors, the real players don't stop at that. They keep working at their craft. They keep readjusting their stance.

They keep sharpening their fielding. They don't let a good day at the plate stop them from swinging twice as hard at batting practice the next day. After all, even if they did make it to the majors, there was always going to be someone sitting there in the dugout—just like I was—wanting to take their place.

All of this became a motivating force for me, even as I watched my teammates play without me.

If I ever get into that lineup, I thought to myself, *I'm never coming out.*

At the end of the season I headed south to play winter ball, more determined than ever to prove myself all over again—to get my confidence back. I played hard and well, leading the league in homers and RBIs, and batting .355. And, more important, whenever I wasn't playing, I was practicing. The work paid off. The following spring, I was named starting third baseman for the Baltimore Orioles. It was my job to lose.

On opening day, I had three hits, then immediately went into a deep slump. But Earl Weaver kept playing me, and eventually I broke out of the nosedive. Then I got beaned and missed one game, caught a fever in Chicago, and missed another. But right after, I decided to make true the promise I'd made to myself in that dugout the previous fall.

On May 30, 1982, I stepped into the Orioles' lineup and didn't come out again for another sixteen years. I played 2,632 straight games.

The press made a big deal of "the streak," and, of course, I was flattered. But what I was most proud of was not the number of consecutive games I played, but the constant work that made it all possible. For that accomplishment, I credit my dad.

There's an old saying that goes, "You can't rest on your laurels," but the baseball variation on the phrase should be, "What have you done for me lately?" I was lucky enough to learn a valuable lesson about success before I'd even had the opportunity to achieve it. My father's words forced me to ask myself a simple question: Why sit back and admire yourself when you could be spending that time trying to get better and better? "The beauty of baseball," he'd say, "is that there's always something to learn."

Cal Ripken Sr. passed away in 1999, but I still think about him in almost everything I do—from the decisions I make, to my approach to life, to my plans for the future.

During the years my father and I were with the Orioles, we used to head into the locker room together. He'd always say, "I can't wait to get into my work clothes," meaning, of course, his uniform. After he died, I would remember him saying those words every time I suited up for a game.

Then I'd grab my glove, run out onto the field, and go to work.

Dennis Rivera

Activist

The words that forever changed my life were not from any book or inspirational speech or poem. They were in a letter I received in 1969 from the United States government. It was addressed to me from President Nixon: "Greetings," it read. "You are hereby ordered for induction into the Armed Forces of the United States . . ."

My first reaction was pure fear. I was nineteen years old, a student at the University of Puerto Rico bound for a solid middle-class future. The most important thing in my life was basketball, and I had few worldly cares. To get a deferment from military service, a student needed to have twenty-four college credits to his name. I had a devastating twenty-three.

Now I was being ordered to risk my life thousands of miles away from home in a war I didn't understand. All I knew about Vietnam was the carnage I saw on TV. I had no idea why the war was being fought and, more important, why I should have any part in it. With one blow, the president's letter shattered the tranquillity of my young life.

But it also generated a crisis that ultimately determined my life's path.

I had no inclination to agree to the draft order, but the first hurdle was my family. They were as determined as Mr. Nixon that I should serve in Vietnam. For them, even *contemplating* refusing the call brought shame and dishonor on the family. My mother could be fierce. "It's your obligation to go," she told me.

"Vietnam isn't my war," I said. "There's no reason for me to die there."

The big problem was that I was living at home at the time, which made them feel they had every right to tell me what to do. Worse, I was forced to stand up to them on a daily basis. Being at war with my family over the Vietnam War was deeply painful. The only positive aspect was that it forced me to appreciate the weight of my decision.

The consequences of refusing to go to Vietnam, of course, were more serious than a family rift. The draft notice ended with the reminder that "Willful failure to report at the place and hour of the day named in this Order subjects the violator to fine and imprisonment."

Although the starting point of my antiwar sentiment had been simple fear for my life, contemplating the consequences of refusing to serve forced me to think about the actual conflict—and I could see no logic or merit in it. To my young mind it seemed nothing like World War II, when we were attacked at Pearl Harbor and had to defend our own country. In Vietnam, it seemed to me, we were the ones doing something to other people five or six thousand miles away. In retrospect, I feel that my youthful judgment was vindicated when even the people who got us into Vietnam, like Robert McNamara, now admit that it was a big mistake—a mistake that cost fifty thousand American lives and a million Vietnamese lives.

At the time, however, it was not an easy choice. My instincts told me not to go, but to follow my gut I had to be ready to face imprisonment. As awful as that seemed, I decided after days and nights of wrestling with the visions of both, that prison was still preferable to participating in a war that I did not think was right.

So I told my parents first and then the military authorities that I chose to be a conscientious objector.

That decision did not send me to prison, in the end. But it did propel me into a lifelong commitment to fight for social justice and, ultimately, led me into trade-union activism. When I decided to object, I needed a lawyer to help me make my case. The only attorneys who would work with the three thousand conscientious objectors in Puerto Rico were social activists. In the process of defending myself, I found myself drawn into the antiwar movement—and the more I learned, the more I embraced the cause with the same passion I had once reserved only for basketball.

My antiwar activism continued even after the authorities dropped charges against us. It connected me to a broader movement for social change. Some of the antiwar people I worked with were also taking up a crusade to organize poor people. Where once I had been bound for a life of middle-class apathy, I now found myself helping to form a trade union for Puerto Rico's garbage workers. Seventy percent of the workers were illiterate. They made almost nothing and had no healthcare benefits. Our success in unionizing some of the island's poorest workers, and the real ways that changed their lives, turned me into a lifelong trade-union activist. I've been fighting for the rights of working people ever since, for the past thirty years.

Would I have found myself in this life's work if I had never been drafted? I don't think so. What got me here was almost a stunning irony. The words in President Nixon's letter made me the full-time activist I am today.

Chris Rock

Comedian

I'm *so* not the kind of guy who can give you an inspirational tale. I just write jokes, cynical bullshit. There's nothing heartwarming about me. But I do remember one thing my dad told me. After I got fired from one of my first jobs, he said to me, "You're going to have to listen to people that you think you're smarter than." And I think that's one of the keys to success—if not *the* key.

My dad was a hardworking guy. He worked *all* the time, driving a truck for the *New York Daily News* and never complained about his job. He didn't go to college, but he made more money than my mother—and she went to college! Still, he was a smart guy, you know? I would imagine anybody who can run a family and keep a house going couldn't be stupid. He fed six kids. The house was warm. There was food in the refrigerator. Where I grew up, not everyone had such things.

Now could I tell you a book my father told me to read? Nah. I've had many an idiot recommend a book to me, but my father gave me the best thing a parent can give you—a good example. You can say anything you want, but kids will ultimately do what they see. That's what they emulate. I emulated my dad in the sense that I've never had a problem with a boss.

No matter how much some job sucked, I couldn't complain. It wasn't like I had some great degree or anything. I saw it like this: If I'm shoveling shit and I dropped out of high school, then I guess I'm *supposed* to be shoveling shit. As opposed to somebody who graduated from somewhere, and they're shoveling shit, then it's like, "Oh, this is horrible. This is a travesty." I was practical that way, just like my father was and a lot of other people are, too. Go to your favorite restaurant right now and say hi to the dishwasher: Unless he's a college graduate, he's not complaining that much. I mean, he doesn't want to *be* a dishwasher, but he's not indignant about it, you know what I mean? Not unless he's crazy . . .

Once I started doing comedy, I learned quickly that I was going to have to take notes from people who had never written a joke in their lives. In show business, you're always getting advice about some *thing* from somebody who hasn't done that thing.

As you get older, you realize that none of it matters. These people really don't care if you're going to be funny or not. They're just concerned about their own comfort level, planning everything out so they'll run smoothly and all. You just have to listen and not have an attitude, because your people skills will take you as far as you can go. Even comedians who can't write jokes still have careers because they listen to people.

Some people let everybody upset them, and the truth is, only a few people have the power to really mess with you—and the boss is one of those people. So just suck it up.

That's really kind of it—just listen to people that you're

smarter than. That's how you eat. That's how your bills get paid. The people with real problems are the ones who can't knock those two things out. If you can, everything else is just God given, you know?

Ray Romano

Actor and Comedian

The first comedy album I ever bought was Bill Cosby's *To Russell, My Brother, Whom I Slept With*. I was fourteen years old and living in Forest Hills, Queens. I remember running the two blocks to my friend Bill Canning's house to listen to it with him. He had the same love of comedy I did and that album blew us away.

That was my introduction to storytelling comedy. I'll never forget the routine about Cosby and his brother jumping on the bed and breaking it. Their father came in right after their bed crashed to the floor and Cosby and his brother were scared, "Who broke this bed?" his father asks.

And Cosby as a child answers, "Some man came in the window, Dad, and he just started jumpin' on the bed, and he broke the bed."

"What do you mean some man came in?"

"Yeah, Dad, some man came in the window, he started jumpin' on the bed. Some man."

His father goes up to him and says, "You want to know what happens to kids who lie? When they die, they go to hell. You want to go to hell?"

"No, Dad."

"Do you know what happens in hell?"

"No, Dad."

"In hell you burn and it's hot and do you want to burn in hell forever?"

"No, Dad."

"Is that what you want?"

"No, Dad, I don't want to burn in hell."

"Then tell me how the bed broke."

"The man came in the window. . . ."

That album not only made me laugh; it changed how I viewed my own life as a kid. A lot of Cosby's stuff was about family competition. He had a bit about him and his brother sleeping in the same bed together and how they would say, "You're on my side of the bed. Right where that pillow creases." That hit close to home. My brother was a year and a half older than me, and at that time we were severe sibling rivals. We hated each other then. I was scared of him. He had a mental edge over me. He could threaten me. There was a lot of pushing and shoving.

On a subconscious level I can see now that the Cosby album helped change my perspective—that the fear I felt from my brother could also be funny. I'm not sure how funny I felt at the time, but that was the big appeal. There was another way to look at family dynamics that made them less scary.

Cosby was the first guy to talk about his life and his family and that influenced me. His material is not setup, punch line. It's not topical or political.

From the moment I started in comedy, I never did jokes about the news. I knew I was naturally funny when I was talking about what happened with my father, my brother or my mother. Or my wife's Italian mother. Whenever something happened in real life, I could use that as material.

The Cosby album also turned me on to other comedy albums, and from those I began watching stand-ups. I listened to Cheech & Chong, and George Carlin. I went to Steve Martin's concert at the Nassau Coliseum.

My first time onstage doing stand-up was audition night at the Improv in New York City in 1982. I needed three to five minutes of material. I did something about my family.

Eventually stand-up led to my TV show. When we were pitching the concept and interviewing writers, we discussed stories about my family. One was about my older brother Richard being a cop, saying sarcastically, "Look at what I do for a living. People with guns chase me. And look at what you do. *Everybody* loves Raymond." Which is how the title came about. From these stories, we built a show. Years later, I'm telling stories about my family the way Cosby did about his.

Ray Romano

Carlos Santana

Musician

When I was growing up in Tijuana, Mexico, my dad was in bands and orchestras all over Mexico. He passed his love of music on to me and he taught me everything: how to play the guitar, how to read, how to play violin. I started playing guitar when I was eleven or twelve on Revolution Street in strip joints. I would play for an hour and the strippers would strip for an hour. We'd go back and forth until six o'clock in the morning. And then on Sundays I would play violin in church. That contrast gave me a nice balance. That's where I learned about dignity. A woman can work at night doing what she has to do, and on Sunday morning she's dressed in white, her kids are dressed in white with white candles and they go take confirmation. If we taught dignity in school we wouldn't need so many jails.

When I moved to the United States I was held back because I couldn't speak English. I was already eighteen or nineteen and the only words I knew were *stick 'em up.* I swear. Not because I ever held anybody up, but from watching Roy Rogers on TV in Tijuana. So I was put in junior high school, even though I finished high school in Mexico. Going back to junior high was terrible. It was like being in college and then being told you've got to go back to kindergarten all over again.

I used to draw and paint all the time, mainly because I was bored out of my head. One day Mr. Knudsen, my art teacher, took me aside to the supply room because he didn't want to embarrass me in front of the whole class. He said, "Santana, I took the liberty to check out your grades since you've been in the United States and they're pretty lousy. You're getting F's and D's, but you're getting a lot of A's in my class. I can see you have a talent for it but I've also heard you're a musician and you play in the streets. If you want to be an artist I want to take you to the art institute here in San Francisco so you can see what you're up against."

And he took the whole class on a field trip to the art institute. When I saw what other people were painting—I mean they looked like photographs—and my shit looked like a doodle, man, I was like, *Ohh,* okay.

And that's when Mr. Knudsen told me, "There's no room for anyone giving 50 percent. You should do 150 percent. Whatever you're doing or whatever you're trying to be. Whether you're a painter or a musician or a fireman."

And when he said this I felt embarrassed and I started to cry. Because I thought that a person was seeing right through me for the first time. I felt really awkward. This guy really penetrated something in me. I took a deep breath and started to cry. He made me aware that I have this potential. He gave me a quantum leap right there. He pushed me into this reality. So I'm really grateful to him.

And that's when I started hanging around the Fillmore where all the great musicians of that time were hanging out. People like Bill Graham and B. B. King and Michael Bloomfield. When I found that I could fit in there it gave me the confidence to follow my own path. I stopped drawing. I didn't feel confident enough to go into the art institute and pull out my stuff. But with music I could fit in. So Mr. Knudsen did me the biggest favor. He directed my energy in the right place.

After that I spent more time at the Fillmore than at school. It had matinees, so there goes school. That was my school. I'm pretty sure I had graduated with highest honors when John Lee Hooker, B. B. King, Miles Davis took me under their wing. Along with Bill Graham they taught me the subjects of music and business. I learned to balance emotions and numbers.

At the time I was living with my mom. She was washing my clothes and cooking for me. It was a comfortable cushion. I left my house almost right after Mr. Knudsen gave me that wisdom and started living in the streets. I went to Haight-Ashbury. When I was in my house with my mom I didn't have a clue about asking questions, or even why to ask questions. But after a while living in the streets you learn. I learned that there's a bigger picture. I arrived right on time because after the assassination of John F. Kennedy, a consciousness revolution was born here in San Francisco with the hippies and the Black Panthers, and then it spread. It was like a river of cultures merging. And it was all deep.

You can't play at life unless you live it. I'm not saying you have to suffer, but you can't play the **blues eating** home cooking and getting your clothes washed. You have **to leave** your nest in order to fly. You might fall on your face, but you have to try. How can I convince anyone that my music is true if I'm still living with momma? Firsthand experience is firsthand experience. You don't learn it from a book or from having your momma regurgitate it to you. You have to go out and get it.

Diane Sawyer

Broadcast Journalist

I stumbled back home to Louisville, Kentucky, after college, where I had spent four years majoring in Identity Crisis and Self-Absorption, with a minor in Poetry and Daydreaming. I was stuck. No plan, no driving impulse. No idea what should come next. It didn't help that I was moving back in with my parents, just as the great horizon was supposed to beckon. But Eudora Welty was right, of course: "All serious daring starts from within." I still remember exactly where we were sitting in the living room, my father and I, when he asked the questions that still seem to me so simple and profound.

"What is it you love?" he asked. And then, "Where is the most adventurous place you could do it? And are you certain it will serve other people?"

That was a quiz I could ace. And just giving the answers had the effect of a bolt slipping purposefully into its place. I loved stories, writing them, sharing them. Later, when I made a foray into law school for a semester, I knew instantly, again, I didn't want to litigate. I simply wanted to corner people and say, "You won't believe what happened in this case."

And adventure? There were no women doing TV news reporting in Kentucky—this was back in the Bronze Age—so I showed up at one of the local news stations and offered to start anywhere. Anywhere was as a weather girl—hairspray, tight sweaters, map and all.

I was a disaster—famously a disaster, I might add. I was distracted and didn't know what I was doing. To complicate matters, I was nearsighted. Without contact lenses, I couldn't see the West Coast of the map from my perch on the East Coast. I always seemed to be taking wild guesses at the weather in San Francisco.

Then, of course, there was the night I signed off by saying, "The high temperature for today was 78 degrees. Currently it's 85."

But right across the hall was the newsroom. And before long, I wheedled my way into a story or two or five or ten. Our news director, Ken Rowland, was a man actually radiant with curiosity, compassion and love of the truth. He showed up every morning to make it matter. So I knew I was home.

Not that I always stayed there. I took a break from television to work in the press office of Richard Nixon; I wanted to see politics and passion from the other side, the inside. Those turbulent years of Vietnam, then Watergate, were a new palette of gray hues for me—no more simple theories about good/bad, or stories with the logical beginning, middle, end.

After four years in the White House I left on the plane with a president who had resigned in defeat and disgrace. I went to San Clemente because it seemed to me, if you were present for the good times, you owe something in the bleak and shattered hours too.

Over the years, others in my life have said things that remind me of my dad's advice. A minister once told me that if you have to make a difficult decision and want the best shot at happiness—hour by hour, day by day—you need to "find the place where your greatest love meets the world's greatest need." Another friend said once, "Keep it simple. Just try to nudge the world, a little bit at a time."

My father died a few years after that winter-night conversation, but it's him speaking every time I am asked by a kid or new graduate or friend for career advice. "Three questions," I say. If you can answer the first two, and you're sure about the third, it will be like one of those global positioning satellites—take the road ahead and love the ride.

Diane Sawyer

Martin Sheen

Actor

Many powerful words from heroes and saints whose lives spoke volumes have inspired me throughout my life: Gandhi on the absolute necessity for nonviolence; Mother Teresa's assurance that we are never asked to be successful, only faithful; and Dorothy Days's belief that the only solution is love, to name a few. But no one spoke more clearly or more personally to me than Daniel Berrigan.

I returned to Catholicism in 1981, but becoming a practicing Catholic again meant far more than Sunday mass and the Sacraments. Indeed, my decision began a long and difficult journey toward involvement with social justice through nonviolent action by way of moral obligation.

Daniel Berrigan is a Jesuit priest in New York City. During the 1960s he and his brother, Philip, who was also a priest, began organizing nonviolent protests against the war in Vietnam. They were the first to burn draft cards, and in what would become a famous case, they and seven others raided a draft-board center in Catonsville, Maryland, in 1968, hauling many files into the parking lot and burning them with homemade napalm.

They became known as "The Catonsville Nine," and their action was arguably the single most powerful antiwar act in American history. It was simple and direct. It was nonviolent and it spoke a powerful truth to power.

The Berrigans reasoned that it made far more sense to burn the draft cards of young American men than permit the American government to burn Vietnamese children with real napalm while remaining legally unaccountable and morally unchallenged. But they paid dearly for their action. Found guilty and sentenced to several years in prison, Dan held a farewell gathering, and it was at that event that he made a simple but powerful statement that changed my life forever. While he was explaining the many different ways in which nonviolent actions can work to help end the war, he advocated that everyone involved should seriously consider the risk of going to prison. Suddenly, he was interrupted by a reporter who challenged him. "It's fine for you to go to prison, Father Berrigan. After all, you have no children. What's going to happen to our children if we go to prison?" To which Daniel Berrigan calmly responded, "What's going to happen to them if you don't?"

When I read that statement in the newspaper it hit me like a thunderbolt. I was in Los Angeles at the time pursuing an acting career and had not been active at all except for some work I had done for the civil rights movement. But reading Dan's statement—he was already in prison by then—he became an ideal and an inspiration as his one comment forced me to reevaluate everything about myself and the world in which I lived. Eventually it forced me to look at social justice in an entirely different light, and that light illuminated every political and social stand I would take for the rest of my life.

What is the personal cost of activism for social justice? After all, if our ideals are of any true value they have to cost us something, and the more lofty the ideal, the higher the price.

I didn't meet Daniel Berrigan until 1981 while filming a docudrama on "The Plowshares Eight." Dan and Phil were on trial again, this time for symbolically trying to disarm a nuclear weapon. These two extraordinary brothers were still working nonviolently for peace and social justice and still risking prison long after the war in Vietnam had ended and the nation was lulled into a false sense of Cold-War peace and well-being. After befriending Dan and returning to Catholicism I began involving myself in many different types of activism, demonstrating on behalf of issues from nuclear disarmament, farmworkers and the homeless, to the environment and the death penalty. Along the way I have been arrested sixty-four times, and although I am currently on probation for three years following a nonviolent protest against SDI (Star Wars) at Vandenberg Air Force Base in California, I've never gone to prison . . . yet.

Activism for social justice is not always a popular option, of course, especially for actors whose success or failure often depends on public approval, and I am very well aware of the toll it can take on those special people who choose to take the road less traveled. Ed Asner, Mike Farrell and Edward James Olmos come to mind, and recently the name of Richard Gere should be added. Shortly after the September 11 attacks I saw a TV news account of a fund-raiser at Madison Square Garden to benefit the families of the NYPD personnel who lost their lives at the World Trade Center. Richard Gere was to introduce a documentary film at the event and used the opportunity to speak about the war in Afghanistan and how Americans need to concentrate less on military might and more on its capacity for compassion and forgiveness.

Unfortunately, he was nearly booed off the stage, but he calmly held forth in the face of overwhelming disapproval and finished his statement with elegance and grace. Then he introduced the film. I was so deeply impressed with his courage and commitment that I tracked him down on the phone several days later where he was filming in Canada. "You are the only one among us with the courage to speak the truth in public. Thank you," I said, "and would to God I had such courage."

Martin Sheen

Dr. Ruth Simmons

President of Brown University

When I was a junior at Dillard University, I left my home campus to study for a year at Wellesley College. This experience was my first real opportunity to study outside a segregated environment and the change brought with it great apprehension. As a visiting junior, I was one of a small group of African Americans at Wellesley. Having chosen to major in French, I was doubly isolated as few minority students took upper-level French courses. So here I was in 1965, a black student from a black college studying at Wellesley where I was feeling isolated in many ways. The fact that I did not speak or understand spoken French made me feel even more alien because my French classes were taught in French.

Having had no international and few transcultural experiences as a child, when I became a college student, I sought out foreign language study because I felt it would liberate me intellectually as well as socially from the narrow racial and cultural horizons to which the South of the fifties and early sixties consigned me. Most language instruction of that era was in English. As a result, I had mastered French vocabulary and grammar without having encountered native speakers or been afforded the opportunity to become proficient in understanding spoken French. I had not been introduced to a high-level program in language study where oral proficiency was expected. In my junior year, when one takes more advanced courses, this proved to be a problem.

Dillard, a historically black college in New Orleans, was a familiar, homogeneous, supportive environment for me. Wellesley was an entirely different world where wealthy students studied in an isolated, though beautiful environment steeped in New England white culture. As an impoverished, young, urban black woman, I felt that I stuck out like the proverbial sore thumb.

After several weeks of sitting through classes in a fog and missing all French assignments, I summoned the nerve to inform one of my instructors that I could not continue. I stated firmly that I could not understand lectures and that I had to drop his course. To my surprise, he stated rather matter-of-factly: "Don't worry. Just keep doing the work and attending class and eventually you'll understand the lectures."

Discouraged by his apparent insensitivity to my plight, I was doubly disheartened. However, I continued the work.

His advice, it turned out, was extraordinarily correct and even inspired. Had I left that course, I would have left French behind and changed my intellectual direction. I would also have been persuaded that there were some endeavors that lay outside of my range of intellectual ability. Because of his insistence that I could do the work, I stayed in the course and, with time, I came to understand and speak French, achieving fluency much more easily than I thought possible. Eventually I earned a Ph.D. in French at Harvard and served as a professor of French like the Wellesley instructor who taught me how to have confidence that I could stand up to intellectual challenges.

Most important, since that moment, I have never felt intimidated by any problem that could be solved by intelligence. There have been many moments in my life when I have been tempted to declare that success was impossible. Inevitably, I remembered the words of my French professor and the glorious feeling of freedom and empowerment that I felt when the impenetrably foreign sounds of spoken French gave way to a clear matrix of meaning no longer closed to me.

Every time students come to see me to proclaim that they wish to drop a course because they do not understand the material, I tell them this story. In many ways, this simple advice given to me by my French instructor empowered me in my lifelong quest for education and convinced me that the most important thing one can do for children is not accept the limitations they are so willing to impose on themselves.

Carly Simon

Singer and Songwriter

My son likes to say that my nervous system does not live inside me. Instead, he says, it exists outside my body, in a plume.

I was born with an interestingly different brain, and as a consequence, I had many emotional problems growing up. I stuttered and stammered. I had phobias and tics and all sorts of anxious habits. I was chronically nervous.

By the time I was in the fourth grade, the problem had reached a critical level. I was living in Riverdale, New York, and was so disabled by my fears that I would actually become sick in the morning before I went to school, simply because I knew I would have to be who I was in front of my classmates. I dreaded them making fun of me.

I would have stomachaches or a knot in my throat that made it impossible for me to speak without gagging (my mother called this a "worry lump"). It was awful. I'd hide in my bedroom, under my bed, anything I could do not to have to go to school.

My stuttering was the most tormenting problem though, and my mother spent a lot of time helping me to face the music. I remember once sitting at the dinner table and literally being unable to speak the words, "Pass the butter."

"Puh . . . puh . . . puh," I tried again and again, ultimately collapsing in failure when I couldn't get the words out.

So my mother said, "Sing it." And even though it was embarrassing to break into song in front of my family, I did just that, completing the sentence in one try. That single incident momentarily lifted a tremendous burden from my shoulders, proving to me that, if worse came to worst and I couldn't speak, I could always sing. Eventually, I would teach myself other little tricks to overcome my stuttering, such as emptying my lungs completely before answering the phone, so that I could properly say the *h* in "hello."

My mother also began intervening at school on my behalf, frequently speaking with my fifth-grade teacher, Pappy, about my problems. Pappy was a wonderful man. He'd meet me outside my classroom every day and teach me new yo-yo tricks as a way of wooing me inside. He also stopped asking me to read out loud in class, which was the most traumatic thing for me. Pappy was a godsend.

My mother gave me the most valuable advice of all during that year. One day when I was going through a particularly bad patch, she sat me down and said to me, "If you can start thinking about other people rather than yourself all the time, you may begin to lose your self-consciousness." In other words, she thought that I might be able to wage a better battle with my insecurities—my fears, my flaws, my self-criticism—by focusing on how other people were feeling, and what their needs might be.

This turned out to be a brilliant strategy, because by the end of that school year—and well into the next—I began growing interested in other kids in the most extraordinary ways. It was a mind-blowing transformation. How many fifth or sixth graders really know how to reach out to other kids and help them with their problems? And yet I did just that, in a very conscious, very parentally encouraged way.

Once I got out of my own head and began lending a hand to

friends, I became the most popular girl in my class—or the "hub of the wheel," as my teacher liked to say. If any of my classmates had to go to a doctor, for instance, or to the principal's office, I was the one chosen to accompany them. If a student had a problem that had to be dealt with, I was the emissary. I was even voted queen of the fair.

By the time I got to sixth grade, I had become the frog who turned into a prince. This is not to imply that I was suddenly able to get up in front of the class and recite Walt Whitman, but I began to feel some sense of my own power through caring about other kids.

Another huge breakthrough occurred when I was in the eleventh grade. By then, my stuttering was pretty subdued, but I still stammered—which is different from a stutter. I was so embarrassed I couldn't even write about it in my diary. Instead, I referred to my stammer by a code name—"stamform"—believing that if anybody read my journal, they wouldn't know what I was talking about.

At the time, I had a boyfriend named Nick, and I remember going to his house for the first time to meet his mother. By then I was in love with him, and terrified that he or his mother would pick up on my stammer. Sure enough, my worries were realized. Nick and I were talking one day—we were in his Chevy convertible, out by the reservoir in Larchmont—and he told me that his mother thought I might have a stammer. I immediately burst into tears. Here I had so desperately tried to keep my stammer a secret and had failed. As I cried and cried, Nick just held me in his arms. Finally, he said, "But I think it's so charming."

Amazingly—and not surprisingly—that was the turnaround. After that, I realized, I didn't have to hide my stammer anymore. Nick had given me a new name for it. It was *charming*.

If my childhood taught me anything, it's that everybody has

problems, and learning to share them is essential. Hiding pain requires an enormous amount of energy; sharing it is liberating. By identifying with someone else's struggle, you learn that you're not alone, that your fear isn't some great big Hefalump out there, tormenting only you.

Just as my mother had taught me, the laws of compensation are critical. If you can't do something well, focus on something else. If the path you're following doesn't inspire you, try following your imagination. If you can't say an *h* well, start working on an *s*.

Today, I consider myself a work in progress. My stutter is still there, though very subtle and barely perceptible. My "worry lump" eventually gave way to a performance anxiety that has plagued me on and off throughout my career. But my mother's advice continues to help me through all this, reminding me that whenever I find myself too much in my own head and overly self-conscious, I need only direct my energy elsewhere.

Carly Simon

Sammy Sosa

Athlete

Every time I hit a home run I touch two fingers to my mouth and blow kisses to my mother and say with my lips, *"Para ti Mami. For you, Mommy."*

I hadn't always wanted to be a baseball player, even if everyone is crazy for baseball where I am from. That is the Dominican Republic. It is a very small country but we have many players in the major leagues. From San Pedro de Macoris, my town, come eight major leaguers like Juan Marichal, Joaquin Andujar, Rico Carty and George Bell. All the boys, *todos los niños*, dream of becoming a pro and play *bitilla*, like street baseball, but a bottle cap for the ball and a stick for the bat. For me, I didn't dream of being a baseball player.

My life when I was a boy was kind of a struggle. My father died when I was seven and my family fell to poverty so I had to work. It was tough on me; I didn't have a chance to play as a kid or be with my friends. I would go to Parque Duarte, the plaza in the center of town where there were newspaper vendors, people selling tickets for the *lotería*, food stands and betting parlors. I shined shoes, I washed cars, I sold oranges and watched parked cars in the night. My brothers and sisters worked also and *Mami* cooked for the prison and sewed for other people. Sometimes we didn't have any food—a good meal was rice and beans, maybe an egg. All the money I made went to *Mami* so she could buy us food. There were many people like us in San Pedro, working hard to survive. People lived in shanty housing surrounded by heaps of garbage and packs of dogs. Sewage sometimes seeped into the drinking water.

But our family had pride and hope, and love too. My family was very loving and has always been the most important thing to me. I always told *Mami* I was going to get her out of there.

I thought when I grew up I would work in the oil refineries or sugar cane fields, but that's not what I wanted to do. When I got a little older, twelve or thirteen, almost a man, I started to practice boxing. I dreamed of being a great boxer so I could help my family. I was strong and physical, though a little skinny. My mother found out what I was doing. She called me to her. She said, "Sammy, they tell me you are practicing boxing."

I said, "Yes, it is true."

And she said, "My son, I want you to know that if you ever become a big-time boxer, I will never watch you on television."

I didn't understand. *"Porque Mami?* Why Mommy?"

She put her hand on my face and said, "Sammy, do you think I can watch you hit someone and watch someone hit you?"

I shrugged and told her it was nothing. I liked boxing. My mother thought she would have to see me get hit in the face. She didn't know that I punched a lot of people in the face, that I was a good boxer.

"No," she said loudly, "don't say it is nothing. That is something that would be too much for a mother to endure."

When my mother said she would never come to see me box, that was it. I knew I would never do something I could not share with her. It was a big blow, but I didn't get depressed, or angry, as if an opportunity had been taken away. As if boxing was the only thing in the world that I could do. I realized, okay, I have to figure something else out. I know that a lot of times when people are told that they can't do something that they really want to, they feel defeated. They only think how they missed their chance or opportunity. But there is never just one answer. There is always another way.

I didn't know what it was going to be, but then my brother Luis said to me, "Why don't you come play baseball." I said okay, I can give that a try. Luis took me to see his friend Hector Peguerro, who had a baseball league. It was called *La Liga Mexicana*, The Mexican League, even though we lived in the Dominican Republic.

Hector put me in left field and I swung the bat and Hector said to my brother, "We have a chance."

I was fourteen years old. Since that day I started working hard. I got up early in the morning and did exercises; I went to the beach and ran in the sand. By our house there was a truck tire embedded in the ground, and I used to swing at it every day. That work ethic is still with me today. I take nothing for granted. I always run hard. I run from the dugout to the outfield to start the inning, and I run back when the inning is over.

I was lucky my mother told me how she felt. And then I was lucky my brother took me to play baseball. Maybe I would have been a good boxer. I know I would have been good, but I wouldn't have been able to share it with my mother. Instead another opportunity opened up, and I became a baseball player and so many wonderful things have happened to me. I've been playing baseball ever since that day and my mother watches me on the TV. That is why whenever I hit a home run I blow her a kiss.

Steven Spielberg

Director

In 1954, I walked from my parents' house on Crystal Terrace Avenue to the movie theater twelve blocks away. I was going to see Disney's *Davy Crockett, King of the Wild Frontier.* My parents had a rule about movies; we weren't allowed to see anything violent or sensational, but I had decided that Davy Crockett was neither and set out on my own to see the film.

I loved it, but what struck me more than anything else was when Davy Crockett said, "Be sure you're right, then go ahead." I was eight years old, sitting in the Haddonfield, New Jersey, movie theater by myself, but I knew those words were important. They resonated with me.

About a decade or so later, I had an opportunity to use Davy Crockett's advice. I was a junior studying English at Cal State Long Beach, but spent all of my free time hanging around on the Universal lot. I found an empty room, set up an "office" for myself, and watched as they edited movies, mixed sound, corrected color—I took in all the information I could get. I also made movies of my own; one of them was a short film called *Amblin,* that I handed off to an editor friend who managed to get it in front of Sid Sheinberg, the head of Universal Television. Not long after, I got a phone call from his secretary. "Mr. Sheinberg has seen your film and would like to meet with you." It was the golden opportunity I'd been hoping for.

On the day of the meeting, I drove over to Universal and prepared to enter the black tower of power: the home to the studio executives, the hub of all important decision making, and the one building that had, until then, been off limits to me.

I stepped into the elevator and rode the fourteen floors up to Sid's office alone. The door opened onto an expanse of cubicles and I found my way to Shirley, his secretary, who invited me to sit down and wait. "Mr. Sheinberg is in a meeting." Fifteen minutes later I was escorted into his office—totally terrified.

Sid Sheinberg's office looked out over the 455 acres of studio grounds—the soundstages, the commissary, Western Street, Spartacus Square. It was the factory of dreams, and as I looked out at the view, I realized that I had entered the throne room of King Arthur.

Sid got right to the point. He was impressed with my film and offered me a seven-year contract directing television. I wanted to say, "yes," immediately, but I knew that it was very important to my father that I finish college and accepting the offer would mean dropping out forty-seven units short of a degree. I didn't know if I could do it. I wanted to be sure I was making the right decision, so I hesitated.

Sid misread my hesitation, thinking I was weighing his offer (something that no twenty-one-year-old kid could reasonably do). In his low, radio announcer voice he said, "Sir, there are a lot of places in this industry that will abandon you the first time you fail, and you will fail, but I won't abandon you. You will always have a job here." It was the assurance I needed to feel that I was making a decision that I could live with for the rest of my life, so I went ahead.

I accepted Sid's offer. I went to my father and got his blessing, and within a week I had a contract, an agent, and a real office on the lot. I made the right choice, and thirty-three years later I got my degree.

Steven Spielberg

George Steinbrenner

Owner of the New York Yankees

I grew up with a very strong six-foot-four German father and a wonderful five-foot-two Irish mother. My father expected me to do well in everything. He was a big man, a great athlete, and a fine student. He graduated from MIT near the top of his class and became the school's only NCAA champion in track and field ever. That's what I was up against. I was an only son, and I knew he was always watching.

My father didn't believe in giving his children an allowance. My sisters and I never got one. Instead, he believed in a person earning money on his or her own. I was ten years old when he told me how it was going to be. He said, "You'll learn to work and to earn for yourself." I can still hear him saying that to me.

At the time, we lived on a nice rural place eleven miles outside Cleveland in an area called Bay Village. To start me out, my father lent me money to buy baby chicks. I raised one hundred chickens, ducks, geese, and guinea hens and sold the eggs, and on weekends I dressed chickens to sell for eating.

I'd wake up early, feed the chickens, and scrape the roosts, and then I had to reach into all the little compartments where the chickens laid their eggs. The same thing happened every time: I'd reach under a hen and—boom! Those hens would peck at my arms. If they didn't want you to get the eggs, it could get fierce. When I was done, my arms were pecked up and down.

My father was a proud and very disciplined man whose mother was an immigrant from Germany. He used to make me wear a coat and tie to school. I was the only kid in school so attired, and if you think that was easy, you're crazy. I used to have a corduroy coat, and sometimes when I'd collect the eggs I'd forget and stick the eggs in my pockets. Once, in the sixth grade, I was sitting at my desk, when all of a sudden wet stuff started dripping out of my pockets. It was the broken eggs; I had forgotten all about them and left them in my coat. The other students kidded me regularly, but I just tried to ignore it. A grade below a B brought my father to school with me and my report card to find out why I had gotten a B and not an A—if you think that didn't build character!

Each night I added up the money and put it in a small, wooden-like barrel. Whatever I made on the chickens was my allowance. Once I was finished with my evening chores I would dress for dinner.

When I left to go away to Culver Military Academy, I sold my egg company to my sisters. It became the S & J Egg Company, after my sisters Susan and Judy. My sisters and I still joke about it. I overcharged them and they still hold it over my head to this very day.

Out of this experience working with my chickens, I learned two things. I learned the importance of a dollar, how hard it is to earn and keep. It made me understand how we can never take much for granted. My folks used to tell me, "Assume nothing."

I also learned what farmers are up against. My father used to teach me that the farmer is the first man up in the morning and the last man to go to bed at night. So I always respected farmers. They never get enough credit.

To this day I can tell you all about poultry. I was chairman of the Florida State Fair for about seven years, from 1994 to 2001, and to this day I can go into the poultry exhibit—which I love—and say, "There's a Rose-Comb Bantam, there's a Plymouth Rock, a White Rock, and a Buff Leghorn," but today there are so many new hybrids that it's difficult to keep track.

I even impressed Frank Perdue, the chicken man. He's a nice guy. One day he asked to sit in my box at Spring Training. It was a thrill to meet him. I started to talk chickens to him. He couldn't believe I knew anything about chickens. Of course, he really knew his baseball too, which amazed me.

The bottom line is I learned discipline and duty at a young age. You'd be hard-pressed to find another organization that believes in discipline, respect, and neatness the way we do. I walk around the grounds, and when I see wrappers on the ground, I pick them up and put them in a wastebasket. People come up to me and say, "Hey aren't you George Steinbrenner?" And I say, "Do you think if I was George Steinbrenner I'd be picking up wrappers like this?" That usually ends the conversation.

I appreciate discipline, focus, and duty in other people as well, people who work tirelessly for what they believe in.

So my father and mother changed my life with simple words and meaningful lessons, including a great quote from *Hamlet*, "This above all: To thine own self be true."

Gloria Steinem

Author and Activist

> The universe as we know it is a joint product of the
> observer and the observed.
>
> —Teilhard de Chardin

I was only half kidding when I used to say, "An examined life is not worth living." That was the degree to which I felt impatient with introspection, and suspicious that it would displace activism.

Only after I had got burned-out several times by this imbalance in my life did I begin to wonder if externalizing everything was so wise after all. It dawned on me that my upbringing in a factory-working neighborhood might have had something to do with it—which was a step toward introspection in itself. After all, men worried about making a pay envelope stretch for a week, women about the same thing, plus worrying about the men, and both were more concerned with bread than roses.

Still, I didn't really pay attention to the inner half of reality until a wise woman came along and asked me a question.

I was explaining to this older friend that I had gone to New York's Cathedral of Saint John the Divine for its annual celebration of Saint Francis of Assisi's birthday. Given his devotion to the four-footed and the winged as well as the human poor, many people brought their companion animals to be blessed. For a few hours, the traditional space of the cathedral turned back to a more universal and pagan time.

When I entered the cathedral's lofty arches, hundreds of pews were already dotted with animal lovers. Some had cats perched on their shoulders, or nestled in carriers at their feet. Others sat with dogs sleeping or listening attentively. Many children had hamsters rattling treadmills on their laps, rabbits on leashes, goldfish bowls balanced on their knees, or tropical and domestic birds in cages. One tall man had a very large snake curled around his body, another walked in with a huge owl perched on his arm, and yet another was leading a very pink and flower-bedecked pig down the aisle.

During the service, the dean of the cathedral walked among the congregation with microphone in hand, a modern Pied Piper who told the life story of Saint Francis of Assisi as children trailed behind him. After he finished his account of this rich man's son who had renounced everything for the poor, the members of his procession gathered around the main altar. As they turned to look up the aisle, I followed their gaze.

Two camels with flowers around their necks, each led by a costumed keeper, emerged from the shadows. Then came goats with bells tinkling at their collars, tropical birds perched on the shoulders of women and men in choir robes, Shetland ponies prancing on multicolored leads, fat white geese that elicited laughter with their waddle, and a pig so enormous that his harness looked like ribbons on a duffel bag. All these were part of an animal delegation that the cathedral itself had gathered.

But the best and biggest came last—an elephant that may have been small by her species' standards, but was very big compared to everything else. A wreath of flowers trailed from her neck as her mahout led her down the aisle. As she glided past me in lumbering slow motion, I saw the depth of her ancient eye. From that moment on, I couldn't take my own eyes off her.

All the birds and animals stood in a semicircle around the central altar. They were a peaceful kingdom of beasts of burden and endangered species, subjects of poetry and slaughter, myth and sadism, each one a miracle of survival. Despite long religious bias that said animals had no souls, they were being blessed. In truth, they all blessed us with their presence, yet my eyes filled with tears only for the elephant.

I told my friend about this, explaining that I was worried about whether the elephant was well treated, lonely, imprisoned in too small a space as so many are; all perfectly good externalized reasons. Still, as my friend pointed out, the same worries could have applied to almost any of the living things in that cathedral.

"So the question is," she said thoughtfully, "what about you is the elephant?"

Images rushed in unbidden. *Living in a world not one's own . . . vulnerable . . . gentle . . . unable to hide . . . strength for others but not for oneself . . .* I thought: *No wonder women especially tend to identify with this gentle, communal, and endangered species—not to mention the unique reasons that each of us may have.*

My friend's question reminded me that I had no idea what the elephant felt or truly needed. As long as I couldn't admit what part of her was me, I couldn't know what part was really her. Had I acted on such unexamined feelings, I might have been a danger to us both.

So now, I try to remember: My inner world is no more important than the outer one, but no less important either.

I always ask myself, "What part of me is the elephant?"

Gloria Steinem

Martha Stewart

CEO and Entrepreneur

In January 2002, *Martha Stewart Living* was about to celebrate its one-hundredth issue, and I needed to write my editor's letter that would somehow explain what this meant to all of us at the magazine and what motivated us each month. A difficult task. One of my editors walked into my office and handed me an old document she had dug out of a file cabinet that she thought might be useful in writing my letter. I glanced at the old memo and instantly broke into a huge smile.

Before I reveal the contents, let me tell you a story.

I grew up in Nutley, New Jersey, the second oldest of six children in a family that had absolutely no money for "extras"—no expendable income for "luxuries," only day-to-day basics. And yet the remarkable thing is, it didn't even occur to us to worry about money, because the work ethic was instilled at a very early age. If you needed new clothes, then get a job and pay for them. College costs a certain amount of money? Go earn a paycheck.

This is not to suggest that our household was some sort of heartless, pecuniary factory. It was fascinating actually because everyone was busy and productive. We were all occupied twenty-four hours a day. I baby-sat first, and soon after, I created children's birthday parties, helping parents make the events special, with craft projects and other unusual ideas.

Meanwhile, if my chores were done and I wasn't at work, I was allowed to go to the library as often as I wanted. If I wanted to read in bed, before I went to sleep, nobody came along and told me, "Lights out." Shutting off the TV is one thing but you never turn out the lights on a reader.

Because my parents had both been educators—my mother, a sixth-grade teacher in a local grammar school, my dad a physical education and Slavic languages instructor—they were natural-born "encouragers." Although I can hardly recall a day I didn't feel an over-whelming sense of optimism from my parents, I do remember the first time that hope was crystallized into actual words.

I was fifteen years old, and my teacher had assigned us a book report. For some reason I decided to write about *The Scarlet Letter* by Nathaniel Hawthorne. I quickly regretted my choice. This book was not easy for a ninth grader.

What does A stand for? Oh, adultery. (Pause.) *What's adultery?*

If this wasn't hard enough, imagine having your father—not your mother—explain to you what this very grown-up novel was all about. Then imagine trying to write a paper about it. Naturally, I was a mess, worrying and crying and telling my dad that I'd made a big mistake in choosing the book.

"It's way too hard to understand!" I protested. "I won't be able to write anything that makes sense!"

My father listened carefully as I listed all of the reasons Nathaniel Hawthorne and I simply weren't going to hit it off.

"Martha," he said, "you can do anything. If you put your *mind* to it. *Anything.*"

Something in that fleeting moment crystallized for me. Because I trusted my parents without exception—and because my dad was an educator, after all—I accepted his words as gospel and sat down to write my paper. My father had revealed the key to accomplishing difficult tasks: Setting your mind to something could make it happen. One week later I got the paper back from my teacher with a huge A written on it (in scarlet, no less). I think I still have that paper somewhere.

After that day, I shrugged off any self-doubt I may have felt, newly emboldened by my father's decree that anything was possible. Around this time a neighbor of mine, a ballerina, had become a model, and I decided that this sounded exciting. So with my parents' blessing, I went to New York with this girl, her agency signed me up, and I began going to auditions. It could be pretty scary, climbing onto a bus and going into the city to apply for work, and the modeling business was brutally competitive. But, again, I remembered my father's advice, and I was on my way.

I began making TV commercials shortly afterward. Funnily enough, I wasn't cast as a child, but instead as a woman. In fact, one of my first jobs was playing a young wife in a Lifebuoy soap commercial. I was fifteen—*a baby*—and playing a married woman! Where did I get the self-assurance to pull off such an outrageous transformation? From the words, "You can do anything."

I've lost count of the number of times my parents' support came back to guide me through life, from applying to college to raising a child to starting my own company. But once that kind of self-confidence is instilled in you, it's with you forever. What's more, you can pass it on to others. That's what I do now in all of my businesses. I'm constantly encouraging people to do, to learn, to accomplish, to create. And I continue to push myself, as well.

Which brings me back to the memo. When my editor handed

it to me, I immediately recognized it as something I wrote back in 1991, when *Martha Stewart Living* was approaching its first anniversary. It was called "Tenets for a Good Business," and it included a list of goals I set for myself—and the magazine—such as, "We must establish and maintain a standard of perfection," "We must remember our reader," and "We must provide information that inspires."

What made me laugh was that I had just been writing the same exact words for my one-hundredth anniversary issue letter. Here ten years had passed, and even with all our successes, we were still setting goals, still pressing forward, still believing in the limitlessness of our potential. Having a dream is one thing. Putting your mind to it to accomplish it is what makes it come true.

My only problem? What am I going to write for our two-hundredth issue?

Martha Stewart

Amy Tan

Author

The most hateful words I have ever said to another human being were to my mother. I was sixteen at the time. They rose from the storm in my chest and I let them fall in a fury of hailstones: "I hate you. I wish I were dead . . ."

I waited for her to collapse, stricken by what I had just said. She was still standing upright, her chin up, her lips stretched in a crazy smile. "Okay, maybe I die, too," she said between huffs. "Then I no longer be your mother!" We had many similar exchanges. Sometimes she actually tried to kill herself by running into the street, holding a knife to her throat. She, too, had storms in her chest. And what she aimed at me was as fast and deadly as lightning bolts.

For days after our arguments, she would not speak to me. She tormented me, acted as if she had no feelings for me whatsoever. I was lost to her. And because of that, I lost, battle after battle, all of them: The times she criticized me, humiliated me in front of others, forbade me to do this or that without even listening to one good reason why it should be the other way. I swore to myself I would never forget these injustices. I would store them, harden my heart, make myself as impenetrable as she was.

I remember this now, because I am also remembering another

time, just a couple of years ago. I was forty-six, had become a different person by then, had gone on to become a fiction writer, someone who uses memory and imagination. In fact, I was writing a story about a girl and her mother when the phone rang.

It was my mother, and this surprised me. Had someone helped her make the call? For three years, she had been losing her mind through Alzheimer's disease. Early on, she forgot to lock her door. Then she forgot where she lived. She forgot who many people were and what they had meant to her. Lately, she could no longer remember many of her worries and sorrows.

"Amy-ah," she said, and she began to speak quickly in Chinese. "Something is wrong with my mind. I think I'm going crazy."

I caught my breath. Usually she could barely speak more than two words at a time. "Don't worry," I started to say.

"It's true," she went on. "I feel like I can't remember many things. I can't remember what I did yesterday. I can't remember what happened a long time ago, what I did to you . . ." She spoke as a person might if she were drowning and had bobbed to the surface with the force of will to live, only to see how far she had already drifted, how impossibly far she was from the shore.

She spoke frantically: "I know I did something to hurt you."

"You didn't," I said. "Really, don't worry."

"I did terrible things. But now I can't remember what . . . and I just want to tell you . . . I hope you can forget just as I've forgotten."

I tried to laugh so she would not notice the cracks in my voice. "Really, don't worry."

"Okay, I just wanted you to know."

After we hung up, I cried, both happy and sad. I was again the same sixteen-year-old, but the storm in my chest was gone.

My mother died six months later. By then she had bequeathed me her most healing words, those that are as open and eternal as a clear blue sky. Together we knew in our hearts what we should remember, what we can forget.

Julie Taymor

Director

One afternoon I found myself crawling along the rim of an erupting volcano in Indonesia. I was twenty-one years old. I had just finished producing and directing my first puppet-mask trilogy with Balinese performers and was on my way to a village in the north to see an initiation ceremony for the young men of Trunyan. The population, called the Bali Aga, considered themselves to be the original Balinese, not descended from another culture or another nation, but mythologically born out of the water. I was traveling with a friend, a wild French gypsy named Roland, who had dropped from an airplane into the jungles of Sumatra and joined my theater troupe as an actor.

Roland decided to scale the mountain, even while the volcano was spewing flames, and I was game to join him. Going up wasn't too hard. We were only wearing rubber thongs, but we could climb by grabbing on to roots. The problem was we would have to find another way to get down.

At the top, on the rim of the dead crater, we stopped to eat food we had brought in banana-leaf packages. Roland said he wanted to see the inside of the erupting volcano, about forty feet from us, that was spewing fire every fifteen minutes. He rose and disappeared into the sulphur smoke. The only safe way to descend the volcano was a trail that started at the rim of the live crater. I would have to follow Roland, but the rim of the dead crater that led to the erupting one was about six inches wide and pointy, more like a tightrope than a walkway, and the wind was blowing hard. There was a sheer rock face on one side, and on the other, the infinite abyss of a sulphurous hole. I was terrified. I shed myself of everything I was carrying and let it all fall into the crater, even my camera. I got down on my hands and knees.

Images of "the end" invaded my imagination. Then I remembered words from Carlos Castaneda's *A Separate Reality*. The essence was that "to get to your impossible destination, you have to focus on only the immediate point in front of you; forget everything else surrounding that point, and you will get where you're going." I held that in my mind, and on all fours, like a cat, I started across, looking directly in front of me at the line of the crater beneath my eyes. If I had gazed to the left I would have been too terrified to move. If I had looked forward and seen how far I had to go, I would have been afraid that I wouldn't make it. But by concentrating on this line and moving slowly, I was able to get there without any feeling of fear.

When I finally reached Roland, he was standing at the edge of the live crater, wearing a turban and holding a stick. With the sulphur smoke swirling around him, he looked like Moses on the mount. I went to the edge and looked down into the molten red and yellow lava: an unbelievable sight. Just as I turned to walk away, I slipped. Volcanic rock had carved a hole out of my shin that was the spitting image of the inside of that crater.

That night in the village I saw another demonstration of letting everything but the moment fall away. I was sitting underneath a gigantic Banyan tree, alone in the darkness, listening to the surrounding sounds of village gamelans. Overlapping orchestras, like a Charles Ives concert. After a while it was quiet. There was no electricity, but the moon was full. All of a sudden, in the dead of night, I saw the moonlight bouncing off little glimmering mirrors, and twenty or thirty old men in full Balinese warrior costumes, spears in hand, danced into the empty square.

For the next half an hour amazing musical sounds emanated from their bellies as they performed an extraordinary war dance with no spotlight but the moon and no audience but myself, hidden under the tree. As soon as they finished, they disappeared. It was a ritual they had to do for a purpose that belonged to them, for an audience that needed no light to see: a spirit larger than life itself.

Many of the travails in my life in the theater and film worlds bring me back to these two experiences and the words of Carlos Castaneda: When it all seems impossible, focus on the point in front of you, follow it like a hawk and forget everything else.

Twyla Tharp

Choreographer

Quite a while ago now, a newspaper reporter was writing a story about me and my work. Martha Graham was interviewed for the article. I was well on my way in my dance career by then. I had done a lot of work, enough so that a newspaper was doing a big story on me and called to talk to Martha about me. She told the reporter, "I'm a rebel and she's a rebel."

Those words were absolutely validating. Here was someone I had great regard for, and she thought I was going in the right direction. In essence, she was certifying me as a breaker of the law like she had been. I was breaking the rules about what a dance is, how dances are made, and what they look like.

But in another deep sense, I realized I had never been a rebel. I might break the rules of what had been done in choreography, but my career itself has been a lot of hard work, step-by-step. My career was not a one-off kind of thing, but a day-in, day-out commitment to trying to be the best. My mother saw to it that I was dedicated to excellence from the age of two.

First, you have to understand my parents' own devotion to the arts. My mother trained to be a concert pianist, but when World War II came, she started teaching music. So she was a frustrated concert pianist. My father was a painter and an architect, who sold cars. Both of them would have preferred to have artistic careers, but they felt it was incumbent upon them to supply their children with college educations. To do that, my father could not be a painter and my mother could not be a concert pianist. They sacrificed their desires because their deeper desire was to give their children hopes and dreams.

When I was born, my family lived on a farm in Indiana. The town wasn't a place that understood the arts much, but my mother did. I was the eldest of four, and when all of us were less than a year old we were already ear training—my mother would play a note and we would sing it back. When I was two, Mother began sending me to a woman who specialized in teaching babies at the keyboard, a form of pre-Suzuki. By the time I was four, I was studying lots of things, including violin and different kinds of dancing with formal teachers. We eventually moved to San Bernardino, California, and there she found a pair of sisters from the Paris Opera and sent me to them when I was ten. When I was twelve, I went to a woman who had studied with Pavlova. My piano teacher was a woman who had gone to Juilliard.

I didn't get patted on the back that much for whatever skills and techniques I learned studying under that impressive array of teachers. We children were expected to do well. More important, failure was not an option—that was my parents' main thing. There was not a big reward system for us children. My parents' clear mandate was excellence: to be thorough and demanding and rigorous in one's pursuit of whatever we eventually chose to do.

My father and mother always said, "We don't care what you do. We don't care if you dig ditches, as long as you dig the best ditches anybody has ever dug." Those were truly the words that set the course of my entire life.

I always attempted to fulfill my parents' expectations. They told me I should practice my piano an hour and a half every day; I should practice my violin forty-five minutes every day; I should do X, Y, and Z. And I did. But I always recognized there was a reason for it all, and that it was up to me to figure out how it all connected and what to do with it.

In all this encouragement and expectation, there was love; I knew that, in all of these demands, someone cared. It was my mother loving her children in this way that gave me the resources to make my career what it has been. I'm not saying I played piano for my mother. It was clear I was playing for myself, to develop these skills and to become a pianist. And that carried over to dancing, to everything. Everything I did, I did very seriously, even if it was studying shorthand, because who knew when the bottom might fall out of the possibility of playing the piano? It wasn't about pleasing my parents. It was serious business.

My mother gave me the wherewithal to do what I do today. There are no miracles in this business. Each dance has to get a little stronger, a little better, a little closer. My mother's encouragement is one of the most loving things I can possibly imagine. I felt that love in the ongoing push and daily insistence that one can accomplish. It's an amazing investment in another person, whether it comes from a teacher or a parent or whomever. And we who receive that attention in our lives should be very grateful, beyond gratitude.

Ted Turner

Founder of CNN and Philanthropist

Iwent to school for fourteen years before a teacher actually said, out loud, that he was going to "put a premium on thinking for yourself." I couldn't believe my ears. I was a sophomore at Brown University in 1958 when, for me, the sun finally came up on my life as a student. There were about fifteen in the class and we sat around in a circle discussing the *Aeneid*. It was the class of the teacher I remember best, classics professor John Workman. Here I was, encouraged to discuss a work that the old school of listening and taking notes would have made me squirm with edginess as I tried to store the material long enough to last until exam time.

Professor Workman was different. The difference he made for me could be written large on a bumper sticker: "Think for Yourself." This may not sound like a revolutionary banner, but it was to me. I will never forget the thrill of actually being encouraged to think for myself. It was exciting being in that circle and popping off about a Roman epic that would have, in the old school of rote learning, sent me running away with a headache. In Professor Workman's class our own views, arrived at by our own thinking, were actually respected. The whole class actually listened! And it was fun. Ted Turner was having fun! And it was happening in school!

It would be thirty years before I was granted a diploma from

Brown University. Even though I did not have enough credits to graduate, in the eighties I was given the equivalent of a Battlefield Commission. (I also have an honorary degree from Brown.) But it's the Battlefield Commission I treasure. It was offered "without reservations," which means I am a graduate of Brown and I can prove it. Not your regular route to a sheepskin, but a diploma nonetheless.

About fifteen years ago, Professor Workman came to Atlanta to address a Brown alumni meeting. After the event I drove him to the airport and we spent most of the time in the car talking about the good old days at Brown. I just couldn't thank him enough for being such a powerful influence on me. He was the first teacher to encourage me to speak my own thoughts, do things my own way. Today it's called "thinking outside the box." Maybe that circle of students in Professor Workman's class at Brown was the place where I began to think that even edgy, impatient Ted Turner was capable of creating something great. Maybe not a civilization; how about a cable TV channel that would bring the news of the day to all the civilizations of the world?

Maybe, I thought, just maybe I could pull this off; as long as I could think for myself, no telling what I could accomplish.

Mike Wallace

Television Journalist

Martha's Vineyard, Massachusetts, has somehow always been the only place I have felt genuine roots. For a few years, starting when I was ten, my folks would rent rooms in a rooming house in Vineyard Haven, and the day after summer camp, we'd drive from our house in the Boston suburb of Brookline to the ferry in Wood's Hole and cross the Vineyard Sound for our two-week vacation on the Vineyard. From the moment I saw the seagulls and smelled the salt water, I was hooked.

I adored everything about the slow rhythms of the island, its fishing docks, stone-fenced farms, woodsy roads and rolling beaches. But after college, my broadcasting jobs took me to the Midwest and then hurled me east to New York, and I didn't get back to the Vineyard for some thirty years. Once I rediscovered that summer routine, my wife and I would rent a house for a couple months in either Edgartown or Vineyard Haven, near my close friends Art Buchwald and Bill Styron.

On a breezy afternoon in the summer of 1990, Artie and I were taking a walk up Main Street in Vineyard Haven. As we were approaching the West Chop Lighthouse, we passed a small colonial cemetery. Artie turned to me and said, "You know, we can buy plots here for five hundred bucks." He paused and arched his eyebrows. "Perpetual care . . ."

I'd never considered buying a plot. Who thought about such things? "Are you going to buy one, Artie?" I asked. "Is Styron?"

He nodded.

"Maybe I ought to," I said. "Tell you what. You know how I feel about this place. What kind of epitaph might I have if I came here for my final rest?"

Artie smiled. "Here lies Mike Wallace. He was always a renter."

With those words, Artie turned a near-certain morbid discussion of mortality into a commentary on whether or not I had committed to a place I considered the most beautiful on earth. His comment, oddly enough, changed my life profoundly, in a way that no epitaphic summary of my career could have. Despite the fact that we were talking about cemetery plots, I didn't attach any meaning of life or death to being "a renter." Instead, it made me an outsider, not a real "Vineyarder."

So I stopped renting and bought a house about three hundred yards up the street from Artie. The property had belonged to Kingman Brewster when he was president of Yale. He used the main house for living and the smaller, adjacent house for his summer office. To create more space and a unified feeling, Mary Yates, now my wife of sixteen years and dear friend of four decades, and I had a hole dug next to the old house and built a new two-story structure that connected the smaller house with a breezeway.

But here comes the important part: The finished structure brought my entire extended family together under one roof. We open up the house in May and there's a steady stream of family flowing informally through the doors until we close it in October. I'm off work six weeks, from June 15 to August 1, and I spend the entire time on the island, as well as scattered long weekends through the rest of the summer and the fall. Like the kitchen at Thanksgiving, the house on the Vineyard became a gathering place for the Wallaces and Yateses. When we rented, the scheduling that went into family trips made them feel like obligations for all parties. Now people come and go as they please.

Between Mary and me, our family and extended family of children, stepchildren and grandchildren has grown since we bought the house. We now have eleven grandchildren, and they all come with their parents during the summer, and for me, it couldn't be better. I get to see my stepson, Eames Yates, catch fish where there are no fish. I wouldn't trade for anything the time I've spent there with my beloved stepdaughter of almost fifty years, Pauline Dora, her husband, Dick Bourgeois, and their kids Nadina, Wallace and Lowell.

But on a special level, the house has also helped mend some broken bridges between my son Chris and me. We had gone through a long patch when we weren't close. Both of us were busy, running from story to story and sorting out our own immediate family matters, and to my dismay a kind of disconnect grew between our families.

Now Chris and his wife and four kids come for a week every summer, and I get to see what a truly wonderful father he is. We sit on the lawn and have those casual conversations that for years we weren't able to have. By bringing our families together, the house helped bring Chris and me back together.

All that's left now is for Artie to come up with a new epitaph.

Mike Wallace

Barbara Walters

Broadcast Journalist

In 1976, I left my job at NBC's *Today* show, after spending thirteen happy years there. My destination was ABC, where I would become the first female coanchor of a nightly network news program.

Now, in a way, that's a dubious honor. To my mind, it's much tougher to cohost one of the morning programs than it is to do an evening news broadcast. There's a certain spontaneity to the morning shows—a fly-by-the-seat-of-your-pants format that doesn't really exist on the evening programs. And yet the *Nightly News* had always been considered *the* place to go for a serious newsperson.

At ABC, I was hired to coanchor the evening program with veteran newsman Harry Reasoner. At one point during his tenure at the network, he had worked with a partner, then eventually returned to doing the program solo. But now—horror of all horrors—Harry was informed that he would not only once again be sharing the news desk, but with a female, to boot.

To complicate matters, I had not come into journalism the traditional way—as a wire reporter from AP or UPI, for example—but instead had received my training on television. I had been a writer on the *Today* show before becoming an on-air reporter, then cohost.

When I finally arrived at ABC, I was greeted by the most

awful press imaginable. According to reports, I was a prima donna, demanding, among other things, a pink typewriter. What seemed to aggravate the media most, however, was my salary, which was said to be $1 million—the largest paycheck for any newsperson ever.

Not so. In truth, I was making the exact same salary as Harry—$500,000 a year—with another $500,000 being paid by the entertainment division for four one-hour, prime-time specials. It was actually a bargain for ABC.

But beyond the matter of salary, what really weighed against me at ABC was the fact that I was a woman. This was an era, remember, in which it was believed that women didn't belong in the so-called "hard" news business, and Harry clearly didn't want to work with a female, no matter who she was.

To say that I was not an instant success at ABC is an understatement. Everybody watched us the first night, but nobody tuned in for the second, other than to see how these two uncomfortable people were behaving. And we weren't behaving all that well. Harry could not hide his displeasure at having to share the program with me. For my part, whenever I walked into the studio, no one would talk to me, not even the stagehands and cameramen.

Years later I interviewed Harry on the air while I was hosting the ABC news magazine *20/20,* and I couldn't resist asking him about this time. His answer was, if nothing, frank. He told me that I had simply been the wrong face in the wrong place at the wrong time. "It was nothing personal," he said.

But back in 1976, it was very personal. I was crushed, to say the least. I remember I would go home every night, and my only comfort was my then seven-year-old child. In fact, one of the reasons I had moved to ABC in the first place was because I had wanted to spend more time with my little girl. I was tired of getting up at four in the morning and falling asleep in my soup every night.

Another thing that kept me going during this tough time was the endless stream of letters I would get from women all over the country. "Hang in there," they would write. "If you can do it, we can do it, too." All of that gave me strength.

But the real turning point—and what I will always remember most—was the arrival of a telegram one day. I was sitting at my desk when it was handed to me. I opened it, and began to read. The wire simply said: DON'T LET THE BASTARDS GET YOU DOWN. And it was signed, JOHN WAYNE.

Reading the telegram, I felt as if the cavalry was coming. More than offer much needed solace at a moment of crisis in my life, John Wayne's words eventually taught me that you can't live your life around what other people may say about you, no matter how critical those comments are. You've got to keep your chin up. You've got to raise your head high. To put it in John Wayne terms, if you fall off that horse, you must get back on again.

And that's exactly what I did. After I was on the program for a little more than a year, ABC hired a new president for its news department, Roone Arledge. Roone had faith in me. He made the choice to keep me on the air, and Harry went back to CBS, where he had worked before ABC. Then, little by little, I worked my way up. I interviewed Egypt's President Anwar Sadat and Israeli Prime Minister Menachem Begin at the time of the Egyptian-Israeli peace treaty signing; I talked on the air with Cuban leader Fidel Castro and did a whole series of news-making interviews. In a sense, I had grown into my work, a process that began with John Wayne's telegram.

Ironically, I was able to thank John Wayne personally for his valuable words years later when I interviewed him for an ABC special. Before we began taping, I told him how I had never forgotten the wire he sent me. Our subsequent interview turned out to be moving and, as fate would have it, the last he would ever do: The next day John Wayne went into the hospital and never came out.

His inspiration lives on. As for Harry Reasoner's words, I learned that I hadn't been in the wrong place at the wrong time after all. More important, I also discovered that by hanging in there and working hard, I could make the time and the place my own.

Vera Wang

Designer and CEO

Iwas standing in front of Ralph Lauren, about to break the news that I was leaving his company. I had heard Ralph already knew what I was going to say—office grapevine, and all—but what he didn't know was that my decision was forty years in the making.

Let me back up.

As a young girl, I had been a figure skater—a *serious* figure skater. I competed in singles and pairs, and over the years was ranked among the top dozen skaters in the United States. That's a pretty decent achievement. Unfortunately, people only remember the champions, never the runners-up. I had set my sights on the Olympics, and the American team selects only two or three skaters every four years. Timing is everything; consequently, I never made it to the Games.

So at the age of nineteen, having skated competitively for twelve years, I left the sport and never talked about it again. It broke my heart to give up something I loved so much, and I felt like a failure for not making it to the pinnacle before I walked away.

When I graduated from college, I decided that my true fantasy, second only to being an Olympic champion, was to become a fashion designer. For as long as I could remember, I harbored a passion for all things related to fashion and style. My father didn't exactly warm to this idea. "I'm not paying for you to go back to undergraduate school to take design courses," he said, "and I don't want to hear about it. You think you're so gifted—go out and get a job."

Well, I did. I went to *Vogue* and became one of the youngest fashion editors in the magazine's history. I stayed for sixteen years. It was the perfect job for me. I was on the move constantly, supervising fashion shoots, traveling the world. The job didn't pay a lot—averaging $30,000 a year—but it wasn't about money for me. I was passionate about the work. I also was confident that someday I would land the job as editor-in-chief. I wasn't alone in these aspirations. There were several of us princesses-in-waiting at the magazine, all of us convinced that one day we would top the masthead.

Unfortunately, just like in my skating career, the big win never materialized: When *Vogue* needed a new editor-in-chief, they hired someone from the outside and, suddenly, there I was, having spent more than a decade and a half of my life working like a dog for that one triumph—my personal Everest—only to have it elude me once again.

And so, at forty, I moved to Ralph Lauren's company, as a design director. I was one of Ralph's trusted sergeants and he assigned enormous responsibilities to me. But I was newly married and wanted to start a family. I was very torn. Two years after joining the company, I walked into Ralph's office to tell him I was leaving. Looking back, I had no idea I was quitting to start my own business. I remember thinking perhaps it just wasn't meant to be for me, that I wasn't going to achieve my dreams.

It was impossible to tell Ralph I was leaving. He had put a lot of trust in me; I had nothing but enormous respect for him and I didn't want to let him down. But I also knew I was making the right choice. I told Ralph, assuring him that my departure wasn't because of bad feelings. "I just need to take some time for me."

Ralph listened patiently. Then he started to speak.

"I never say this to anybody," he began, "so you'd better take it seriously: Although I don't want you to go, I understand. So hear these words and take them to heart: If anyone ever doubts you, if you're discouraged or frightened, always remember that you have talent. Never forget that."

I don't remember what I said when Ralph finished—if I said anything at all—but I recall being shocked by the supportiveness and generosity of his words. I had always known that he believed in me when I worked for him, but here I was leaving him, and he still believed in me. Given his success in the fashion industry—which is, I think, historic—to hear that kind of encouragement at such a crucial moment was nothing short of overwhelming.

I've come to discover that Ralph's advice wasn't so much about having talent as it was about having confidence. Quite often, we are the last to know that we possess a reservoir of strength, an ability to persevere. We're all frightened. We all have self-doubts. But I think what I have learned most from my forty-year journey is that sometimes we have to dig a little deeper to find that last bit of power that keeps us moving toward whatever dreams we have.

Within two years of leaving Ralph Lauren my own name was appearing on labels, and I was running a business I built from scratch out of a tiny storefront office on the Upper East Side of Manhattan. To say that the work was hard is an understatement: The job is twenty-four hours a day and now I have financial burdens and creative pressures I never imagined. But the rewards are boundless; and whenever I become unhinged or disheartened—when I feel as though I can't go on another minute—all I need is to summon Ralph's words and they give me a kind of courage, a mental strength.

Ralph believed in me, I think to myself. *He saw something there. Maybe I can, too.*

Wendy Wasserstein

Playwright

Before I was a woman and a writer, I was a girl who was sweet, smart, funny, and chubby. And when you're all of those things, let's be honest, you're not at the big people's table.

In 1967, I went off to college at Mt. Holyoke in South Hadley, Massachusetts. But in my junior year, I transferred to Amherst College as part of an experiment in coeducation; the school was admitting women from various colleges for the first time in its history. When I arrived at Amherst, the makeup of the student body was, to say the least, lopsided: there were twenty-three women and twelve hundred men.

One evening shortly after the start of the first semester, I was sitting on my bed, talking with my roommate, Mary Jane, when a fellow we'd seen around campus wandered into our room. He leaned against the doorway and, after a few minutes of conversation, revealed to us an unusual hobby of his.

"You know, my friends and I rate the girls at Amherst," he informed us—meaning, of course, that they had ranked the newly admitted women according to their looks. "Care to hear the top ten?" he asked.

Yes, we wanted to hear.

Topping the list was a girl name Maria (pronounced MAHria)—she was number ten. Maria was one of these artsy-looking girls who had beautiful straight hair and olive skin and always wore a shawl. Right behind Maria on the list—pulling in at number nine—was my roommate, Mary Jane. A good choice, actually. Mary Jane was great looking.

The guy rattled off the rest of his list and, naturally, I wasn't even close to being on it. This didn't really bother me, as appearance had never played a big part in my childhood. Growing up, I was always considered *funny* and *nice* and *sweet* and *smart,* while my sister, Gorgeous (that's really her name), was the one with the looks. Because things like weight and femininity had never been my best assets, after a while I didn't give them much thought.

Consequently, when this boy excluded me from his Amherst Top Ten, the only thing that really bothered me was that he had rated my roommate *behind* Maria.

"What do you mean?" I asked the guy indignantly. "Mary Jane should be number ten." My protests fell on deaf ears.

Now, around this time, Mary Jane and I were frightened to eat in the college dining room. Because of our tiny minority status at the school, as soon as we would walk through that door, twelve hundred heads would turn in our direction. This didn't make for a very relaxing meal.

So Mary Jane and I developed a system: I'd go to the dining room, where I'd quickly make us peanut-butter-and-jelly sandwiches at a side table, and then bring them back to our room.

But one day while I was in the middle of this procedure, a sandwich fell to the floor. I stooped down to retrieve it, but as I stood back up, my head banged into the tray of a student who happened to be walking by. Well, not just any student. It was Maria. Number ten. In a single heart-stopping moment, Maria's pancakes went flying into her face, syrup shot off in all directions, and I ran back to my room crying.

When I breathlessly recounted all of this to Mary Jane only minutes later, she couldn't stop laughing. "That has to be the funniest thing I have ever heard in my life," she said. Me, I was still in shock. I just kept repeating over and over again, "I hit number ten in the face with a pancake. . . . I hit number ten in the face with a pancake. . . ."

Not long after this incident, however, it began to dawn on me: *You know, all of this is just ridiculous.*

In one of my favorite lines in *The Heidi Chronicles,* the central character says, "What do women teach their sons that they never bother to tell their daughters?" Back when I was nineteen, this question was always on my mind. The boys at Amherst had all of this confidence. They always talked in class, whether they had read the book or not; they were loud and outgoing; they felt comfortable with themselves, at least enough to walk into a stranger's room and begin boasting about how they rated the girls.

All of this made me wonder, *Why is there such a difference between the genders when it comes to this kind of outward self-assurance? Where do these guys get all this confidence?*

The only answer I could come up with was that the mothers of these men must have taught them something—some secret to life, perhaps—that they never bothered to teach their daughters. Slowly my feelings about women—and particularly women's voices—began to awaken. "Daughters deserve confidence, too," I decided. "Maybe I can write for them. Maybe I can put women onstage and give them a voice—one that was, at the very least, equal to the kind of voice men seemed entitled to."

Alas, by the end of that school year, all twenty-three girls were sent back to their original colleges. As an experiment in coeducation, we'd been a failure, and Amherst wouldn't officially go coed for another four years. I did get an honorary degree from the school many years later, however. I brought Mary Jane and her husband and children with me, and in my speech at the alumni dinner, I recalled the pancake story. Then, holding my diploma in the air, I announced, "This is not just for me, it's for The Amherst Twenty-Three—the women you sent back."

If the remark by that odd fellow who came into my room that day began a chain of events for me—one that would lead me to my career—one other comment completed the journey. In 1982, I was walking down the street with my friend Andre Bishop, who was the artistic director of Playwrights Horizons Theater. At the time, I was mulling over an invitation Andre had given me to rewrite my play *Isn't It Romantic,* which had previously gotten mixed notices. Andre said that he'd be thrilled to stage a new version of the play, but being a Libra, I was waffling over whether or not to take him up on his offer. That's when Andre lowered the boom.

"You have the chance to redo this play and be taken seriously," he said, "and, in my opinion, the way to be taken seriously is to take *yourself* seriously. If I were you, I'd take the chance at the rewrite—because I, for one, take you seriously."

Even now, when I think about this comment, I want to cry.

For a comic writer whose greatest fear is not to be respected—perhaps because she's too sweet or too funny or too chubby—when a friend turns to you and says, "I take you seriously," it guides the rest of your life.

Maxine Waters

United States Representative

The James Weldon Johnson Elementary School stood at the corner of Laclede and Ewing Streets in St. Louis, Missouri.

A three-story building of brown brick—and home to some of my fondest childhood memories—the school sat on a modest tract of land and was completely surrounded by a fence. There were two entrances and two exits to the school, where teachers greeted students in the morning, monitored their activity at recess, and waved good-bye to them at the close of day.

Most of the faculty at James Weldon Johnson lived in the neighborhood, allowing teachers to visit students from time to time, perhaps to take them on a picnic or, on other occasions, meet with their parents to discuss the occasional bad deed.

Our teachers were passionate about their work. They spanked us when we were bad; but when we were good, they rewarded us with special lessons that went beyond the typical three-Rs curriculum. They taught us old Negro spirituals; they recited great oratory and took us on journeys through the world's rich cultural arts.

My sixth-grade teacher was Miss Stokes, an immaculate, middle-aged lady with gray hair who had devoted the entirety of her life to education and learning. Blessed with an excess of energy, Miss

Stokes had never married and gave all of her time to her students. My classmates and I secretly called her "Old Maid."

And yet there was nothing old about Miss Stokes. She was full of warnings and advice. She was stern and loving. She was as critical as she was complimentary. And she had a keen, almost clairvoyant, sense of her students.

Most important, though, Miss Stokes helped us to develop confidence in ourselves.

I'll never forget the day I handed in my health report. We'd been given an assignment to write about health and nutrition, and even though we were only in grammar school, Miss Stokes had told us that she expected our reports to be thorough, informative, and "presentable to any person in the City of St. Louis."

Ordinarily, most of my classmates submitted their reports in fancy, store-bought notebooks or binders. But because I was poor, I never had the means to purchase such extravagant supplies. Naturally, I fretted that my report would not have the visual flair of my classmates' submissions. But I was determined to do a good job and immediately set about the task of designing a folder that would show the best of me.

I began with two pieces of construction paper that had been given to me by Miss Stokes. Fashioning one of them into a front cover, I decorated it with a collage of fruit and vegetable pictures that I had clipped from magazines. Neatly sliding my report between the covers, I punched holes along the left side and then tied it all together with brightly colored yarn that was given to me by a classmate, who had been knitting a scarf.

Before I knew it, my health report was completely done, in all its homemade splendor.

Now, Miss Stokes knew I was from a large family of twelve brothers and sisters and that we didn't have any money. So when I handed her my report, she gave it a good, long look, then broke into a huge smile. She faced the classroom.

"Look at this, class," she said, holding my report high up in the air. "Where there is a will, there is a way."

No other words of explanation were needed. Everyone knew what she meant, including me. When I saw the looks on the faces of my friends and classmates—and the unmistakable pride in my teacher's eyes—I felt no less than ten feet tall. I felt smart. I felt confident. I felt special.

Miss Stokes's words and the glory of that single moment have seen me through the most trying times throughout my life. Whenever tasks are too complicated to perform, or problems too daunting to solve, I suddenly find myself transported back to that small room in that old building on Laclede and Ewing. "Where there is a will, there is a way," I hear my teacher say, and once again I am moving forward.

Although neither Miss Stokes nor I knew it at the time, the can-do spirit she instilled in me that day prepared me to tackle the huge public policy issues and exhausting legislative battles I would encounter later in my career. In the end, these rocky political confrontations would end up actually changing lives around the world.

Prior to my election to Congress, I served as a member of the California State Assembly, where I introduced legislation that required all retirement funds of public employees and state teachers be divested from companies that did business in South Africa. I wanted to ensure that California would not support the brutal apartheid system.

This was no small fight. For seven years, I pressed my eighty colleagues to vote for divestment. I constantly talked to them about the hateful scourge of apartheid. I sent them chilling items I clipped from newspapers and magazines. I traveled around the country helping to organize a national "Free South Africa Movement." The work never stopped.

I sometimes feared the worst—that our battle would fail, that apartheid would hold fast, and that blood would continue to flow in the streets of South Africa. But then I would remind myself of the struggles and sacrifices of the South African people themselves, and the way they were standing up to their oppressors by sheer will alone. I would then remember my teacher's words, and I'd take a breath and go at it again.

At last, unbelievably, I collected the votes I needed: After more than seven years of pitched political battle, my divestment bill was signed by the governor of the State of California in September of 1986. Ironically, he had initially opposed the legislation all those years before.

If I thought my proudest moment would forever be that day at James Weldon Johnson Elementary School in St. Louis, I was wrong. On February 11, 1990, Nelson Mandela, South Africa's leading political activist, was freed after twenty-seven years in prison. Not long after that, he made his first visit to the United States, where I had the honor of hosting a reception for him in California. He would, of course, go on to be South Africa's president.

I produced a welcome rally and concert at the Los Angeles Coliseum attended by ninety thousand people. When I escorted the guest of honor onto the stage, the audience rose to its feet, greeting Mr. Mandela with a long and thunderous ovation. It was one of the most memorable moments of my life.

Success is often about stepping back, taking deep breaths, and devising new and creative strategies to confront obstacles. If my life—and Miss Stokes—taught me anything, it's that dreams can be realized with little more than a stretch of yarn and imagination. A child who can't afford school supplies can become a United States congresswoman. A political prisoner can rise to the presidency of his people and then stand as a symbol of freedom around the world.

Where there is a will, there *is* a way.

Maxine Waters

Venus Williams

Athlete

It's not often you hear someone admit to getting advice from a kid sister. But to be honest, Serena's words changed my life.

I started playing professional tennis when I was fourteen years old. I did well my first year and moved forward pretty quickly. When I began playing full-time, I was ranked at number 204; by the end of the year I was in the top twenty. My hot streak continued the next year. I ended up fifth or sixth in the world.

After that, my progress was pretty much steady. I'd win some titles; I'd make it into the semifinals and finals. But when it came to the big victory, I'd fall short. Most important, I wasn't winning any Grand Slams.

This wasn't the case for my sister, Serena. She is a year younger than me and joined the tour only nine months after I did. Serena started well, too, and in 1999 won a Grand Slam, by grabbing the women's singles title at the U.S. Open.

Around this time, I found myself playing in a doubles match one afternoon with Serena at one of the big tournaments. I don't remember where we were, but I do know that I wasn't on top of my game, specifically my service game. In tennis, a player's service is crucial to his or her performance. When you're serving the ball, you're basically in control and have a slight edge over your opponent. So of all the times there are to lose in the sport, your service game can't be one of them. But at this point in my career, I was losing my service game all the time.

To make matters worse, on this day I was playing in a doubles match, and doubles isn't really Serena's and my game. Doubles is something that definitely requires practice—you have to rely on your partner a lot, know their strengths, and sense their next move.

So not only did I feel the pressure of performing well for the team, but I also didn't want to let Serena down by making mistakes.

We were in the middle of the match, sitting on the sidelines during a changeover, which is the one-minute break that players are allowed when they switch sides of the court. Ordinarily, you talk to your partner during a changeover. If you're winning, you talk about anything—a movie, the weather, the news. If you're losing, you talk about tennis.

On this particular changeover, Serena and I were talking about tennis. It had been a tough afternoon and we were trying to grind the match out. For my part, I wasn't focused or doing my best, and Serena knew it.

"Listen," she said, almost jokingly, "I don't care what you do on your side of the court, but I'm not going to miss on my side. We will not lose this match."

I didn't say anything. Then Serena got serious.

"Look, Venus," she said, "no matter how you feel about your game, you have to show up at the court, right? You're here to play tennis, after all. But you *do* have a choice about whether you want to compete well or compete badly. I'm going to make the choice to compete well. Why don't you do that, too?"

Although Serena's advice may now sound like a simple pep

talk, on that day—at that moment, sitting at the side of the court—it made so much sense to me, it was almost unreal. It summed up everything I'd been struggling with. When you commit yourself to something, you can't find a way out of it. You can't say, "Oh, I don't want to play today." You have to go. And as long as you have to be there, why not give it your all? Why not give it the best you can?

In other words, don't overlook the opportunity to achieve something, don't be nervous, don't hold back, give it all that you've got, because the moment may never come again.

I'm not sure if we won the doubles match that afternoon—though I believe we did—but after that day my game got better and better. In a difficult time in my career, Serena gave me good, valuable words, and I've taken them to every match I've gone to since.

Although as I write this I'm only twenty-one, I've already learned that if you don't give yourself the chance to do something new, something daring, who knows what you could have achieved? So what if you fail? At least you'll know what *not* to do when you try again.

Oprah Winfrey

Talk Show Host and Entrepreneur

I had come to Chicago on Labor Day weekend 1983 to audition for a new position as host of a local morning talk show.

All of my colleagues said don't do it. . . . "You're walking into a land mine. There's no way you can survive in Chicago. The competition will make mincemeat out of you." The show was called *AM Chicago*. It had a revolving door of previous hosts, and ratings so low they were barely countable. The show was positioned against the most formidable competition, the king of talk, the man who actually created the genre of open, candid discussion for a daytime viewing audience and made it popular: Phil Donahue.

Phil's show was based out of Chicago and broadcast nationally. He reigned in the ratings and basically had no competitors. He had been a mentor to me for many years. I watched his shows daily, first as a fan. Then later for instruction. When I was offered a cohost position on a show in Baltimore in 1978 called *People Are Talking,* I watched Phil every day to see what I could learn. I learned a lot. How to listen and interrupt only when necessary. In fact, I learned so much, I stopped watching after I heard myself on the air one day repeating a Philism, "Is the caller there?"

Coming to Chicago was a giant step for me. I would be competing against Phil Donahue in his home-base town. His was a national show. I was on a local station, with a budget that could only afford fake geraniums for the set. I told Dennis Swanson, the general manager of the station, I had many concerns. First of all, I would be the first black host of this show in a city known at the time for racial volatility. I was not exactly svelte. At my previous job, station management had wanted me to change who I was—my hair, my face, my weight, even my name.

I said, "I'm black and that's not going to change. I'm overweight and that's probably not going to change either."

He said, "I'm aware of that. I'm looking at you, young lady. You have a gift, a way of connecting with people. I don't expect you to change, just to use your gift."

Then he offered this gift to me. He said, "Donahue is killing us every day . . . we don't expect you to beat him, of course. Just go on the air and be yourself."

Those words freed me and set the trajectory for what unfolded to become *The Oprah Winfrey Show.*

No doubt if he had said the opposite, "We want you to beat Phil Donahue, . . ." I wouldn't have known what to do or how to do it and would have been doing the work for the wrong reasons. Instead, I felt completely uninhibited to speak with my own voice. To create my own path. Those were the right words at the right time. Every time I get a chance, I say, "Thank you, Dennis."

Tom Wolfe

Writer

London, April 21, 1894, the Avenue Theatre, packed practically up to its Mannerist ceiling moldings for the opening night of George Bernard Shaw's new play, *Arms and the Man,* and the curtain has just come down upon the final act. Tremendous applause, sustained applause, curtain call after curtain call, bow after bow, the entire cast, then one by one, then the entire cast again, and still they applaud, until finally the cry rings out, "Author! Author!" and a tall, pinch-shouldered man with a beard and a half and a mustache from here to there, the thirty-seven-year-old Shaw, critic, essayist, podium provocateur, and now fabulously successful playwright, brilliant young comet among Britain's men of letters, comes out from the wings to the center of the stage to yet more intense applause, to applause and bravos, and starts to take a bow, when—

"BOO! BOOOO! BOOOOO!"

The audience goes silent. All heads swing up toward the gallery for a look at the man with the astonishing lungpower who is on his feet, his hands cupped about his mouth like a megaphone. It's a fledgling drama critic named Reginald Golding Bright up there bellowing out this utterly insulting critique of the great Shaw—

"BOO! BOOOO! BOOOOO!"

Shocked, appalled, all eyes stare at Bright, and then all turn back toward the stage, where Shaw stands, alone, victim of a violent ambush. What would he do? What would he say?

Shaw was renowned for his wit, but the use of wit to deal with a face-to-face insult is a highly specialized branch of the art. The literature on this specialty is not vast, but I daresay anybody's study of it would lead him to the same conclusion as mine, which is: to be successful, wit used for this purpose must be akin to the Japanese martial art of jujitsu, in which he who is attacked uses his assailant's own power against him. In any sudden violent assault, the attacker will likely have an overwhelming advantage in terms of power and momentum. Seldom is there any way the victim can mobilize his own strength fast enough to resist head-on. So if, for example, a man with a knife hurls himself toward a jujitsu adept, he neither fights nor flees. Instead, at the last possible instant he rolls backward from a standing position onto his upper back—the adept is trained, needless to say, in basic tumbling skills—and thrusts both feet upward into the midsection of the attacker, whose own momentum, own highly mobilized power, own violent aggressiveness send him hurtling toward the wall behind, upon which, if the adept is adept enough, he breaks his neck.

The English have been the traditional masters of jujitsu wit, as in the famous instance in which Oscar Wilde, wearing mauve velvet jacket and knee breeches, white silk stockings and silver-buckled shoes, lollipop-collared and lily-cuffed ruffled shirt and a pageboy bob, was seated at a London dinner party when a reigning dowager said in a voice that took command of the entire table, "Why, Mr. Wilde, you look almost like a woman."

Without skipping a beat, Wilde said, "Oh, thank you, Madame. So do you."

But Shaw was Irish, proving that, in fact, jujitsu wit knows no nationality. Every eye was pinned upon this not very sturdy stalk of an Irishman as he stood alone onstage that night at the Avenue Theatre. The last round ripe boo had barely left the mouth of Reginald Golding Bright when Shaw looked up toward his assailant, smiled, and in the most congenial of voices said:

"My dear fellow, I quite agree with you. But what are we two against so many?"

The audience rose to its feet, applauded, cheered, all but tore the Mannerist moldings off the ceiling with their bravos. Had he wanted to, George Bernard Shaw, the Irish jujitsu witmaster, could have stood there and taken a hundred bows . . . that fateful night in London in 1894.

Or fateful for me, it was . . . me, the man who fortunately knew his Shaw when the time came. One evening in Montreal some eighty years later, I was at the center of a stage, too, having just concluded a public lecture. My platform panache and profundity were exemplary that night, or at least I had no difficulty interpreting the sustained applause that way. I was bathing in the blissful sound, floating in it, swimming in it, wallowing in it, when—

"BULLSHIT! BULLSHIT! BULLSHIT!"

It was a young man in the next to the last row of the auditorium, standing up, a very tall young man, hands cupped about his mouth like a megaphone, and Reginald Golding Bright's lungs couldn't have been any more powerful—

"BULLSHIT! BULLSHIT! BULLSHIT!"

The great hall grew silent. Every eye was pinned upon me, a foreigner alone in the middle of the stage. What would I do? What would I say?

The last cloacal insult had barely left my towering attacker's lips when I looked toward him, smiled, and in the most congenial of voices said:

"My dear fellow, I quite agree with you. But what are we two against so many?"

The audience rose to its feet, applauded, cheered, shook the roof with a thousand bravos. Had I wanted to, I could have remained on that stage taking bows from that night to this, so fantastically adept had I proved to be in the teeth of a surprise attack.

Scholarly protocol dictated that my newfound Canadian fans be informed of the actual originator of such a masterful jujitsu maneuver—but who was I to play killjoy and encumber a climactic moment like that with a footnote?

THE DALAI LAMA

The following verse from the *Guide to the
Bodhisattava's Way of Life* has been one of the most
inspiring prayers for me:

> For as long as space endures,
> And for as long as all living beings remain,
> Until then may I too abide
> To dispel the misery of the world.

March 2, 2002

The children of St. Jude Children's
Research Hospital

Memphis, Tennessee
February 25, 2002

(Photograph by Jere Parobek)

Marlo Thomas

Dear Reader,

When the hardcover edition of *The Right Words at the Right Time* was released in the spring of 2002, I knew in my heart that readers would be as captivated as I was by the compelling stories told in its pages. After all, who wouldn't be moved by the survival story of a war hero, or the thrilling tale of a sports star's victory, or the wisdom of a Supreme Court Justice? Who wouldn't be swept up in the drama of a struggling actor's ascent to stardom, or a courageous astronaut's ascent to the stars? Who couldn't find inspiration from the life and words of the Dalai Lama?

But what was really exciting to me was how personally the readers of *The Right Words* identified with the book's theme. Everywhere I went, people came up to me, eager to share those special "right words" stories from their own lives, and to explain to me how the perfect turn of phrase—spoken at precisely the right moment—had made such a difference to them.

I remember one fellow from Chicago who called into a radio station where I was the guest on a local talk show. He told me (and about a million listeners) how, without his father's constant reminder—"You can be anything you want to be"—he might never have had the courage to start his own business, an enterprise, incidentally, that he's now been running successfully for more than twenty-five years.

Then there was the recent high school graduate from Baltimore who confided to me that, just the year before, her teacher had taken her aside after she'd failed an exam and said, "Remember, in real life, it's the work that matters, not the score. And no one works harder than you." Those words, said the girl, convinced her to apply for college.

And I'll never forget that lovely senior citizen from Phoenix, who, after I'd done a book signing, walked up to me, took my hand, and softly recounted the last thing her mother ever said to her. So special—and so secret—were those words, that the woman could only whisper them into my ear. When she did, both of us began to cry.

The appeal of *The Right Words at the Right Time* became even more evident when editors at *Parade* asked readers to submit their own "right words" recollections to the magazine, some of which *Parade* went on to publish. That was almost a year ago, and the stories are still coming in.

That's why I'm so excited about our next project. Inspired by the touching and heartfelt response to *The Right Words at the Right Time,* we are compiling a second volume of stories and I'm hoping you'll be a part of the adventure by sharing a story of your own. If there's one thing we learned from the first book, it's that you don't have to be a prizefighter, or a world-renowned architect, or a concert violinist to have been affected by the power of words, and to have experienced firsthand how those words can change a life in an eye-blink. I'll bet you have a story just like that.

Maybe somebody gave you just the right bit of encouragement as you stepped up to the plate at a softball game, or before you made your entrance in a school play. Perhaps someone offered you an unforgettable piece of advice before you got married or began your first job.

Maybe you heard a song lyric on the radio—a simple line that instantly spoke to you. Or perhaps it was a phrase you read in a book, or something someone said in a magazine interview.

Maybe somebody shouted at you in anger, prompting you to respond not with like words, but instead with positive, life-altering action.

Whether you were consoled in a time of grief, or buoyed in a moment of triumph, I'm sure you have a memory that's worth sharing, and I'd love to hear it.

On the following pages, you will find a form on which you can tell me a little bit about yourself, then simply attach another page and write down your story, just as you remember it. Don't worry, we're not giving grades here—we're more interested in what you have to say. So write from the heart.

And, by the way, just like with the first *Right Words,* proceeds from the sale of the new book will go to St. Jude Children's Research Hospital, the hospital that my father founded in 1962, which, to this day, continues to provide care for children all over the world who suffer from catastrophic diseases. And no child is ever turned away for a family's inability to pay. The kids of St. Jude benefited enormously from the sales of the first book, and we look forward to providing even more help with the second one.

But enough from me. Now it's your turn. Sit back for a moment, reflect a bit, then turn the page and write me your story. I can't wait to read it.

Marlo Thomas
New York City
November 2003

Call for Entries

Share your story for possible inclusion in an all new volume of
The Right Words at the Right Time

Was there a moment when words changed your life? Whether they
were spoken to you by a family member or friend; whether you
read them in a book; whether you heard them in a movie or on the
radio; we'd like you to share your story with us. Selected entries
will be included in a forthcoming book of stories compiled by
Marlo Thomas.

- In 550–1,500 words, tell us about the words that had a profound effect on you and how they changed or influenced
  your life. (For examples of the kinds of stories we are looking for please refer to the stories in *The Right Words at the
  Right Time.*)

- Include the following information along with your submission: first and last name, postal address, email address, age,
  occupation, telephone number, title of your story, and any
  background information that may be relevant to your story.

• Enter on the web at www.rightwordsbooks.com or mail entries to: Right Words Books, Atria Books, 1230 Avenue of the Americas, New York, NY 10020.

Official Rules

NO PURCHASE NECESSARY.

The following Contest is intended for participation in the U.S. and Canada (excluding Quebec) only. Do not enter the Contest if you are not located within the U.S. or Canada. The Contest begins at 9:00 A.M. EST on January 6, 2004, and ends at midnight EST on April 16, 2004.

1. **How to Enter:** In order to be eligible for THE RIGHT WORDS AT THE RIGHT TIME Contest, you must submit your own true story about the words that had a profound impact on you. Entries must be fully original, no less than 550 words, no more than 1,500 words, written in English, typewritten and double-spaced, and must have never been published or professionally developed. Entries can be submitted on the website: www.rightwordsbooks.com or mailed to this address: Right Words Books, Atria Books, 1230 Avenue of the Americas, New York, NY 10020. Online entries must be received by midnight EST on April 16, 2004, and mailed entries must be postmarked by April 16, 2004, and received by April 20, 2004. Limit one (1) entry per person. All entries become the sole property of Simon & Schuster and will not be acknowledged or returned. Simon & Schuster reserves the right, in its sole discretion, to disqualify any entries that it deems inappropriate for any reason, including but not limited to entries containing references to drug or alcohol use, sexually explicit activity, or violation of laws. Entries must not

violate the rights of any third parties, including copyrights, rights of privacy, or rights of publicity, and entries must not be defamatory, as determined in the sole discretion of the judges. In the event an insufficient number of entries are received, Sponsor reserves the right to cancel the Contest. Limit one entry per person or household.

2. **Eligibility:** Open to legal residents of the U.S. and Canada (excluding Quebec). Parental consent required for entrants under the age of 18 as of January 6, 2004. Employees and immediate family members of employees of Simon & Schuster, its parent, subsidiaries, divisions, and related companies and their respective agencies and agents are ineligible. Void outside of the U.S., in Puerto Rico, and wherever prohibited or restricted by law.

3. **Judging Criteria:** All submissions must be a true story that is the fully original work of the entrant and the sole property of entrant. Please retain a copy of your submission. On or about August 16, 2004, stories will be evaluated by a panel of judges, on the equally weighted criteria of human interest, expression of thought, creativity, and originality. The decision of the judges will be final and binding in all respects. Entries must not have been previously published, must not have won any awards, and must never have been professionally developed. By entering, all entrants assign and transfer all rights, title, and interest in and to their respective submissions to Simon & Schuster. By entering, all entrants agree to abide by these guidelines and grant Simon & Schuster all rights to the entries to be used throughout the world in any and all media. Entrants agree that Simon & Schuster has the right to copy, rewrite, revise, edit, publish, promote, broadcast, and otherwise use

in whole or in part, in perpetuity, their entries in any manner without further permission, notice, or compensation.

4. **Selection of Entries:** Approximately one hundred entries will be selected based on the above-stated judging criteria, from among all eligible entries, to be published in a forthcoming book. Entries may also be selected for subsequent books compiled by Marlo Thomas. No prizes, payment, or compensation of any kind shall be awarded to Selected Entrants, other than inclusion of the selected entry in the forthcoming or subsequent books compiled by Marlo Thomas. Simon & Schuster may disqualify a potential entry at any time during the selection process. Simon & Schuster is under no obligation, and shall not be subject to any liability, in the event the book is not published and/or a particular entry is not included in the book. By agreeing to have his/her entry (if selected) included in the book, each Selected Entrant grants to Simon & Schuster the right to use his/her entry, name, and likeness for any advertising, promotional, trade, or any other purpose without further compensation or permission, except where prohibited by law. If the Selected Entrant is a Canadian resident, then he/she will be required to answer a skill-testing question administered by mail or email. Only those short-listed for inclusion in the book will be notified by mail or email, on or about October 16, 2004. Selected Entries are non-transferable; no substitutions or cash redemptions permitted.

5. **General:** Each Selected Entrant will be required to execute and return an Affidavit of Eligibility, Release and Transfer of Rights, within 15 days of attempted notification or an alternate Selected Entrant may be selected. In the event any Selected Entrant is con-

sidered a minor in his/her state of residence, minor's parent/legal guardian will be required to sign and return all required documents, within the prescribed time period, or an alternate Selected Entrant will be selected. By entering this Contest, participants agree to be bound by these official rules and Simon & Schuster's decisions, which are final in all matters relating to this Contest. Simon & Schuster and its parent, affiliates, subsidiaries, and employees, officers, directors, shareholders, agents, and advertising, promotion, legal advisers and any person or institution connected with publication are not responsible for and shall not be liable for: (i) lost, late, misdirected, incomplete, illegible, damaged, mutilated, or postage-due entries; (ii) any injuries, losses, or damages of any kind caused by or resulting from participation in this Contest; or (iii) any printing or typographical errors in any materials associated with this Contest. Entrants further release Simon & Schuster and any person or institution connected with publication from any liability for claims based on publicity rights, defamation, invasion of privacy, or the violation of any intellectual property rights, including but not limited to copyright infringement. Any dispute arising from this Contest will be determined according to the laws of the State of New York, without reference to its conflict of law principles, and the entrant's consent to the personal jurisdiction of the State and Federal Courts located in New York County and agree that such courts have exclusive jurisdiction over all such disputes.

6. **Internet:** If for any reason this Contest is not capable of running as planned due to an infection by a computer virus, bugs, tampering, unauthorized intervention, fraud, technical failures, or any other causes beyond the control of Simon & Schuster, which

corrupt or affect the administration, security, fairness, integrity, or proper conduct of this Contest, Simon & Schuster reserves the right, in its sole discretion, to disqualify any individual who tampers with the entry process, and to cancel, terminate, modify, or suspend the online portion of the Contest. Simon & Schuster assumes no responsibility for any error, omission, interruption, deletion, defect, delay in operation or transmission, communications line failure, theft or destruction or unauthorized access to, or alteration of, entries. Simon & Schuster is not responsible for any problems or technical malfunctions of any telephone network or telephone lines, computer online systems, servers, or providers, computer equipment, software, failure of any email or entry to be received by Simon & Schuster due to technical problems, human error, or traffic congestion on the Internet or at any website, or any combination thereof, including any injury or damage to participant's or any other person's computer relating to or resulting from participating in this Contest or downloading any materials in this Contest. CAUTION: ANY ATTEMPT TO DELIBERATELY DAMAGE ANY WEBSITE OR UNDERMINE THE LEGITIMATE OPERATION OF THE CONTEST IS A VIOLATION OF CRIMINAL AND CIVIL LAWS AND SHOULD SUCH AN ATTEMPT BE MADE, SIMON & SCHUSTER RESERVES THE RIGHT TO SEEK DAMAGES OR OTHER REMEDIES FROM ANY SUCH PERSON(S) RESPONSIBLE FOR THE ATTEMPT TO THE FULLEST EXTENT PERMITTED BY LAW. In the event of a dispute as to the identity or eligibility of a Selected Entrant based on an email address, the winning entries will be declared made by the "Authorized Account Holder" of the email address submitted at time of entry. "Authorized Account Holder" is defined as the natural person 18 years of age or older who is assigned to an email address by an Internet access provider, online service provider, or other organization (e.g., business, education institution, etc.) that is responsible for assigning email addresses for the domain associated with the submitted email address. Uses of automated devices are not valid for entry.

7. **List of Selected Entrants:** A complete list of Selected Entrants for the forthcoming book may be obtained after April 16, 2005, by sending a stamped, self-addressed envelope to: Right Words Books, Atria Books, 1230 Avenue of the Americas, New York, NY 10020.

8. **Sponsor:** Simon & Schuster, Inc.
1230 Avenue of the Americas
New York, NY 10020

Marlo Thomas graduated from the University of Southern California with a teaching degree. She is the author of two bestselling books, *Free to Be . . . You and Me* and *Free to Be . . . A Family.* Ms. Thomas has won four Emmys® and the Peabody Award and has been inducted into the Broadcasting Hall of Fame for her work in television, including the long-running hit series *That Girl,* which she conceived, produced, and starred in. She serves on the Professional Advisory Board and as the National Outreach Director for St. Jude Children's Research Hospital. Ms. Thomas lives in New York with her husband, Phil Donahue.